The Complete Landlording Handbook

By the Editors of Socrates

SOCRATES™
KNOW HOW TO DO MORE
AND SAVE

Socrates Media, LLC
227 West Monroe, Suite 500
Chicago, IL 60606
www.socrates.com

Special discounts on bulk quantities of Socrates books and products are available to corporations, professional associations and other organizations. For details, contact our Special Sales Department at 800.378.2659.

The Complete
Landlording
Handbook

Special acknowledgment to the following:

Jane Jerrard, Managing Editor; Lucas Otto, JD, Editor: Chip Butzko,
Encouragement Press; Jeannie Staats, Product Manager; Derek Vander Laan,
Cover Art; Peri Hughes, Editor; Alison Somilleda, Copy Editor; Kristen Grant,
Production Associate; Edgewater Editorial Services, Inc.

Get the most out of
The Complete Landlording Handbook.

Take advantage of the enclosed CD and special access to the
Landlording resource section of Socrates.com that are included
with this purchase.

The CD and Landlording resource section offer readers a unique
opportunity both to build on the material contained in the book
and to utilize tools such as forms, checklists, spreadsheets and
appraisals that will save time and money. More than $100 worth of
free forms and content are provided.

The CD bound into the back cover contains a read-only version of
this book as well as a variety of fillable and savable forms,
spreadsheets and checklists formatted in Microsoft® Word and Excel.

Readers can access the dedicated Landlording resource section by
registering their purchase at Socrates.com. A special eight-digit
Registration Code is provided on the CD. Once registered, a variety
of free forms, checklists, appraisals, research articles, government
forms and other useful tools are available at:

www.socrates.com/books/landlording-handbook.aspx

From time to time, new material will be added and readers will be
informed of changes in the law, as well as updates to the content
of this book.

Finally, readers are offered discounts on selected Socrates products
designed to help implement and manage their business and personal
matters more efficiently.

Table of
Contents

Section One

What Are You Getting Yourself Into?

Chapter 1: The Pros & Cons of Landlording

Chapter 2: Do You Have What It Takes?

1 The Pros & Cons of Landlording

You may be new to the role of being someone's landlord—or perhaps even new to the idea of landlording—but this handy guide will show you the ropes. You will learn everything you need to succeed at renting your property, from choosing the most profitable property to building a rental agreement that covers your assets.

You can skip from section to section to learn what you need to know on a particular subject or study the topics you are most interested in. Just be sure that you are well informed and as knowledgeable as you can be before you take your first big step, whether that is buying your rental property or looking for your first tenant.

Reality Check

You may believe that being a landlord is nothing more than a means to extra income. But being a landlord is much more; entailing work, time and worry. Even if your rental property is in tiptop shape and all your tenants pay promptly and take care of your property, you will still face expenses and time-consuming duties each month. You should know that up front. Simply put:

> **landlording can be lucrative and rewarding,
> but it will always require effort and time.**

Now let us take a look at some of the factors you should consider before you jump into renting your property.

Landlords of All Sorts
You may be considering renting out the second floor of your two-flat, or buying a 10-unit apartment building in another state. No matter what the size and scope of your plans for buying and renting property, the rules, guidelines and advice in this book will still apply—though you may have to consider how certain factors fit your landlording situation.

Financial Factors

Everyone who picks up this book is interested in landlording so that they can make money. There is really no other reason or benefit for becoming a landlord. You can make money on real estate appreciation, on rental income or on both. Generally speaking, your goal is to:

a. take in more money in rent than you spend on the mortgage and your expenses and/or

b. let your tenants' rent pay for a property's expenses so you can reap the appreciation.

Buying the right real estate is a secure investment that can provide a solid income and pave the way to more property purchases.

The advice in this book should help you choose the best property for your goals, set your rents correctly and earn money. However, before we get into the details, consider these advantages and disadvantages:

Financial Advantages

- Investing in the right rental property can be the wisest thing to do with your money. You might say, "It is not the rental—it is the real estate." Choose your property (or properties) wisely and you will be financially secure for life.
- You can take advantage of tax write-offs and deductions for your rental properties, which can add up to huge savings on taxes.
- You can use the equity you build in a rental property to invest in more property, and thus expand your "landlording empire" without spending all of the money in your bank account.
- As long as you have paying tenants in all your rental units, landlording ensures a steady income.

Financial Disadvantages

- The initial buying or converting of rental property is a huge investment for most people. Unless you have a spare condo or house ready to rent, you are going to spend a lot of your money on real estate.
- Maintaining that property—and your new landlording business—will also require some money. You will have expenses for decorating, repairs and maintenance; possibly for hired help such as an accountant, lawyer or maintenance help; and general business expenses.
- Over time, you may find that your property value is not increasing as much as you thought it would. It is crucial that you continually look at the "big picture" value of your property, along with your current and potential rental income, to make sure you are coming out ahead.

Taking Time

In a perfect world, you will end up with rental properties that are in great condition and never require repairs, tenants who are happy and complaint-free and never leave. Even in these ideal conditions, you will still need to devote some time every month to the following tasks:

Accounting	Make sure rents are paid and deposited, and taxes and insurance are up-to-date.
Maintenance	Is the grass mowed or the sidewalks shoveled? Gutters or furnace filters cleaned? Smoke and carbon monoxide batteries working?
Communications	Is everything OK with your tenants? Check for problems with the property or with neighbors, along with any other nuisances. Also stay informed on issues with the neighborhood, rents/expenses in your area and other landlord issues.

And if conditions are not ideal, plan on spending a great deal of time advertising and showing the property, screening tenants, keeping your rental units in good condition and handling repair issues. Depending on the size and condition of your property, and the turnover rate of your tenants, landlording could become your full-time job. That is OK—as long as your salary for that job is acceptable!

You Are the Boss

When you become a landlord, you become a business owner. Whether you incorporate and give your new business a name, or simply rent out property as a side job, you become responsible for tracking your finances, paying your taxes, getting appropriate insurance coverage and generally staying on top of every detail.

And, as the business owner, you are liable for any failures or penalties. If you do not declare income taxes on the rents you receive, you are personally liable to the Internal Revenue Service (IRS). If you forget to renew your homeowner's insurance (usually includes liability coverage) on the rental unit and your tenant falls down the stairs you were meaning to fix, you may be faced with an expensive lawsuit. Owning your own landlord business means the freedom to make the decisions, but also the burden of responsibility.

Get Your Game Face On

Another aspect to being the boss is dealing with tenants in difficult situations. Every landlord has a different approach to dealing with tenants. You can be friendly or aloof—whatever works best for you and comes most naturally. But remember, from the first moment you talk to or meet potential tenants, there may come a day when you have to be all business with them. When the rent is late or an eviction warning is in order, you need to be the boss, the bad guy and the disciplinarian.

Losing Your Personal Life

It is 10:00 p.m. on a wintry night and you are just sitting down to watch the news when the phone rings. It is your tenant, calling to say that the toilet is overflowing all over the bathroom. What is your first inclination?

a. Tell them you will be over tomorrow morning to take a look and hope the water damage does not cost more than $1,000.

b. Pretend to be the babysitter and say the landlord is out for the evening.

c. Grab a plunger, pull on your boots and head over to fix the problem.

No matter what your inclination, the correct answer is C. Once you become a landlord, you will lose at least a little of your personal life. Even if you hire a management company to handle those 10:00 p.m. calls, you will still want to be notified about emergencies and any major decisions. So brace yourself for a new way of life: The landlord lifestyle!

Still Interested?

So now you know: Landlording will take work, special skills and commitment. But the good news is that this handy guide, and the Web landing page www.socrates. com/books/landlording-handbook.aspx will help you prepare for the necessary work and master the skills that will help you make the commitment. It will also help you make the most profit on your rental properties while minimizing the problems that many landlords have with their tenants, properties and more.

Do You Have What It Takes?

Now that you have been warned about the hardships of being a landlord, let us take a detailed look at what it takes to run a rental property. You will need certain resources, qualities, contacts and preparations in order to succeed at making money on your property without running yourself into the ground.

One basic rule to keep in mind is that every task or aspect of landlording will either cost you time and effort or money out of pocket. Example: You can take the time to do your own accounting or you can hire a professional bookkeeper to do it for you. If you do not have the skills for a task, or if you cannot afford the time, consider hiring outside help.

This chapter will reveal what it takes to be a landlord and, if you do not have it, how to get it!

Time Commitment

As you saw in Chapter 1, being a landlord requires time commitment. At a minimum, you need to run your rental business, even if that means just giving other people orders to carry out the work. But it is likely that as a new landlord, you will be doing all the work yourself.

If you hold a full-time job, make sure you are ready to devote some of your off-hours to being a landlord. If you own just a few rental properties, you should be able to do what needs to be done in the evenings and on weekends. If you are working with a spouse or partner, this will be even easier. And if your full-time job offers flexible hours, that too will help.

➡️ **Real-Life Experience**

"It is easy to handle everything myself, especially because all my properties are in the same area. I have more flexibility with my [work] hours than most people, so I can make appointments in the middle of the day."

—Mark Berlinski, Owner of Multiple Rental Properties, Chicago, Illinois

Not counting the scouting and purchase of new rental properties, your time as a landlord will be spent on the following tasks:

- advertising and showing property
- screening potential tenants
- moving in tenants (organizing rental agreement, keys, house rules, etc.)
- collecting/depositing rents, paying bills and other accounting
- general maintenance and cleaning of the exterior of property
- maintenance and repairs on each unit
- tenant communications, as necessary
- renewing leases or starting over with advertising property
- staying informed on landlording laws, policies, rents and advice

How much time each of these tasks will take depends on the state of your property and how efficient you are. But you can see from this list that most of these tasks can be handled on weekends or in the evenings. And you can shave time off most of these duties with the advice in this book.

Time Savers

Here are a few tips on how to reduce the number of hours you spend on your regular landlord duties:

- Have tenants mail rent, or set up a direct debit to your tenants checking account or credit card. Do not waste time collecting checks in person.

- Schedule a time once a month when you sit down and pay all your bills and settle your accounts. Make this date about a week after rents are due so you can see immediately if a check is late.

- Batch as many landlord-related phone calls as you can and make them in one sitting.

- Set up a weekly and/or monthly maintenance schedule so you can batch small repair jobs to avoid multiple trips—your time is money!

- Bring something to do while you are waiting to show a unit or meet a repairman. If the person you are meeting is late or does not show, you will not have wasted time. Make phone calls, do paperwork or check out the unit or building for necessary repairs and/or improvements.

Financial Commitment

Let's say you have spent the money to acquire your rental property and to get it in shape for your tenants. Now you are ready to start getting a return on that investment. But keep in mind: you are not finished spending yet. In fact, you are never finished spending.

Be sure you have enough cash at hand to cover both regular landlording expenses and unexpected emergencies. Use these charts to calculate how much ready money you will need.

Minimum amount you should keep in a reserve fund:

	<write amounts here>
One month's mortgage on the rental property.	
One month's cost of utilities/other expenses on property.	
One month's property taxes on rental property.	
Total:	

Recommended amount you should keep in a reserve fund:

	<write amounts here>
Three month's mortgage on the rental property.	
Three month's cost of utilities/other expenses on property.	
Three month's property taxes on rental property.	
Total:	

You can anticipate major expenses by either examining the building yourself or having a professional home inspector go over the property if you are not confident. Consider the following:

- When will the roof need to be replaced?
- When will the furnace or the hot water heater need to be replaced?
- How is the building's foundation?

Also consider:

- How long will the major appliances last? When do the warranties run out on each?
- When should the floors be refinished or the carpets replaced?
- When should you paint the interior?

Take the information you gather and list a 3- or 5-year schedule of when major and minor repairs are expected, as well as maintenance work. Create a long-term budget around those repairs so you can start saving. And do not forget to update that budget every year!

Warranties and Guarantees

Keep a file of all receipts and warranty information on appliances and other major expenditures for the rental property. Check that file first when any repair work is called for on a washing machine, refrigerator, etc.

Set Up Separate Accounts

Open a new checking account to use for your landlording business. Deposit rent checks in this account and use it to pay any related costs. This is an easy way to keep track of your rental income and expenses. It also keeps your personal money out of the mix, as it should be.

Consider setting up a separate savings account or money market account to hold security deposits. This money, which tenants turn over as part of their rental agreement, is to be held by the landlord to cover expenses such as skipped rent or damages.

> ### Note
> Many states require landlords to keep security deposits in a separate account and, if some or all of the deposit is returned to the tenant, to provide the interest as well. Check your state law on this or with your local landlord association or housing authority.

But what if you are just starting out and have no reserve funds, liquid cash or any cash for that matter? Well, the good news is you may not need a lot of money right away. However, it does not hurt to consider how you might get some ready cash if something unexpected comes up. Here are some options to keep in the back of your mind:

1. Refinance your rental property (or your residence) for a lower interest rate and pocket as much money as you can on the deal.

2. If you live on the premises of a duplex or three-flat, you can take out a home equity loan on the rental property (or your separate residence) if you have some equity in it. If you own a larger property, take out a line of credit using the property as collateral.

3. Get a second mortgage on the property. This is a last-resort step, to be undertaken only if you are 100 percent positive you can assume the additional debt.

Personal Commitment

A successful landlord—especially one who is a do-it-all-yourself type of landlord, needs certain skills and personality traits. A list of these characteristics can be found on the next page.

Free Forms and Checklists
Registered readers can visit **www.socrates.com/books/landlording-handbook.aspx** for free forms, letters and checklists. See page iv for details on how to register.

Organized and detail-oriented	A landlord needs to keep track of dozens of details, including accounting, record keeping, maintenance schedule, etc. If you are not good at staying on top of details, find a system that shapes your schedule and your to-do list.
Good with numbers	You will need to track several bank accounts and make sound decisions on spending and making money, including calculating how much rent you can charge and how to make a profit.
Good people skills and intuition	Can you tell when someone is trying to manipulate you? Are you skilled at settling arguments and deflecting anger? Landlords need to know how to read and handle current and prospective tenants.
Handy around the house	Most maintenance issues are small—stopping a toilet from running all night or tightening doorknobs. Handling these quick fixes yourself will save you a lot of money. If you do not know how to handle basic maintenance, learn! Take a class, read some books or ask for help from a handy friend.

Landlord Central: Setting Up Your Home Office

You will need to devote part of your home to your landlording workspace. It does not have to be fancy or take up a lot of space, but as a working landlord, you should have:

- a computer with Internet access and a printer;
- a small file cabinet or other means of keeping paper records;
- dedicated space for maintenance supplies and tools; and
- a cell phone or dedicated phone for your business.

You do not have to have a dedicated computer just for managing your rental property; the family PC will do. Just keep separate folders or directories for your landlording, and be sure to back everything up regularly to safeguard it!

Discounts on Other Socrates Products

In addition to a variety of free forms and checklists, you will find special offers on a variety of Socrates products. Visit www.socrates. com/books/landlording-handbook.aspx for more information.

In order to gain access to free forms, dictionaries, checklists and updates, readers must register their book purchase at Socrates.com. An eight digit Registration Code is provided on the enclosed CD. See page iv for further details.

Using Your Computer

Of course, you can rent property without using a computer. All tasks can be done with a pencil, paper and calculator, but with a computer you can:

1. Keep track of your accounts. Use standard off-the-shelf accounting software to enter deposits and payments and sign up for online banking.

2. Perform credit checks on prospective tenants. It is fast and easy to request credit checks online.

3. Create advertising signs, flyers and classified ads. Once you have written them, just update as needed. (Examples can be found on the Web landing page www.socrates.com/books/landlording-handbook.aspx.) Create or revise rental agreements, notices, policies, etc. Download templates and customize on your computer.

4. Send and receive faxes. You can buy software that lets your computer act as a fax machine. This might come in handy for receiving completed rental applications and leases, and it is cheaper and takes up less space than a fax machine.

5. Educate yourself. Stay up-to-date with state and federal landlording laws, research local rents and real estate prices, and chat with other landlords across the country—it is all on the Internet. You will find a list of recommended sites at the end of this chapter, as well as the Web landing page www.socrates.com/books/landlording-handbook.aspx.

Find enough space for all the paperwork that comes with being a landlord and develop a filing system that makes sense to you. Your paper files will include:

- signed rental agreements and leases
- up-to-date contact information on tenants
- building records
- receipts and bills
- insurance policies
- maintenance schedules
- tax records
- tenant correspondence, such as rent increase or lease violation notices

Long-Term Record-Keeping

Paperwork involving anything you declare on your federal income taxes (rental income or deductions) should be kept for 7 years. If you are limited on space, box up each year's receipts and forms after you pay taxes and store it in a safe, dry place like the attic or a closet shelf.

What should you keep and how long should you keep it? Use this chart as a reference.

Signed leases or rental agreements	Keep these as long as you own the building. Once a tenant leaves, you can move his or her lease from your active files to a storage area, but it is a good way of keeping track of who lived in your building.
Contact information on tenants	Keep cell phone numbers, work numbers and emergency contact numbers for 2 to 3 months after the person leaves, in case you need to reach him or her.
Correspondence with tenants: Their letters of complaint and requests for maintenance or letters to them regarding broken house rules or policies	Keep these throughout their tenancy until approximately 6 months after they leave. You may need a paper trail in case a dispute arises, or if you need to prove why a security deposit will not be returned.
Receipts, bills and other tax-related documents	7 years for anything declared on your taxes.
Records of purchasing property and making capital improvements	Keep these as long as you own the building. Eventually you will need these for tax purposes.

Tools to Go With You

Put all your most commonly used tools in a portable toolbox and have them ready to go. Keep the tools in your garage, some other area of your house, in the trunk of your car or consider leaving tools on-site at your rental property. Perhaps you can keep a locked box in the basement of your multi-unit building where you can access wrenches, a plunger or a putty knife, as needed.

A Dedicated Phone Line

One area where you definitely want to keep your personal life and your landlord life separate is the telephone. Having a separate phone for your business helps you control communications with tenants, prospective tenants and contractors, and also provides a more professional sound on your voice mail message and when you answer.

The best way to have a landlord hotline is to get a cell phone devoted (or partially devoted) to managing your property. Use this number as your landlord hotline and give it to tenants and your professional contacts. Make sure to list the number in rental ads and on your business cards and forms.

If you prefer not to use a cell phone for your landlording business, you can either install a second phone line in your home or use your home number. Either way, make sure you have an answering machine or voice mail that you can check when you are away.

> ### Note on Getting a Second Telephone Line
>
> Telling your phone company you want a business line installed is like asking them to charge you more. Make sure you request a second personal line, like you did for Internet access or to handle your teenager's calls, or you will pay more for installation and calling charges on a business line.

24/7 Availability

Landlords must be available to their tenants (or their management company) round the clock. If you go out of town for a week, or just a day, people should have a way to get in touch with you. If you will be unavailable—in the hospital or backpacking across Europe—appoint a contact person for emergencies and let your tenants know how to reach that person.

Building Your Rolodex® of Contacts

Even if it makes good financial sense to do everything yourself, from balancing the books to installing a deadbolt lock, you should know some skilled professionals you can call on in an emergency. They include:

- an accountant and/or tax preparer who specializes in property management
- a lawyer who can handle liability suits and questions
- an insurance agent
- a plumber
- an electrician
- a carpenter
- an HVAC contractor

How can you locate contacts in these areas? One way is to join a local association of rental property owners. These associations are terrific ways to network, get answers to your landlording questions and stay abreast of your local laws and rental market.

To find a landlord association in your area, visit www.realestateassociations.com/index.html or www.landlord.com/assoc_main.htm. Either site lets you look up associations by state, then city or region.

You can also network through your community by contacting your local chamber of commerce, or joining a group such as the Kiwanis Club, which is sure to include professionals from various industries. It is obvious: The more people you meet, the better your network of contacts.

Landlord Resources

Reading this book and browsing through the information on the enclosed CD and the Web landing page, www.socrates.com/books/landlording-handbook/aspx, can get you up and running as a landlord. But if you want to excel as a property owner and manager, your learning should not stop here. You can continue your education through several avenues: reading books and periodicals, browsing the Internet and talking to other landlords and related professionals.

Here are some suggestions of resources you might find useful:

Web sites

National Apartment Association—www.naahq.org

This association is an advocate for quality rental housing, serving the interests of rental property owners, managers and others. Landlords can get insurance through NAA, get information on vacancy rates, the rental housing market and other indicators.

MrLandlord.com—www.mrlandlord.com

Ask questions, sign up for the free WEEKLY RENTAL OWNER e-newsletter, access a free special Real Estate Report each month and more.

Landlord.com—www.landlord.com

Full of resources from listings of landlord associations to links to appraisers, contractors and handymen, state laws and much more.

National Association of Residential Property Managers—http://narpm.net/

Looking for a property manager? This is a terrific resource.

Now you have an idea of what you need to be a successful landlord: money, time and skills, as well as an office setup, a phone, a Rolodex of contacts and continuous education. If these items are all within your reach, let us get started on the nuts and bolts of how to start your new rental property business.

Section ■ Two

Property

3

Which Rental Property Is Right for You?

Being a landlord covers everything from renting out a room in your home to owning a building with dozens of apartments. Which end of the scale is right for you? You are probably somewhere in the middle. Of course, you may already own your rental property at the time you are reading this. If that is the case, this chapter still contains some pertinent information for you. If you are in the process of making a buying decision, you will definitely want to read on to make sure you make the right choice.

Choices, Choices

If you want to buy rental property, the type of building will be guided by your finances (how much you can afford) and your abilities (how much you manage to maintain and run).

Here are the basic categories of property to choose from:

Property Type	Definition
Single-family home	A free-standing house or a townhome. Typically includes a yard and often a garage.
Condominium or co-operative apartment	A single apartment within a multi-unit building, which you own and rent at your discretion. Can be anything from an efficiency to a large apartment.
Duplex or two-flat	A building that includes two separate apartments, whether a single-family home has been split in two, or an apartment building with an upstairs and a downstairs unit.
Multi-unit building	A building that is set up for multiple apartments, from two or three to dozens.
Furnished apartment	A rental that includes all or most furniture, which is provided by the landlord.
Single room	A bedroom or suite within an existing home.

You can also rent commercial space, or storage or garage space, but here we will deal with residential rentals.

As mentioned earlier, the type of property you decide to rent will depend on what you can afford and how much time and energy you can devote to being a landlord. Obviously, owning a building with 20 apartments will require considerable time in bookkeeping alone, not to mention finding tenants and showing vacancies. An undertaking of that size will turn your landlording business into a full-time job.

If you are just starting out as a landlord, it is best to start small, with a single rental property. That gives you a chance to get it right, whether it is buying the right place or dealing with tenants. If you plan to build a landlord empire, you can do so after you are comfortable with your starter rental, and when you have the hang of making money and avoiding mistakes.

Meanwhile, your first step is to understand what you want and what you can handle.

A Steady Source of Wealth

Investing in real estate is a terrific way to make money. Choose your rental property or properties wisely, and you will find that it is easy to start with a relatively small outlay of cash, and build solid financial security that will last a lifetime. The real estate market may experience a temporary decline, but over the years the appreciation on your investment is sure to grow. And that equity is like gold—it will outlast inflation, rocky stocks, bonds and any retirement plan or pension you are enrolled in. With careful consideration of the area in which you buy and the specific property you buy, you can turn your first landlording venture into a wealth-building investment that you can grow as you add properties.

Know Your Long-Term Plan

Before you make your first commitment to becoming a landlord, you should understand your goals. Ask yourself these questions:

- Why do you want to be a landlord? Is it to make extra income now or to have some security when you retire? Are you planning on relying on instant cash flow or property appreciation? Unless the market is exceptionally good or exceptionally bad, you will get one or the other—not both.

- How long do you want to be a landlord? Are you in this for the long-term or the short-term?

- Do you plan to stay in the same geographic area for a while? If not, are you willing to be a long-distance landlord if you move?

- Would you prefer to live on your rental premises—either in half of a duplex or in one of the apartments in a multi-unit building?

- How much of your savings are you willing to spend on your first rental property? How much of your retirement accounts? Life insurance policy?

- Can you afford to lose money over a period of time if you have trouble finding a tenant? Could you still afford the mortgage on your rental property?

- Is your spouse or partner willing to help you in your new endeavor? If not, are you sure this is something you can do by yourself?

- If you cannot afford to buy a property alone, would you consider finding a partner who would help with expenses and share the profits?

Your answers to these questions will help narrow down what type of property you buy, where you buy it and when. However, the most important determining factor for most people is money.

Appreciation vs. Cash Flow

What is your investment strategy? According to Catherine Brouwer of Blue River Properties in Memphis, Tennessee, you can invest in real estate for appreciation or cash flow. You can get both out of the same property, but when you are starting out, you are likely to get only one. A smaller property such as a duplex or single-family home will realize faster appreciation in value, though you will only net enough cash flow from renting to cover the mortgage and maybe your expenses. The good part is that you can pull out some of your equity in the property after a few years and purchase another…then another.

Investing in a larger multi-unit building will bring immediate cash flow from all of those rent payments, but appreciation will be negligible for years if not decades. The only way around this is if you make major improvements in the building— and that is costly.

It is up to you. Your goals, finances and personality will dictate what type of property best suits you.

Real-Life Experience

"Keep your resale in mind. A two- or three-bedroom apartment will be easier to make a profit on than an efficiency or one-bedroom. Those smaller places can only go so high."

—Catherine Brouwer, Founder, Blue River Properties, Memphis, Tennessee

Figure out Your Finances

Real estate prices will vary greatly depending on where you are looking (general geographic area, city or town and even neighborhood), what the market is like at the time and sheer luck. (The same is true on how much rent you can charge.) Determining if you are getting a fair market value is covered in the next chapter; first you have to know how much you can afford.

Any lending institution you approach for a mortgage or other type of loan will let you know what they think you can afford. Your first step should be applying at one or two lending institutions to be pre-approved for a mortgage. This does not lock you in with a particular lender or for a particular loan; you simply provide your financial information and the institution will tell you how big a mortgage they would give you. Your pre-approval amount will help set your expectations for how much you can spend on your rental property.

> **Note**
>
> To apply for pre-approval, start by contacting the bank where you hold your checking and savings account, and select two or three others. Let them know that you are interested in purchasing a rental property. Each will run a credit check on you and add up your assets, then report if you are pre-approved for a mortgage and if so, what types of loans you can get and the maximum amount.

Finance Formula

One tool lenders use to determine the maximum mortgage an individual can afford is a debt-to-income ratio. Lenders generally allow the following percentages for residential mortgages:

A maximum of 28 percent of your monthly gross income (before taxes) goes to housing expenses, including property taxes and insurance.

A maximum of 36 percent of your monthly gross income goes to housing expenses plus recurring debt, including credit card payments, car loans, student loans, child support, etc.

Calculate your debt-to-income ratio and see how much you should spend on your rental property each month. (Remember to include expenses associated with your own home.)

Keep in mind that the institution's idea of what you can comfortably pay each month, or pay down initially, may not be realistic. It is best if you can estimate your own comfort levels for cash. Here are some tips for doing so:

Down Payment

The more you can put down on your initial payment, the lower the amount you will have to borrow for a mortgage. A larger down payment can also save you in closing costs—think of this as a reward for giving your bank so much money upfront. So the larger a down payment you can make, the better. But do not spend too much of your savings on this—you will need money for closing costs (your real estate agent can give you an estimate on this), for getting your new property ready to rent and for starting up your landlord business.

Mortgage lenders typically require at least five percent down on residential property. That percentage refers to the purchase price of the property. Any rental property from a single-family home to a four-unit building is considered residential property.

If you purchase a property that contains five or more units, you will need a commercial mortgage. This requires a higher down payment—typically 25 or 30 percent, more paperwork and more time to process. Your lender will want to examine the rental income and other financial factors to ensure that your income will be sufficient to cover the mortgage and all other operating expenses.

> **Attention Homeowners**
>
> If you own a home and have enough equity invested in it, you may be able to pay for your rental property with a home equity loan rather than a new mortgage. In this case, you would get a tax-deductible loan from a bank, which you would then pay off monthly as you would a mortgage.

Monthly Mortgage Payment

The amount of your monthly mortgage payment will depend on your purchase price, your down payment and the interest rate you get on your mortgage. Check comparable rental properties in the same area to estimate how much rent you will be able to ask for regarding your new property. If the rent will cover the mortgage payment, you are in good shape. Ideally, the rent(s) you collect each month will pay for all your monthly property costs with money left over for you. However, this is not always the case. Your main benefit from renting the property may end up being the equity you build by hanging onto it while the rent helps offset your loan and other expenses.

> ## Automatic Calculations
>
> You can find all sorts of free financial calculators on the Internet that can automatically figure out what your monthly payment would be on a particular mortgage, how much you can afford given your income and debt and a lot more. Check the Web site of your bank or lending institution, or try any of these online calculators:
>
> www.mortgage-calc.com
>
> www.jeacle.ie/mortgage
>
> www.calculator.com
>
> www.bankrate.com/brm/mortgage-calculator.asp

Private Mortgage Insurance

This is basically insurance for your lender, and ensures that the mortgage will be paid off if you default on your loan. Unless you pay a hefty down payment—typically at least 20 percent on a residence—your lender will require that mortgage insurance is added to your loan. (Remember that residence can mean a duplex or three-flat.) Your insurance payment will be added to your monthly mortgage payment.

Property Taxes

Find out what the current annual property tax is for comparable properties in the neighborhood where you are looking. Add this to your annual expenses and make sure you can afford the taxes. In high-end areas and urban neighborhoods, these taxes can be surprisingly high. Property tax is considerably less for condominiums and co-op units, because you are not paying tax on land.

Additional Expenses

As you are figuring out how much you should spend on your down payment and your monthly mortgage payment, remember to give yourself enough ready money to cover standard expenses like insurance premiums and costs of maintenance and repair. It is also a good idea to have a safety cushion in your bank account to cover unexpected events like plumbing repairs.

> **Real-Life Experience**
>
> "You have to set aside a substantial account for emergencies—most people do not do this."
>
> —Catherine Brouwer, Founder, Blue River Properties, Memphis, Tennessee

What to Look for in a Neighborhood

Everybody's dream rental property is a low-priced place in a high-end neighborhood. The low-priced part is common sense. And buying property in a good neighborhood is the best way to ensure that the value stays as high as when you buy. But if you can target an area that is just on the cusp of changing from a not-so-great neighborhood into a desirable area and even a future hot spot, consider buying a property there. It makes sense to do this because an investment in a turning point neighborhood is the most profitable one you can make. The value of your property could double or triple, or go even higher. And, you will be able to raise your rents along with the value as the neighborhood becomes more desirable.

How can you identify a turning point neighborhood? Here are some things to look for:

- New construction is starting on homes or commercial development that indicates a new class of homeowners/renters will be interested in living in the area.
- The town or city has set plans to develop new areas within the neighborhood.
- Some apartment buildings are being transformed into condominiums—an increased ratio of homeowners to renters will improve the neighborhood.
- The area has a prime location, near a thriving downtown or other popular neighborhood that is bursting at the seams.
- Property taxes are increasing, revealing that property values are starting to rise.
- Real estate agents are talking about the area and even buying property there.

Note that getting a bargain in a marginal area may not pay off for several years. If the neighborhood is too unsafe or unappealing, you will have trouble getting good tenants at first—and may have trouble getting any tenants at all. But if you can afford to pay the mortgage and watch your tenants closely during those initial years, you should see a dramatic increase in your property value that will make those lean years worthwhile.

➡ **Real-Life Experience**

"It is best to know which neighborhoods are on the edge [of improving]. You may have trouble renting in borderline neighborhoods, but the payoff can be tremendous once they change. In the meantime, you have to be careful about the tenants you choose."

—Catherine Brouwer, Founder, Blue River Properties, Memphis, Tennessee

Start your search geographically. You want your rental property to be close enough to your own home that you can check on it regularly, and you want it in a neighborhood that is good, or going to get good soon. If you have lived in your home for a few years or more, you will know which streets or neighborhoods are desirable and which are not. If you are not sure, do an eyeball check of the neighborhood. Are the homes and yards in good repair? Are there vacant lots or vacant buildings? Is the neighborhood full of rental properties, or are there owner-occupied houses or condos? The more owner-occupied homes in an area, the better: Homeowners will take better care of their own property and will do their best to make sure their block stays crime-free.

Can You Afford the Neighborhood?

The better the neighborhood, the higher the property values and thus the property taxes. Do some research to find out how much property taxes would be on the type of property you want. Count that amount into your projected annual expenses—and keep in mind that property taxes increase regularly.

You can also ask the local chamber of commerce for information on any new developments coming. These can have a positive or negative impact on a neighborhood; if a new super grocery store will be built next year, tenants may want to be near it. If a new jail will be built, you might want to look in a different neighborhood. Your chamber of commerce can also provide information on the overall economic status of the town.

Big City Renting

Keep in mind that properties in big cities are likely to be more expensive, as will the property taxes. But rents will be higher as well, and there is a larger tenant pool.

Another aspect of a community you need to check is the rental market. Are there already too many similar rentals in the immediate area where you are looking? Or more importantly, do those rentals have a high vacancy rate? If so, the market may be flooded and you should consider looking elsewhere or for a different type of property.

Example

You find a great bargain advertised in your local paper: a building with six one-bedroom apartments. You drive past to check it out and realize it is on a block full of similar buildings. Check for For Rent signs, read the classified ads and do an Internet search on rentals to find out how many apartments on that block are advertised. Perform these checks each week to see if they rent. If not, you should consider a different neighborhood, or perhaps a different type of rental so that yours will attract different tenants—like a single-family home.

Of course, what you may be seeing is a market with too many rental properties and not enough tenants. If you change your search to a different type of rental and find the same problem, this may be the case. In a situation like this, you must be very careful—and patient—about choosing what to buy and when. Consider holding off on your decision for a year or so, or looking in a different part of your state or a different state altogether.

Great Rental Neighborhoods

There is a steady market for renters in any neighborhood that is near a university or a hospital. You are almost guaranteed to find quality renters among the faculty, students and researchers that come to work for 1 to 3 years and do not want to buy a home.

What to Look for in a Starter Property

Once you know how much you can afford to spend on a property and the general area where you would like to own it, it is time to narrow your search. Ideally, you want to find a property that is in sound condition, but needs some work. You should get a better price on a neglected building, which is easy to spruce up without spending a lot. (Chapter 6 provides some detailed information on buying a handyman special and increasing the value.)

For your first rental property, a duplex or two-flat is a good investment. Here are six good reasons to start out with a duplex:

1. You can live in one of the two apartments. This saves on your costs and puts you in a perfect position to keep an eye on your new rental property.

2. Duplexes are generally affordable.

3. They are also historically easy to sell. A property that appeals to owner-occupied will double your market, because your potential buyers will include investors and landlords.

4. You can use the rental income from your tenant to help pay the mortgage while you build equity in the property.

5. Maintenance should be easy.

6. You will start your landlording with a single tenant—a guinea pig for testing out your lease, policies, etc.

> ## Should You Rent a Furnished Property?
>
> Renting a furnished apartment or house will allow you to charge more rent, but you will also bear the expense of paying for the furnishings.
>
> The real question is, what kind of tenant would want a furnished home? The answer: someone who has no furniture of their own. Think about this…a tenant renting a furnished apartment is more transient and less likely to stay, lease or no lease.

Where to Look

Finding good rental properties for sale is an art. Here are three main methods for scoping out potential properties and ultimately finding the right one:

1. Networking

If you have connections in your community, use them. Talk to neighbors, other landlords, real estate agents, contractors and friends and family to let them know what you are looking for. This type of networking can help alert you to the perfect property before it goes on the market.

Real estate agents are a very good source, because they often get the word-of-mouth information on sales first. Cultivate relationships with several real estate agents. Let them know that you are just looking, but are serious about buying. If your long-term plans include buying multiple properties, let them know that, as well. Positioning yourself as a potential long-term customer will make them take you more seriously.

2. Newspaper Ads

In addition to networking, check your local classified ads for income property for sale or properties for sale by owner. Read these ads regularly to get a feel for the market in your area—what is available where, how much your targeted property type is selling for there and what amenities are included.

Also check the For Rent section to keep track of what is renting and what is not. If you see a trend of long-time vacancies in the area you are looking, check into it further. Are these properties in good condition? Do they appear to be priced competitively? If the answer to both is yes, there may be a problem with that rental market.

3. Signs

Make it a habit to drive or walk around the neighborhood you are interested in. Read any posted For Rent signs or For Sale signs. Carry paper and a pencil so you can note the addresses of places that do not offer information on the sign.

> ## Nobody Pays Sticker Price on Real Estate
>
> Keep in mind that as you are looking for a property to buy that price is always negotiable. Your real estate agent can help with this, but assume that any advertised price can be negotiated down five to ten percent.

Working with a Real Estate Agent

Once you have decided what type of rental property you want to buy and which town or neighborhood you want to look in, you may want to find a real estate agent who can help you find it. If you are familiar with the area and do not mind doing some research, you can handle this aspect alone, but it will take time. Also consider that when the time comes to make an offer, your agent can expertly guide the negotiation process. So let us assume you are going to be working with a real estate agent. How do you choose one? Here are some ideas on what to look for:

- You want an agent who knows the area well. When you are investigating neighborhoods where you want to buy, look for For Sale signs and note the name of the agent on the sign. If you see multiple signs for a person, give them a call. They are obviously familiar with the neighborhood and know a lot of the properties there first-hand.

- You want a real estate agent with experience buying (and selling) the property type you want. If you are looking for a multi-unit building, make sure they have handled similar property deals and know the ropes! You can rely on a good agent for a lot of advice on financing, legal matters and more.

- You want a real estate agent who understands what you are looking for and shows you appropriate properties. When you first contact an agent, be clear and explicit about what type of property you want, including price, size and location. It is a good sign if they ask you questions that help narrow this down.

- You want a real estate agent who works as your partner, and is enthusiastic about finding a property that is a perfect match for you. Steer clear of anyone who consistently shows you properties that are priced out of your budget or are inappropriate properties. Also monitor how closely they stay in contact with you between showings. If you feel you are being neglected, you may be too low end for them.

The good news is that you are under no contract or obligation to stay with an agent. You can go to see a property or two and if you feel the person is not a good fit, you can let them know you are changing real estate agents and try someone else.

Consider Accepting "Housing Choice Vouchers" (Section 8)

Some landlords are successful at renting to a unique niche audience: tenants who receive government assistance.

The Housing Choice Voucher program, formerly Section 8, is a housing assistance program funded by the U.S. Department of Housing and Urban Development (HUD). Here is how housing choice vouchers work: tenants qualify for the program if their income is below a certain level. This level, plus the number of family members is different in different geographical areas. Qualified tenants rent properties that are pre-approved and qualified. These approved rental properties can be apartments, duplexes, or single-family homes, and must meet requirements for minimal size, amenities and condition. The tenant pays part of the rent directly to the landlord, and the remainder of the rent is paid by the government—specifically, a local public housing agency (PHA). If the tenant has no income and has a family, the PHA may pay 100 percent of the rent.

The benefit of accepting tenants through the housing choice voucher program is that you are guaranteed that at least some of the rent will be paid. Even if the tenant should break their lease or you evict them, the local PHA will continue to pay their portion of the rent. An added benefit: You are likely to have 100 percent rental capacity, because you will always find voucher tenants.

➡ **Real-Life Experience**

"It is not difficult to sign up [for the Housing Choice Voucher program]—the inspection is the difficult part. You have to qualify for HUD's standards and the inspectors go farther than the criteria calls for."

—Anonymous Landlord, Indiana

If you decide you want to enroll as a housing choice voucher landlord, contact your local PHA. They will provide you with paperwork, inspect your property to make sure it meets Section 8 requirements, negotiate the rent and calculate the tenant's contribution, and, ultimately, pay you the government's portion directly.

To find your local PHA office, visit HUD's Web site at www.hud.gov/offices/pih/pha/contacts/index.cfm and click on your state.

You should follow the same methods of screening and approving potential housing choice voucher tenants that you would use for others. The PHA will qualify tenants to ensure they can get assistance, but the rest is up to you. The same rules apply to these tenants as other tenants: You can collect a security deposit (direct from the tenant, not the government), charge them late fees as stated in your lease and evict them, if necessary.

Free Forms and Checklists

Registered readers can visit www.socrates.com/books/landlording-handbook.aspx for free forms, letters and checklists. See page iv for details on how to register. Among the many items available are:

> **Note**
>
> The Housing Choice Voucher program requires a 1-year lease; you cannot rent month-to-month. At the end of the lease, your property will be subject to an inspection again.

Ready to Buy?

Now that you have narrowed down what type of rental property you should buy and how much you can spend, it is time to find out how to purchase it.

4 Buying Your Rental Property

When should you make the move to buy a property? The best answer is whenever the time is right. The best position you can be in when shopping for rental property is to be ready to make the purchase—with all your financial information at hand, at least one pre-approval for a loan, and a knowledge of what type of property you want—but not in any rush. If you can be patient and wait for the perfect property to come along, you are sure to make a good decision. The more properties you look at, with your real estate agent or alone, the better idea you will have of what you want and what properties are worth.

Of course, if you see a property you know is ideal, do not hesitate to act on it. That does not mean putting money down immediately, though. First find out all you can about the property. Here are some ideas of the information you should find out, either from the seller directly (if possible), from their real estate agent or by doing some research on your own:

- Know the neighborhood. Make sure you are familiar with the quality of the area, including crime statistics, school district, and percentage of rentals verses owner-occupied properties. Talk to neighbors (and current tenants) about the area.

- Know the rental market. Are there a lot of similar properties for rent in the area? Can you afford to match their rent?

- If the property is a multi-unit building, confirm that it is legally zoned. If it is a condominium or co-op unit, make sure the building association will allow you to rent to a tenant.

- Schedule a visit—before you bring in a professional inspector—to thoroughly go over the building and note any work you see that needs to be done. Estimate the costs.

- Why is the seller selling? Find out if they are being pressured to leave, say, by a divorce or long-distance move. You may be able to use their situation to negotiate a lower price or a more desirable closing date.

- Know who you are buying from. If the current owner does all the maintenance and repairs you will not have an estimate of the costs incurred for the work done. If you plan to hire help for all or part of these tasks, add that cost to your budget and make sure you can still afford the property.
- If the building is occupied by the owner's tenants, see Chapter 5 for how to handle taking over as their landlord. You will have to honor their existing lease or rental agreements until expiration.

The Buying Process

Once you have done some legwork on researching the property, it is time to begin the buying process.

Making an Offer

If you are working with a real estate agent, they will handle this process for you. Talk to them about the maximum amount you are willing to spend on the property and what each of you thinks the property is worth. Your agent can get information on comparable properties in the area that have sold recently so you can see if the asking price is fair.

Come up with a low-end figure to offer as a first bid. How much should you offer? Know that in real estate, as in purchasing a car, all prices are negotiable. A lot will depend on the real-estate market in the area; if it is a seller's market and there are more buyers than there are good properties, you are likely to end up paying close to the asking price—or maybe more, if you have a lot of competition. If the market is in favor of buyers, meaning properties are on the market longer and are going for less, you are more likely to get a good price.

> **Real-Life Experience**
>
> "Everything is negotiable in real estate."
>
> —Catherine Brouwer, Founder, Blue River Properties, Memphis, Tennessee

Your real estate agent will contact the seller's agent and make the offer. If you are not using an agent, it is up to you to come up with an opening bid and make the offer to the seller's real estate agent. Then it is a game of going back and forth until you reach an agreement.

> **Example**
>
> You are interested in a duplex listed at $500,000. Your research shows that similar buildings are selling for $450,000, but it is a seller's market so you know you might have to pay more than that. You make an initial offer of $420,000, and the seller responds by saying she'll take $480,000. You offer $440,000; she counters with $460,000. After conferring with your real estate agent, you decide to accept.

Hiring an Inspector

Once your offer has been accepted, you need to have the property inspected. It is up to you (or your real estate agent) to arrange for a time when the property can be inspected. As the buyer, you will hire a professional home inspector to ensure the building(s) are structurally sound and report on the condition of plumbing, electrical systems, heating and air conditioning units, etc. You should definitely be present for the inspection, so you can see first-hand what the inspector reports. If any substantial problems are uncovered, you may decide not to go through with the purchase or you may try to negotiate to have the seller pay to fix the problems or bring the selling price down.

Getting an Appraisal

If you get a mortgage from a bank, you are likely to be required to get the property appraised. Typically, the lender will contract with a professional appraiser to officially verify the value of the property, and their fee will be included in your closing costs. If you disagree with the appraiser's findings, you have the option of hiring your own independent, licensed appraiser to verify the value of the property—but you will have to pay the second appraiser's fee as well.

Note that if the appraiser considers the value lower than the sales price, your loan could be declined; the bank wants to make sure that if you default on your mortgage, the value of the property would cover their loss.

Closing

The closing is when you sign on the dotted line (which you will do over and over again) and the property officially becomes yours. At the closing you should receive all necessary documentation, which includes rent rolls and tenant records, as well as the keys.

Who Does What, and Can You Do It Yourself and Save Money?

Who	What They Do	What They Typically Charge	Can You Do It Yourself?
Real estate agent	Find likely properties to show you, make appointments to see property, act as your negotiator on price and other aspects of purchase.	Real estate agents receive a percentage of the purchase price, typically five or six percent.	Only if you can find a good rental property by yourself and are confident that you can negotiate a fair price on it.
Attorney	Read and advise on all legal contracts; represent you at closing.	Attorneys typically charge a flat fee for handling a real estate transaction. Based on your geographic area, fees can range from $200 to $600 or higher.	If it is a standard sale, you might find a knowledgeable real estate agent who can handle the duties of an attorney, but you should always hire either a real estate agent or an attorney—or both.
Home inspector	Inspect the property's overall structure, electrical system, plumbing, roof, heating and AC units, insulation and more to report on the state of the building, including any need for repair or replacement.	Inspectors charge a flat fee depending on the age, size and condition of a property. For a single-family home, fees typically range from $250 to $400.	Only if you are a professional contractor. When buying a rental property, it is crucial that everything is sound and up to code before you take possession.

Show Me the Money

Now we come to the root of the matter: How are you going to pay for this enterprise? The easiest way to is to get a mortgage or a loan to cover the vast majority of the purchase price. You will need enough cash to make a down payment—which can be anywhere from five to 30 percent of the price—or more if you can afford it. This down payment will be due at the time of closing, so have the money ready in your checking account that day.

➡ **Real-Life Experience**

"It is all about credit. A first-time buyer with good credit can get a four-unit property with no down payment. But you have to live on the property, and you have to have good credit! If that is the case, you can get a commercial property for as little as 10 percent down. Your interest rate might be a percentage higher, but it is worth it!"

—Liz Acevedo, Loan Officer, American Banc Financial, Chicago, Illinois

Here are some ways to pay the hefty down payment on your property:

Use Your Savings

This transaction is an investment in your future, and that is what you are saving for, right? If you have enough ready money for a down payment and enough left over to cover the expenses of landlording, then consider this option.

Buying with a Partner or Partners

If you cannot afford to buy a rental property by yourself, consider going in with a partner who can share the expenses and, eventually, the profits. Just make sure it is someone you trust and that you enter a legal agreement. Both your names should be on the mortgage, the title of the property and other ownership documentation. Talk to your partner about how and when one of you can go about buying out the other share if that should become an option.

Take Out a Home Equity Loan

If you own your home and have some equity in it, you can take out a tax-deductible loan in a lump sum (or in monthly payments) and use that towards your down payment. Depending on the size of your loan, you may be able to use it towards some of your monthly mortgage payments as well—or skip the mortgage altogether. Of course, you will still have the home equity loan to pay off. If you are putting a home equity loan towards a mortgage, consider the total monthly payments you will have to make to both lenders.

Borrow Against Your Life Insurance Policy

If you have a life insurance policy with a lot of cash value, check with your insurance agent to see about borrowing against it. The interest in this type of loan is much lower than that of a mortgage or home equity loan. And there is no set payment plan; you can pay it back however it suits you.

> ## Mortgage Glossary
>
> Here are some terms you should know when shopping for a mortgage.
>
> **Fixed-Rate Mortgages**–interest rate does not change for the duration of the loan. This is ideal if you get a terrifically low rate. Of course, you can always refinance to find a better rate, cash out some of your equity or reduce your monthly payments.
>
> **Adjustable-Rate Mortgages or ARMs**–interest rate may change. It is linked to an economic index (such as Treasury securities), and will go up or down with that index. With a 5-1 ARM, your interest rate will remain fixed for 5 years, then you have 1 year to adjust the rate. You can refinance if your interest rate is going to climb, but it may be prohibitively expensive to convert an ARM to a fixed-rate.
>
> **Annual Percentage Rate (APR)**–this includes not only the interest rate, but also points, broker fees and other charges you will pay each year.
>
> **Points**–fees you pay to the lender or broker for your loan. Points are linked to interest: the lower your interest rate, the more points you will pay.

All about Mortgages

You can apply for a mortgage from a bank, a savings and loan, a credit union or a mortgage company. Each lending institution will offer its own terms for a loan and will offer fluctuating interest rates. The most efficient way to shop for a mortgage—and the surest way to get the best terms—is to work with mortgage brokers. Brokers are independent agents who make money off finding a lender for a buyer. They will look at dozens of lenders to find you the right deal. If you have bad credit, a mortgage broker may be able to find a lender who will accept you.

> ## Pre-Approval
>
> If you took the advice in Chapter 3 and got pre-approved for a mortgage, then you will already know at least one lender who will give you a mortgage—assuming the property you decide on is selling for the amount of the loan for which you are pre-approved.

Try to get your real estate agent or another trusted source to recommend a broker—but try to find two or three. That way you are guaranteed to find the best deal for you. You can find a mortgage broker in your local Yellow Pages or through an online search. (Many of the mortgage finder sites belong to mortgage brokers.)

"When you are getting a mortgage, everything depends on the bank. Smaller, local banks can be more flexible while large national banks have more rules and red tape and it is harder to get to the right person to ask for a loan. That is why mortgage brokers have become so popular—it is easier for buyers to work through them and find a good option."

—Delia Peterson, Owner, Mortgage 1 Network, Chicago, Illinois

Once a broker finds a good mortgage for you—with a low interest rate and no or few points, start negotiating. Nothing is set in stone, so ask the broker if that interest rate is the lowest it can be. Ask to cut any points proposed. Select more than one possible lender from the choices your brokers bring you and play them against each other: "ABC Bank is offering me 5.75 percent interest with no points. Can you do better than that?" Use your good credit history, longevity at your job or sizeable assets as leverage in negotiating—whatever your strongest selling point is.

What Is the Best Deal?

Shop around for the best loan you can get. If you are buying property in a not-so-great neighborhood but it is considered an up-and-coming area, you should be able to get a better mortgage, such as an interest-only loan. Study your options, then work with your lender to see what they can do for you.

How Much Will It Really Cost?

Keep in mind when you are estimating your costs of purchasing new property that you will pay a number of additional fees in closing costs. These may include:

- points
- credit report fee
- survey fee
- escrow account deposits
- recording fee
- property taxes (paid in advance)
- mortgage insurance application fee
- lender fees
- appraisal report
- pest inspection
- lender's title insurance
- transfer tax
- mortgage insurance premium

Once you have selected a lender, ask for a good faith estimate of closing costs on the property you are buying. This will give you some idea of how much you will need to pay at the time of your closing. You will be expected to hand over a check at the meeting, so have the money ready.

> **Note**
>
> Some of these fees can be negotiated down, including points, cost of appraisal and legal fees, so try to bring the total cost down by negotiating with your lender.

Every lender will have a different configuration of fees and may set their fees differently.

Residential vs. Commercial Mortgages

If you buy property that contains four units or less, you will get a residential mortgage. The process and requirements are virtually identical to buying a home for yourself.

If you purchase a multi-unit building with five or more units, you will get a commercial mortgage. Commercial mortgages require a higher down payment—typically 25 or 30 percent because these investments represent higher risk to the lender. They will take longer to process and require more paperwork. Your lender will want to examine the rental income and other financial factors to ensure that your rental income will be sufficient to cover the mortgage and all other operating expenses. They are essentially giving you a business loan, and they will want to make sure your business is profitable.

➡ > **Real-Life Experience**
>
> "The guidelines of a bank are totally different for commercial property. We need to find out the amount of rent coming in, the number of vacancies, plus the down payment you can afford."
>
> –Liz Acevedo, Loan Officer, American Banc Financial, Chicago, Illinois

Unlike residential mortgages, there is no regulatory body for commercial mortgages. The rules for residential mortgages do not apply, including laws against discrimination. That means every bank can say yes or no to a loan based on their comfort level. If you go to your local bank where they know you, they can be swayed to give you a loan.

"When you re-finance a commercial property (five units or more), you might have to re-finance your entire loan amount. If this is the case, you have to make sure your original loan does not carry a pre-payment penalty. Another option for financing is to get a line of credit based on the property as your collateral."

–Peterson quote

> **Ready to Refinance?**
>
> When you refinance—that is, pay off your remaining loan with a new one, you will have to pay some of the closing costs listed above.

FHA Loans

Getting a Federal Housing Authority (FHA) loan is a great way to avoid a large down payment, or a great way to get a loan if you have bad credit. With an FHA loan, you can put as little as three percent down. These loans are standard mortgages, but your loan is guaranteed by the federal government. You apply for an FHA loan through a bank or lending institution, and you will need to provide a lot of information, including:

- Two years' employment history in a related field, verified by your employer.
- Two years of income statements, including W-2 forms and/or income tax returns.
- A complete financial statement including your debt, bills and other obligations, and a list of liabilities and assets.
- A credit report.
- A professional appraisal of the property you want to buy.
- Photocopies of your driver's license and Social Security card.

The lending institution will perform a thorough check of your credit and income. While FHA guidelines for acceptable credit are more relaxed, they look at your income closely to ensure that your monthly housing costs do not exceed 29 percent of your gross monthly income.

As you might guess, processing your request for an FHA loan can take a long time—typically 90 to 120 days. If you plan to finance the purchase of your rental property this way, let the seller know that the process may take longer.

Seller Financing

You may be lucky enough to purchase a property and work out a legal agreement with the seller to pay them directly. In a Contract for Deed or Land Contract Sale, you negotiate payment terms directly with the seller, including the size of the down payment, which can be considerably less than you would pay if you went through a lending institution. You would then pay an agreed-upon amount each month at an agreed-upon interest rate. You win because you get better payment terms than you would through a bank, and the seller continues to receive regular monthly income as they did when they rented the property directly.

To find a seller who is open to this type of agreement, check with real estate agents or other landlords, or watch for newspaper ads and signs that advertise Contract for Deed, Agreement for Sale or Installment Contract.

When you find a possible Contract for Deed option, find out why the seller is willing to finance the deal. Viable reasons include older owners who want to retain a regular monthly income from the property, or those owners who bought the property on a similar deal and want to get out with a profit.

Advantages of Buying Direct

Purchasing real estate through a Contract for Deed agreement has several benefits over more traditional financing:

- You can negotiate a smaller down payment—and conceivably no down payment—with the seller than you would with a bank.

- Interest is also negotiable, depending on the price, down payment and length of the contract.

- There are no points or additional closing costs.

- The transaction can be a lot quicker than going through a bank or other lender.

When negotiating the terms of a seller-financed transaction, always have a lawyer represent you. You should also check out the seller by getting their credit report (get their permission first). Finally, make sure you get all deeds and titles to the property.

Free and Clear of Mortgages

Make sure the seller does not still have a mortgage on the property. If they stop paying that mortgage, the bank would foreclose and the bank would own the property—not you. And if their lender finds out that they are selling the building, they may call the loan and ask for payment in full to avoid risk.

Real-Life Experience

"Seller financing, or land contracts, are legal, but the bank that holds the seller's mortgage will not like it. If the bank finds out that the mortgage holder has sold the building, they may ask for payment of the entire loan. This type of arrangement is very risky."

–Liz Acevedo, Loan Officer, American Banc Financial, Chicago, Illinois

Keep on Buying

Once you have acquired the perfect rental property and have been a prospering landlord for a few years, you can start to grow your business. The best part about owning property is that you can cash out some of the equity in your first rental property by re-financing or taking out a home equity loan and use that cash as a down payment on another property. The more equity you build, the less money you will need out-of-pocket to buy another rental property—or, if you prefer, to fix up the property you already have. If you do not want to add rental units, you can continue to upgrade and raise your rents accordingly. Either way, you will make more money as time goes on because you have invested wisely in your initial rental property.

5 Improving & Converting Property to Rental Units

The best way to ensure that you make money on your landlording venture is to get a great price on the rental property. And the best way to do that is to find a property that is priced low because it is neglected or needs some work.

Buying a fixer-upper or handyman's special is a good investment for several reasons:

- With minimum work, you can quickly and easily increase the value of the property for resale.
- You can charge higher rents for a property that has been spruced up.
- Any expense you put into the property will be tax-deductible either the same year or when you sell.

The key, mentioned in the previous chapters, is to find a low-priced property in a good neighborhood. That way your investment is more secure, since you can fix up a run-down property in a desirable neighborhood and be sure to rent it. Fixing up a property in a bad neighborhood, on the other hand, may not pay off. For example, the neighborhood may be in a market for lower rents, or you may have trouble just finding tenants looking to rent.

How to Scout a Handyman's Special

When you are shopping for a run-down rental property, look at what needs to be done to improve it. You want a property that needs general cleanup or moderate maintenance—not an expensive and time-consuming gut re-hab. You want a place you can rent as soon as possible, after or during your improvement work.

You will need to be able to diagnose what needs to be done to improve a property. You will also need to be able to estimate how much time and materials will be needed for each task, so you can calculate how much money you will need to sink into fixing up the property.

If you do not have the skill set to do this yourself, enlist the help of a knowledgeable friend. It may even be worthwhile to hire an independent contractor or handyman who can either come along on a walk-through, or look at photos and draw up an estimate for you. Then you can decide if the purchase price seems fair, knowing how much additional money you will put into fixing up the property right away.

What to Look for	What to Avoid
Peeling paint	Structural problems
Gutters need replacing	Roof needs replacing
Badly stained carpet	Floors need replacing
Neglected but occupied	Abandoned for more than 1 year
Needs decent window coverings	Needs all windows replaced
Minor plumbing repairs needed	New pipes needed throughout

If you have the skills to do some or all of the work yourself, you will definitely come out ahead. The type of fixing up we are talking about here does not require a lot of expertise—just basic handyman skills and some time and effort. Hiring out for painters, cleaners, minor carpentry and plumbing can really add up and greatly extend costs. But if your schedule and skills prohibit you from taking on the work, you do not have much choice. Get estimates on each job before you pay for any services so you can make sure to budget for what needs to be done.

The type of fixing up you are looking for could include tasks like:

- Thoroughly clean the exterior. This includes mowing the lawn, pruning bushes and trees and weeding any garden(s). It may also include painting or putting up vinyl siding.

- Clean the interior, including common areas like hallways and the basement. Rent a dumpster if necessary and get rid of all unclaimed clutter.

- Tear out old carpeting and draperies if necessary.

- Paint the interior and put up inexpensive mini-blinds or window shades.

- Install strong, secure locks on exterior doors and windows.

- Add insulation to save on heating costs.

- Install or replace washing machine and dryer for communal use.

- Upgrade apartments in multi-unit building on an ongoing basis. This can include painting, sanding floors, and upgrading the kitchen and bath.

If you have to replace appliances, fixtures or other components of a rental property, buy those that are inexpensive but sturdy. You do not need top-of-the-line kitchen counters in a rental, but you want those that look nice and are durable.

When you decide to purchase the property, put together a plan, including a rough budget and timeline, for the work that needs to be done and prioritize the tasks.

If the property is empty when you buy it, you need to figure out how fast you can get a paying tenant in. If it is already occupied by tenants, you have to figure out how much work you can do in their homes without totally disrupting their lives.

How Much Is Too Much?
Keep an eye on the real estate market. Do not sink so much money into fixing it up that you cannot recoup your expenses when you sell.

Finding a Fixer-Upper

It may be tough to find the perfect bargain property. Most sellers will fix up a place before they put it on the market—but there are situations where they cannot afford to make the necessary improvements and that is when you will find your opportunity.

The best way to find a fixer-upper is to spread the word that you are looking for one. Use your network of family, friends and acquaintances. Let everyone know the exact type of property you want.

Be sure to tell your real estate agent what you are looking for. And even if you are not a landlord yet, you can join a local landlord's association and network that way. Other members may know of a property that can use some sprucing up. One of them may even own such a property.

You can also check the classified ads under Property for Sale. Some ads will specify that a building is a handyman's special, or they might use other language that will tip you off. Check any prices listed for properties that seem unusually cheap for the area.

You can also drive or walk around the neighborhoods you are interested in buying in. Look for For Sale signs in yards, or checkout the state/condition of each property. If you see one that fits the description of a fixer-upper, you may want to knock on the door or call the number of the management company and ask if they are interested in selling.

Buying a Fixer-Upper

Do not be put off if the asking price for the property does not reflect its neglected condition. After a thorough inspection of the place, put in a low bid and point out the many faults with the property, mentioning how much it will cost to fix each one. The seller may know they have a diamond in the rough, but more likely they will come down in price.

Regardless of the state/condition of the property, you will still go through the usual steps when buying it. Do not get so carried away by the bargain price that you forget to have it inspected, or do not ask for the tenant records from the owner. In fact, an inspection is most important in this case, because you want to make sure the property's problems are only cosmetic or minor. A neglected property may have deeper problems that are too expensive to make it a good investment.

Converting Nonrental Property

What if you want to convert your own home into a rental property? Maybe you are moving and have calculated that you can make more money by renting out your old place than you could if you sold it outright; maybe you want to hang on to your first condo in case you want to move back someday; or maybe your kids have moved out and you want to turn your second floor into a separate apartment. Whatever the reason, first you have to make sure it is legal. Here are the steps you should take:

1. Check with your city council or local zoning department to find out if your property is zoned or can be rezoned as rental property.

2. If you want to transform a single-family home into a duplex, or otherwise add a residence to an existing property, check the zoning on this specifically.

3. Do not cut corners! Follow your local law on zoning—particularly regarding multi-unit dwellings—and on building permits, if applicable.

Once you have determined that you can turn your residence into a rental, take a close look at the property and make sure it is rentable. Ask yourself these questions:

- Does my home need a lot of upgrading and maintenance to be attractive to potential renters? Is that work cost-prohibitive?

- Is my home in a location that is appealing to renters?

- Will my condo or co-op association allow me to rent out my unit? Is my property zoned for rentals or for a multi-family dwelling?

- Does my home have a swimming pool or spa that would be a huge liability issue with renters?

- Can I bear the thought of strangers living in my home and potentially not taking good care of it?

If you decide that your home is rentable, you need to make it safe and attractive to tenants who will live there. Safe means:

- You follow your local and state laws regarding number and placement of smoke detectors and carbon monoxide detectors.

- You provide one or more fire extinguishers that stay on the property.

- You ensure the electrical system uses Ground Fault Interrupter (GFI) circuits.

- You install secure locks on all exterior doors and windows.

- You check the security of stairs and railings and reinforce or replace each as necessary.

Attractive to tenants means:

- You clean and spruce up the exterior of the property.

- You paint the interior and clean or replace carpeting.

- You clean the entire home, paying particular attention to the kitchen and bathrooms.

There are three things you need to do right away when you have tenants about to move in:

1. Change your insurance policy on the home to a landlord's policy. (See Chapter 7.) If you do not do this, you may not be covered for any damage to the property.

2. Strongly advise or require that your tenants provide proof of renter's insurance before they move in. (A Renter's insurance Referral form can be found on the Web landing page www.socrates.com/books/landlording-handbook.aspx.)

3. Have the tenants change the utilities over to their own names. You do not want to pay for their electricity, phone or heat.

If you are turning your single-family home into a duplex, consider whether you want to convert your single gas and/or electric meter into separate meters. It is possible to have direct-vent heaters installed in newly converted apartments with individual meters. Talk to your utility company about the cost of doing this, and then calculate if you would recoup those costs within 3 years. Is it more expensive to pay your tenant's bills?

Money Matters

Owners of new rental properties must walk a fine line when getting a property ready for their tenants. You want to make the property as attractive as possible, while at the same time raising the value enough to charge rents that are as high as the market will bear. On the other hand, you want to spend as little money as possible doing this. You may be tempted to cut corners when making cosmetic improvements. Or, if you are a perfectionist, you may be tempted to buy the nicest fixtures and appliances you can afford.

The best advice on this is:

- Stick to your budget—do not scrimp too much and do not go over.
- Keep decorating simple—white paint is fine and so are plain fixtures. Your tenants will probably prefer this anyway.
- Buy products that will last for years, because it will save you time and money in the long run. Get warranties on everything!

The truth is, you will have to learn this as you go along. Common sense and the advice in this book should help you avoid a lot of the mistakes that new landlords make.

6

Taking over Tenants with a New Rental Property

If the property you are interested in is occupied by the owner's tenants that means more research on your part before you decide to buy. After all, you will take over as landlord to these people, and will be bound by the terms in their current rental agreement—including the amount of rent they pay.

> **Note**
>
> It is important to understand that when you purchase a property that is already occupied by tenants, their lease or rental agreement will stand until the date it expires. After that date you can implement your own lease, rules, policies and rent, but for the duration of the agreement, you must legally abide by the terms set by the previous landlord.

Pros and Cons of Inheriting Tenants

Are existing tenants a value-added bonus to buying the property? Or are they liabilities that you take on? It all depends on the people involved, the rent charged and other factors. Here is an overview of the pros and cons of taking on tenants with your new property.

Pros of Inheriting Tenants	Cons of Inheriting Tenants
You do not have to immediately search for tenants.	You did not screen or select these people, so you are stuck with them if they are problem tenants.
You collect and keep their rent as soon as you take ownership of the property.	The rent may not be as high as you would like or may not cover your costs.
You have some time to get used to being a landlord before you have to begin the process of finding your own tenants.	If a problem arises, you have to address it immediately, sticking to the policies and procedures outlined in the existing lease.
You can implement your own lease as soon as the existing agreement is over—and raise rents as necessary.	You may lose tenants who do not like the changes.

If the property you want is ideal, it should not matter whether or not you inherit tenants. It will definitely be a pro to get the building you want at a good price. That is worth having to cope with the tenants you inherit, no matter how many problems exist with the current lease or rents. And the longest you will have to put up with current conditions would be 12 months—and that is in the unlikely event that a tenant moved in while you were closing.

Before You Buy

You have decided that a particular rental property is your dream come true. In that situation, sometime between the time your offer is accepted and the time you officially close on the building, you need to gather as much information as you can on the tenants, the current rental agreement and how landlordship of the property will be turned over at closing.

Write a letter or e-mail to the seller letting them know what specific information you need before you close. (As you will see, they will need time to gather documents and have them ready for you, so give them as much advance notice as possible.) Set an appointment to sit down in person to ask any lingering questions or perhaps to get additional information. Ask for the following:

- Copies of all rental records for their current tenants. You can check these for the amount of rent paid, the length of the rental agreement and any past problems with late payments.
- An outline of which security deposits you will inherit, and an outline of last month's rent or other deposits the landlord is holding for current tenants.
- A list of everything to be included in the sale: appliances, lawn maintenance equipment, window treatments, etc. You must know what your purchase price includes.
- Copies of all service contracts, licenses and warranties regarding the property and its contents.
- Tax statements for the property.

- Any current insurance policies regarding the property.
- Copies of the latest bill for each utility. This will help you estimate expenses and make it easier to switch the utilities to your name.

After reviewing all the documents, it is time to talk to the tenants. Ask the seller to let them know you will be calling, then try to reach each one by phone in the evening when they are likely to be home. Introduce yourself and ask if they have time to talk to you, and if they do not have time to talk then ask when would be a better time to contact them. You want to find out:

- If the information you received about their security deposit, last month's rent and other deposits is accurate. It would not hurt to review their lease terms as well.

- If they have any maintenance or repair issues that have not been addressed. You are going to inherit these and pay for them!

- What, if anything, they would change about their home or their agreement. Do not make any promises, but find out how you might entice them to stay when you implement your own lease.

Try to interview tenants in each unit of a multi-unit building. Note how willing they are to talk to you. It is not essential that you reach everyone, but you will want to know if you have a tenant who is uncooperative and then keep an eye on them once you take ownership.

When You Close

When you close on the deal, you officially become the owner of the property. By the time you walk out of that meeting, you should be in possession of the following:

- All keys to the property, including keys to tenants' units.

- A check for all security deposits the previous owner collected, with all interest to date.

- A check for all other deposits, including last months' rents.

- Any documentation mentioned above that you have not yet received: complete tenant records, tax statements for the property, insurance policies, service contracts, licenses and warranties.

If you do not get all this material from the seller at closing, it will be harder to get it from them later. They are under legal obligation to turn everything over, but you will have to chase them down in the midst of taking over your new property. It is easiest to make sure you receive everything in advance.

Once You Are the Landlord

As soon as you take ownership of the property, you become a landlord. You are now immediately responsible for those tenants. That means you had better be prepared—and have read every chapter in this book. On the day you close on the sale, you need to have your bank account or accounts set up to accept rent and security deposits, you need to be prepared for dealing with late payments or other tenant problems, and you need to be ready to respond to a call for an emergency repair. To state it another way, you are now open for business.

But let us assume you are ready for anything and everything, and can concentrate on assuming responsibility for the rental property and the tenants. Here are some steps to follow:

1. Before the closing, introduce yourself to all tenants with a letter announcing the change of ownership. Assure them that their current rental agreement and rent is applicable until the expiration date noted in the agreement. Include all your contact information (including emergency numbers) and details on how you want to collect rent. If you accept electronic transfers to your bank account, you can also provide the necessary paperwork for this.

2. Call each tenant and set up an appointment within the first weeks of ownership to come to his or her home and introduce yourself.

3. When you meet with tenants, keep in mind that they are probably anxious about having a new landlord (and eventually having their rent increased). Take some time to set the tone for a friendly but firm relationship.

4. Get their information. Provide a Tenant Information Form to fill out. (This form is provided on the Web landing page, www.socrates.com/books/landlording-handbook.aspx.)

5. Perform a walk-through of their home to check its condition or schedule a time to come back and do this. You may already have done this, but it is good to do it again with the tenant present. This gives you a much more complete idea of the true condition of the property.

6. Check to make sure the keys you received work in the locks. If not, arrange to get a copy of the tenant's keys. This is your legal right as a landlord.

Security Deposits and State Law

Your state law may require that you notify your new tenants that you now have possession of their security deposits. There are many state laws surrounding these deposits—make sure you become familiar with them as soon as you become a landlord.

When the Lease Expires

You will definitely want to implement your own lease or rental agreement as soon as possible. Not only does this allow you to set rents, but your agreement will also include your policies, such as allowance of pets, number of occupants, penalties for late payments and other terms you find essential to renting good property to good tenants.

If tenants are on a month-to-month agreement, you can replace this with your own lease or rental agreement with appropriate notice. Most states require only 30 days notice. It is best to give tenants in this situation a few months before you ask them to switch over to your agreement and rent. That is, of course, unless they are tenants you are anxious to get rid of.

➡ **Real-Life Experience**

"If you rent a duplex, always stagger your leases so your tenants do not move out at the same time."

–Catherine Brouwer, Founder, Blue River Properties, Memphis, Tennessee

Have your lease or rental agreement in order well before the date it will go into effect, and send a copy to your tenants as early as possible so they can study it. Give them a deadline for when they need to sign it and indicate that you do not need to start showing their home.

Know Thy Tenants!

Before you ask the tenants you inherited to sign your lease, make sure you have all their information. You did not screen or choose these people yourself, so get the following information now:

- number of tenants and their names, including any children or pets

- place(s) of employment

- emergency contact information

This information should be provided on the Tenant Information Form you gave to the tenants. Make sure you get the completed form from them.

Changing leases is a delicate matter; any number of factors may cause your good tenants to start looking for a new home when they see your lease. Keep in mind that some policies (besides rent) may be deal breakers for tenants.

Example

If your quiet, reliable, perfect renters own two dogs, they are likely to move if your lease spells out that no pets are allowed. It is best to take a hard look at the tenants you want to keep, and the policies that mean a lot to you, and see if you can be flexible on some matters.

You should be fair to all tenants and have everyone adhere to the same policies and rules. If you decide to waive the no pets clause for those good tenants, leave it out of each lease you send out.

When You Raise the Rent

The only time you can legally increase rent is when you implement a new lease or rental agreement. As mentioned above, you should give your tenants as much time as possible to consider a change in agreement and, especially, a change in rent.

Raising Rent on Month-to-Month Agreements
If tenants are on a month-to-month agreement and you find their rent is reasonable in the current market, leave it as is. You can ask for a cost-of-living increase on the anniversary of their last increase or your anniversary as their landlord.

Do not raise rents just because you can, or to cover your mortgage payments and other expenses. You should do some research to see what comparable properties in your area are renting for—Chapter 11 covers this in some detail. The rental market is self-regulating, and if your property is priced higher than comparable properties, you will not only lose your paying tenants, you will not be able to replace them until you lower your rents.

Once you have confirmed that the rents you are currently charging are too low and you have estimated what they should be, raise them as soon as possible. Let your tenants know why you are raising them or they will think you are being unfair. Of course, once they start looking for a new place to rent, they are likely to find that your new rental rates are comparable.

Ideally, you can make some inexpensive improvements to the property after you take ownership and before you raise rents. Painting an apartment, installing a ceiling fan or redecorating an entryway can go a long way towards justifying a rent increase to tenants.

If you have tenants you really want to keep and you are concerned that a rent increase may send them packing, consider offering them an incentive to stay and switch to your lease. If your good tenants get your lease in advance and let you know that they plan to start looking for a new place, ask them if they would stay if you made an improvement to their home. Check your notes from your initial meeting with them. What did they say they lacked—new carpeting? Better insulation? If there is something you can provide that is cost-effective (compared to advertising and showing the property and finding and screening new tenants), do it!

You Are on Your Way as a Landlord

As the new owner of a rental property and the new landlord of the tenants who live there, you are officially under way as a landlord. However you operate, there is a lot you need to know—so read on to learn the ins and outs of insurance and taxes.

Section  Three

Incorporation, Insurance & Taxes

7 Insuring Your Rental Property

Before your first tenant takes possession of your rental property, you need to beef up your insurance coverage. Even if you are renting one condominium, you will need to take out a new policy and switch from homeowner's to landlord's insurance or rental property insurance. A landlord's insurance policy provides the same coverage as homeowner's insurance—damages to the building and to personal property, plus liability coverage for lawsuits—but it also takes into account that the insured building or property is not occupied by the owner. (Of course, you will still insure the home you live in with homeowner's insurance.)

Not only does a landlord's insurance policy provide more coverage (and more appropriate coverage), if you retain a homeowner's policy on property you are renting, you may run into trouble when you file a claim regarding your rental property because you do not have the right type of insurance. Make sure you have proper insurance on all your rental properties—and make sure you have enough coverage on each.

How Much Will It Cost?

A landlord's insurance policy is considerably more expensive than a similar homeowner's policy, because it must take into account that tenants may not be as responsible with the property as the owner would be. If you live in a single-family home and decide to move and rent it out, your premium as a homeowner may double under a landlord's policy.

Of course, all insurance costs will depend on the size, age, type of building and the area in which it is located, along with other individual factors.

Insurance Glossary

Unfamiliar with insurance? Here are some important terms you will need to understand:

Premium–the annual or semi-annual payment you make to the insurance company for your coverage.

Deductible–the amount you must pay out of pocket before the insurance company begins paying for damage. Typically, the higher your deductible, the lower your premium.

Claim–a claim is filed with your insurance company when you officially notify them of damages you wish them to cover.

Insuring Your Property against Physical Damage

You want to insure your rental property against severe damages and loss, just as you insure your home. A basic insurance policy will cover damage from fire, smoke, wind and hail, lightening, explosions, vandalism, water damage from sprinkler systems or burst pipes, vehicle collision and riot or civil commotion. You can pay more for Special Form Coverage, which covers your rental property against all losses except for any that are specifically excluded.

Are Your Belongings Covered?

If you keep personal belongings on-site at your rental property—like tools, or a lawn mower and snow blower—make sure your landlord's policy covers these things as well as the property.

Also, your insurance may not cover the appliances in your rental—make sure you get a separate appliance policy, if necessary.

Depending on what part of the country you live in, you may also need to buy separate insurance against floods, earthquakes or hurricanes. The problem is that if you live on a flood plain, for example, flood insurance can be very expensive and hard to get. Get some quotes on this specialty insurance and decide if you can afford it.

One decision you will have to make when purchasing insurance is how you want to be reimbursed for damages. Your policy will specify either guaranteed replacement costs or cash value. The example below illustrates the differences between the two:

Your empty rental property was vandalized, and one of the things you need to replace is the front door, which was broken beyond repair. If your landlord's insurance specifies replacement cost, you can buy a similar door and be reimbursed for the full cost. If your insurance specifies cash value, you will be reimbursed for the value of the door, which includes any depreciation. If the door was 10 years old, you are going to receive a check for the value of a 10-year-old door—which is not enough to pay for a similar replacement.

Of course, as with all aspects of insurance, you will pay a higher premium to get the better coverage. In this case, the better coverage is replacement cost. Check your policy to make sure it specifies how you will be reimbursed. Standard Replacement Cost may include depreciation, so check with your insurance agent to verify how you will be paid on a claim.

Coverage on Older Buildings

If you own a rental property that is 20-25 years old or older, your insurance coverage may be limited to actual cost rather than replacement cost for the property. That means if your vintage three-flat burns to the ground, your insurance company would cover the value of the building rather than the replacement cost.

Loss of Rent

If your rental property is damaged so severely that it is uninhabitable, you cannot collect rent until it is rehabbed and repaired. That means you will suffer a loss of income in addition to the loss of property. Do not despair, there is insurance coverage for this as well. Some landlord's insurance policies automatically include loss of rent coverage; others require that you purchase it separately. Loss of rent coverage compensates you for the rent you cannot receive over a specified time period and up to a specified limit. Sometimes this limit varies with the policy, but often it is set by the company at 10 percent of your total insurance coverage on the rental property.

Example

Your landlord's insurance policy on the single-family home you rent would cover $500,000 in damages. That would cap your loss-or-rent insurance at $50,000.

Other Coverage

Consider supplementing your insurance coverage with these additional policies:

Other structure insurance covers garages or carports and any outbuildings on the property not covered by landlord's insurance.

Inflation guard insurance will automatically increase the value of your insurance each year. This ensures that your replacement costs stay current.

Demolition insurance covers the cost for demolition of a ruined building that is still left standing. This is not typically included in basic or extended insurance policies.

Code upgrade insurance covers the additional cost of bringing a new building up to code. This is not typically considered part of replacement cost.

Liability Insurance

Landlord's insurance should include full liability coverage. This type of coverage is extremely important, since it covers your legal costs if you are sued in a personal injury lawsuit. Landlords are especially vulnerable to these types of lawsuits, since tenants can ultimately blame them for anything that goes wrong on the property—from a loose step that causes a fall, to a faulty hot water heater that scalds someone in the shower, to a slippery sidewalk.

In addition to personal injury, your liability insurance should also cover claims of libel, slander, discrimination, invasion of privacy or unlawful eviction.

Note that liability covers legal costs only, not the money awarded to the injured party. But legal defense costs (generally attorney's fees) are often more expensive than the final award for damages.

Experts across the board encourage landlords to buy as much liability insurance as possible, to make sure they are covered for this type of lawsuit. Insurance companies generally cap landlord liability insurance at $500,000 for a single-family home; that means your insurance would pay $500,000 worth of legal costs towards lawsuits in a year. If you purchase insurance in an umbrella policy, you can triple that maximum amount to $1.5 million, and your premium will not be much higher than it would be for $500,000 worth of insurance.

Protect Your Assets

If you are concerned about getting hit up for a lot of damages in a lawsuit, you can protect your personal assets by creating a limited liability company (LLC) for your landlording business. In that case, your company is responsible for paying out judgment awards, not you. Your rental property, business bank accounts and other landlording assets would be on the line, but your own home, personal car, etc., would not.

Of course, incorporating takes time and money, and you would have to set up separate bank accounts and file taxes differently. If you are interested in incorporating, check out the Limited Liability Companies kit at www.socrates.com.

Cover Your Employees

If you hire full- or part-time help for your landlording business, such as a maintenance person, you must make sure they are also covered by your insurance. You will want the following types of insurance:

Workers' compensation: Protects you if an employee is injured on the job. Most states require that every employer carry this insurance.

Nonowned auto liability coverage: Protects you from liability associated with your employees when they are driving to and from work in their own vehicles and when they are driving on the job. This includes accidents and injuries to the driver and to others.

Fidelity bond: Protects you if a dishonest employee steals from you or from tenants. This insurance provides monetary reimbursement for the theft.

Encourage Tenants to Get Renter's Insurance

Your landlord's insurance does not cover the personal belongings of your tenants. It is up to each tenant to buy renter's insurance for this purpose. Many landlords actively encourage their tenants to get insurance, and some even require it. Here is why:

Say your tenant accidentally starts a kitchen fire that causes extensive damage to the kitchen. Your landlord's policy will pay for rebuilding the room and replacing the appliances. Your tenant, who does not have renter's insurance, has lost everything he or she owns that was in the kitchen. Out of desperation to replace his or her belongings, an attempt is made to sue you, claiming you are at fault for providing a faulty stove or unsafe conditions. If you had required that the tenant buy renter's insurance before moving in, the tenant's own insurance would pay to replace the belongings and the tenant would be less likely to sue.

The average renter's policy covers losses from fire and theft, as well as liability claims. So if a tenant's guest injures him or herself due to the tenant's negligence, the renter's insurance would again help protect you from claims.

A tenant can buy a renter's insurance policy that covers the value of his or her belongings. As you can imagine, this varies widely. A college student without much stuff can afford the low premium on a minor policy; while someone more established with more valuable furniture, clothing and other belongings would want a larger policy, and with it, a higher premium.

Choosing an Insurance Company

You probably already have an insurance company or perhaps more than one. If you are happy with the way they have treated you, and think their prices and coverage are competitive, you will probably stick with that company. But regardless of how you feel about your current insurer, when you are ready to start shopping around for your new landlord's insurance, you will want to check out several companies for prices, service and amount of coverage provided. Because there are no standard insurance packages or pricing, it may be difficult to compare companies.

One way is to check with an insurance broker or independent agent—preferably two—who will do the shopping around for you. They have contacts in the industry and know who offers what. They can find the perfect insurance package for you. But it is smart to do some research on your own. By talking to more than one broker, or contacting several insurance companies yourself, you can protect yourself from an unscrupulous broker who gets a kickback from an insurance company for steering unsuspecting landlords their way.

Another way to choose an insurance company is to check their rating. Several firms rate all insurance companies based on their financial stability. Note that this does not reflect their quality of service or customer satisfaction—it specifically tells you if a company is likely to meet all its financial obligations. One of the best-known rating firms is the A.M. Best Company, which provides a Best's Rating on any company at www.ambest.com for no charge.

Check out the insurance company you are interested in and make sure they have a Best's Rating of at least an "A."

Tips on Buying Insurance

When you are ready to buy your insurance, consider these tips:

- You should definitely buy all your insurance from one company, including life, homeowner's, auto, landlord's and anything else you carry. You will get the best price this way, as well as better service. This also helps ensure you are not carrying double coverage or running into problems with claims that might bounce back and forth between two companies—for example, you get in a car accident while on landlording business and your auto insurance carrier and your landlord insurance carrier disagree about who should provide coverage.

- Similar to health insurance, when getting landlord's insurance you will have to decide if you want a higher deductible for a lower cost. Signing up for a policy with a $3,000 deductible rather than a $1,000 deductible should significantly lower your premium—but that means if you need to replace that damaged front door mentioned earlier, you are likely to pay for the entire cost out of pocket. If you are carrying insurance primarily for protection against catastrophes (anything over $1,000), go with a high deductible. You may save money. But check at the end of the year and see how much you spent on insurance verses how much you spent out-of-pocket on damages and legal costs. You can always chance the deductible-premium balance when your next premium is due.

- Ask the insurance company about any savings you did get for insuring multiple properties. Make sure you get the best deal possible, whether you group all properties together and pay a single premium or insure each under a separate policy.

- Ask about discounts for having safety devices at your rental property. Most insurance companies offer discounts if you install things like central fire alarms, smoke detectors, carbon monoxide detectors and fire extinguishers.

- If the building was built in the past 8 years, you may be eligible for a new home discount.

How Much Is Enough?

You will want enough insurance to protect the value of your property and assets. Estimate how much equity you would lose if your building and everything in it were to burn to the ground. That is how much coverage you should have. But keep in mind that you will not be replacing the ground itself, so do not count the value of your land.

How to File a Claim

Your rental property is now adequately insured, and the unthinkable happens—there is a fire or your tenant falls down the basement stairs. What do you do? Follow these steps in filing a claim:

1. Make sure anyone who is injured receives appropriate medical attention.

2. Alert your insurance company. Call up your agent right away and let him or her know what happened. Carry his or her business card in your wallet or have his or her phone number programmed into your cell phone so you will be prepared if you are away from home.

3. If appropriate, call the police. A police report may be necessary in order for you to collect on some claims.

4. Sit down as soon as possible and document everything that happened. If the event was traumatic, you may start to forget or misremember what actually occurred, so it is important to write down the sequence of events as soon as you can.

5. Complete an accident report provided by your insurance company. Sometimes an agent will bring this in person, or it may be mailed or faxed to you.

6. Save copies of all documentation, including the notes you made after the incident. Save receipts for any repairs or purchases that your insurance may pay for.

7. Stay in contact with your insurance company. They may be slow to make a decision or otherwise contact you, so take responsibility for keeping communication open. Call your agent regularly to find out what is happening.

Final Note on Insurance

Finding the right balance of insurance coverage and costs can be very tricky. If you have an insurance agent you can trust, they can help you strike that balance. Otherwise, take a close look at your coverage, and check it each year when your next premium is due. Consider the following:

- Did the value of your property go up? Did it go down? If so, you should increase your coverage.

- Is your insurance company's coverage and price(s) still competitive with others in the market? If you are using a broker or independent agent, ask them to shop around for you.

- Are you meeting your deductible? If you are not using it, consider raising it and thus saving some money on your premium.

Like all aspects of landlording, your insurance should be examined regularly to make sure you made the right choices and that they are still the right choices.

8

Paying Your Taxes

The bad news about landlording is that all the income you make on rents is subject to federal and state income taxes. The good news is that renting property opens up new opportunities for some sizeable tax deductions.

If you are just starting out as a landlord, make sure to hire a good tax professional for at least the first year that you must declare taxes on your property—that way you are sure to stay legal, and you will reap the most rewards from deductions. After you have been in business a year or 2 (or 3), you can consider taking over the task of doing your own taxes, and using the previous year's forms as a template. But tax laws change, so make sure you have the latest version of tax software if you use a computer or that you are up-to-date on any new tax laws.

Income Tax Software

If you are going to do your own taxes, it is easiest to use computer software. That way, you do not have to chase down all the various forms you will need every year, and the software automatically fills in fields with the information you provide.

Leading software packages are TurboTax for the PC and MacInTax for the Macintosh. You can first purchase a software package new, then pay a fee every year to upgrade it rather than buying a whole new package.

Income Tax Basics

You must declare all your rental income for the year on your annual income taxes. Of course, you can also deduct expenses related to landlording to reduce the amount of taxes you pay, and this chapter will outline what deductions you can take.

If you are an individual landlord (as opposed to a corporation), you will declare all the money you have received during the course of the calendar year as that year's income. That means if a tenant pays his or her January 2007 rent early, that money counts towards your 2006 income tax.

If you agree to take goods and services in exchange for rent—for example, letting a tenant paint your rental house in lieu of 3 month's rent—you should include the value of that service on your income tax return.

Similarly, you can take any deductions during the year you pay the services. If you have repair work completed in December 2006, but the bill does not come until January 2007, you would note that deduction on your 2007 taxes.

Security Deposits Are Not Income

A security deposit is money given by a tenant for you to hold to pay for damages or extensive cleaning after they leave. Because you are legally holding the tenant's money in trust for him or her, the security deposit is not considered income and should not be included in your taxes.

However, if you keep part or all of a security deposit after the tenant moves out, that should be declared as income.

Keep careful track of security deposits verses rent—you do not want to pay taxes on deposits that are exempt.

Tax Deductions for Landlords

Simply put, tax deductions are expenses that you can subtract from the amount of income tax you pay, before you pay. Taking deductions on your taxes is like putting (or keeping) money in your pocket—but because it is money you do not have in your bank account, sometimes it is hard to realize the value of deductions. They do have a value: The higher the total deductions you can legally claim, the lower the amount of income tax you will end up paying.

Renting Your Vacation Home

If you purchased a beachfront condo, cottage or other vacation property with the intent of both enjoying it yourself and renting it out, you may be able to take rental deductions on it. How the IRS views this property depends on how often you rent it and how often you use it yourself. The more days you rent it out, the more likely you can treat it as a rental property. Of course, that includes paying income taxes on any rents you receive.

You can deduct 100 percent of the expenses you pay to manage and maintain all rental properties during the year. This is true even if the property is vacant for all or part of that time, as long as it is advertised as available. Possible tax deductions, as well as definitions of each, are included on the next page.

Deduction	Deduction Defined
Cleaning and maintenance	Salaries of employees or contractors hired to clean and maintain properties, and/or materials purchased for cleaning and maintaining. Includes yard maintenance.
Management fees	Money you pay to a property manager or property management company.
Professional fees	Fees you pay to your tax accountant, bookkeeper, attorney and other professionals hired to help your landlording business.
Pest control	Cost of exterminator service(s).
Supplies	Price of tools used to maintain rental property, landscaping supplies, cleaning supplies, etc.
Equipment	Machinery purchased for your rental property, including lawn mowers, snow blowers, etc.
Repairs	Bills for outside contractors hired to make repairs.
Advertising	Costs of advertising your rental property (fees for classified ads, materials for signs, even the cost of hiring someone to create a Web site for you).
Utilities	If you pay for utilities such as electricity and/or gas and water, you can deduct these expenses.
Assessments	If you rent a condominium, you can deduct your assessment payments—but not special assessments for improvements to the building.
Professional association dues and educational materials	Cost of membership for any landlord's associations you belong to; cost of books, magazine subscriptions, classes and other education on landlording.
Insurance premiums	Premiums paid for any insurance on your rental property.
Mortgage interest	Annual interest paid for mortgages on rental properties.
Property taxes	Any property taxes you pay on rental properties.
Home office expenses	Costs of having a home office; auto mileage on business travel.

As you can see, there are a lot of opportunities to find deductions and bring your income tax payment down. But do not go overboard and count more deductions than you should; all expenses you deduct must be ordinary, necessary and directly related to your landlording business. A tax accountant can help you steer clear of tax-related trouble in this area.

> **Note**
>
> You cannot deduct the value of your own work unless you are a professional contractor, painter, plumber, etc. If you are a landlord who is handy around the house, but not a professional contractor, you cannot deduct the value of the time and work you put into sanding the hardwood floors in your rental, although you can deduct the cost of renting the sander. You could also deduct the cost of hiring a professional to sand the floors.

Depreciable Items

Some big-ticket items can be counted as tax deductions, but must be spread out as a depreciation over more than 1 year. These expenses, such as installation of a new roof or patio, are written off in increments over a period of years, regardless of when you paid them. For residential rental property, these expenses are generally depreciated over a recovery period of 27.5 years using the straight-line method of depreciation.

Home Office Deductions

Deductions you can take for using a home office for landlording include:

- Home expenses: if your office is 10 percent of your home, you can deduct 10 percent of your mortgage, homeowner's insurance, electric and heating bills.

- Purchase of business machines such as computer, printer, copier and fax machine.

- Purchase of office furniture.

- Telephone expenses (including a cell phone dedicated to business use).

- Purchase of office supplies used for business purposes.

Deducting the Cost of a New Computer

If you buy a computer for your landlording business, you can claim the entire cost as a deduction for the year you buy it if the computer is used more than 50 percent of the time for business purposes. Or you can depreciate the cost over several years.

Use of Your Car

You can deduct some automobile expenses if you use your personal vehicle to travel to and from rental property, or for other landlord business, such as taking deposits to the bank or going to the hardware store for supplies. Other automobile deductions include:

- Mileage on business travel—deduct 36 cents per mile.

- Interest expense related to financing your vehicle, as well as depreciation—deduct an additional 15 cents per mile.

Keep a daily log of mileage covered for business travel and add this to your tax records at the end of the year.

Tax Records: What to Keep

For every deduction you take, you will need paper documentation. That means keeping an ongoing file or files for sales receipts, invoices for services performed, utility bills, bank statements and canceled checks.

Once you pay your income taxes, you can box up all this documentation and file it by year. The IRS requires that you keep these records for at least 3 years, because that is the period of time in which they can audit those taxes.

Consider which of your tax records may be needed when you sell the property (for instance, proof of repair), or for evidence in a lawsuit. Ultimately, it is best to keep all the documents for as long as possible, given the amount of space you might have for storage.

Keep your actual tax returns forever, both in hard copy format and on your computer, if applicable. These documents can be requested for a number of reasons, including proof of income if you are purchasing a new property, and proof that you paid your taxes 10 years ago.

Are You Passive or Active?

If you register a loss on your rental cash flow, whether from inability to rent a vacant property, or having so many deductions that they exceed your income, you should be concerned about your status as an active landlord.

When it comes to declaring a loss on rental properties, the IRS makes an important distinction between active activities and passive activities. If you can prove you actively participate in renting your property—meaning you make management decisions on setting rents, selecting tenants and improving the property—this will probably qualify as an active rather than a passive activity. (Active participation also requires that you own at least 10 percent of the property.) If you actively participate, you can deduct up to $250,000 of a rental loss. If you hire a property manager and do not make enough decisions to be seen as actively participating in your rental, you will have strict limits on how much of a loss you can deduct.

Rules on active activities are quite complex, and if you have a loss on rental property, you should hire a professional tax attorney to make sure you adhere to what the IRS dictates.

The Advantage of Depreciation

Taking depreciation on your rental property in your annual taxes is one of the most lucrative rewards of being a landlord. It amounts to an automatic—and sizeable—tax deduction every year you own rental property.

The IRS has deemed that all residential rental property depreciates over 27.5 years. This is true for every property, whether it actually depreciates in value or not. That translates into a 3.64 percent tax deduction on your rental property every year. (This is prorated for the first and last year you own it.) Basically, you are deducting a portion of the value of your rental property each year, resulting in a loss on paper that helps offset your tax payment.

> **Note**
>
> Nonresidential real estate depreciates over 39 years.

Example

You typically pay 28 percent income tax each year on the $150,000 condo you rent out. With depreciation over 27.5 years, you end up with a $1,527 tax deduction for depreciation every year. That is your annual tax payment (28 percent of $100,000) multiplied by the depreciation period of 27.5.

When you sell the rental property, you will pay income tax on the total depreciation you took while you owned it. This is called a depreciation recapture. You will pay a lower tax rate on that recapture—but you were not paying taxes on that depreciation money while you owned the building. Depreciation is basically an interest-free loan for the entire time you own a property.

Improvements vs. Repairs

Improvements to your rental property will be taxed differently than repairs. So what is the difference between the two? An improvement adds to the value of your property and must be depreciated over the life of the improvement. (See page 66.) Repairs, on the other hand, keep your property in good condition. Repairs can be deducted in the year they are paid for.

Here is an overview of what is considered an improvement and what is considered a repair:

Improvements	Repairs
Modernizing a kitchen	Replacing broken fixtures
Adding new siding	Repainting
Installing new windows	Replacing broken windows
Adding a new roof	Fixing a leak
Installing central air conditioning	Fixing an existing air conditioning system
Having the yard relandscaped	Seeding bare patches in lawn

Filing Your Rental Income Tax

Landlords should report their rental income and expenses on the IRS form "Schedule E" (Form 1040). If you provide significant services for your tenants' convenience, such as regular cleaning or maid service, you should report your rental income and expenses on "Schedule C" (Form 1040). You will also use ancillary forms to report expenses for home office, auto use and other factors. For more information on forms, along with several IRS publications that provide in-depth explanations of your tax requirements, visit the Web landing page www.socrates.com/books/landlording-handbook.aspx.

Capital Gains Tax

You will pay capital gains tax only when you sell your rental property for a profit. This tax is on the amount between your original purchase price and your selling price.

The IRS classifies capital gains and losses as long- or short-term, depending on how long you own the property. If you own it for more than 1 year, your capital gain or loss is long-term. If you own it for 1 year or less, your capital gain or loss is short-term. For more information on the tax rates, refer to IRS Publication 544, Sales and Other Dispositions of Assets.

If your capital losses exceed your capital gains, the difference is subtracted from other income on your tax return, up to an annual limit of $3,000 or $1,500 if you are married filing separately.

Property Taxes

It goes without saying that in addition to income tax, you will have to pay any state and/or local property taxes on your rental property. These taxes are typically based on the value of your property, and the value is determined when your community is assessed by the taxing entity (usually state or county). This will occur every few years. If you feel your property value has declined over time, contact your assessor's office and request a new appraisal; you may end up with lower property tax payments.

Property taxes are usually paid in two installments each year. If you neglect to pay your property taxes, a lien will be placed on your property and you may end up losing it.

Do Not Tax Yourself over Taxes

Depending on how many rental properties you own, what your cash flow is like, and how intricate your expenses become, handling your landlording taxes can be complicated. As mentioned earlier, you are best off if you hire a professional tax accountant with experience working with landlords to keep you legal and on track.

However, if you are not intimidated by the prospect of learning the latest tax laws and filling out your own tax forms—go for it! (But remember, this is not a good idea if this is your first time filing taxes as a rental property owner.) Your local landlord's association may be able to provide helpful resources. That, coupled with a reliable income tax software package, should make do-it-yourself taxes less taxing.

Section ■ Four

Paperwork:
Rents & Leases

9 Rental Agreements & Leases

Your lease or rental agreement is extremely important. It is a legal contract that binds your tenant (and you) to specifics including payment of rent, use of property and penalties for late payment and other problems. It is your protection against a lawsuit, and it will further protect you if you are hauled into court. It also contains your official policies and house rules, which protect your interests and your property.

You should put a lot of thought and care into your official lease, and continue to update and add to it as time goes on and you learn from your experience. Yes, you can start with a standard lease template like the one found on the Web landing page www.socrates.com/books/landlording-handbook.aspx but each lease may be tailored to a specific property. That means you can add a clause about lawn care on the lease you use for the single-family home you rent or add a stricter policy on noise for a multi-unit building.

> **Stay State Specific!**
>
> Your state and county laws—and even city laws—may dictate certain policies, rents and other major factors. Make sure you are using a lease template that is specific to your state and local laws. (Many state-specific leases are available on Socrates.com.) If in doubt, have attorney look over your final draft.

Types of Agreements

As the landlord, you can set up a rental agreement for any time frame you like. Typically, leases are for 1 year, but you can write a 6-month lease, a 9-month lease—whatever you prefer. Of course, prospective tenants might find such an agreement a bit unusual, but more importantly, really good tenants—the reliable, pay-on-time type—are most likely looking for a year commitment.

If you do not want to commit to a year, you can offer a month-to-month rental agreement. This type of agreement is as legally binding as a lease, but either party can get out of the contract with 30 days notice. If you rent to a new tenant with a month-to-month agreement starting May 1, they can tell you on August 1 that they are moving at the end of the month, and you will have to let them go and start looking for new tenants. Similarly, on August 1 you can tell them to get out at the end of August if you want to.

Some landlords prefer the flexibility of renting month-to-month, pointing out that if tenants want out of a yearlong lease they are likely to break it anyway with no repercussions—except the landlord's mad scramble to find new tenants. Also, a month-to-month agreement gives you more opportunity to increase rents, as opposed to a lease that will lock you into a monthly amount.

Others prefer the security of a yearlong lease, which is more conducive to long-term tenants. This translates into less time and effort spent on advertising and showing the property and screening and choosing tenants.

The choice is entirely up to you. Consider your options, and go with whichever method suits your personality. You can always change your mind down the road—as long as you stick to the time frame outlined in your existing agreement.

Lease-to-Buy Arrangements

If you are willing to sell a rental property, you can offer a lease-to-buy agreement (also known as an option to purchase), which allows a tenant to rent the property that they ultimately plan to buy. This type of arrangement would include a standard rental lease along with a separate legal document that offers the tenant the option of buying the rental property during a specific time frame—typically a year. The price of the property is listed in the contract, and if the tenant buys the property, you must sell at that price. However, the tenant can decide not to buy at any time with no penalty.

Here is an example:

> You are renting out the one-bedroom condominium you lived in before you got married. You are considering selling the property, so when you get a new tenant, you ask if he might be interested in purchasing the condo at the end of his lease. He agrees to the terms and the fact that he is not obligated to make the purchase. He then signs a standard 1-year lease, along with a lease-to-buy contract that states he has 1 year to purchase the condo at the fair market value of $100,000.
>
> The tenant pays rent, which includes a monthly nonrefundable fee—outlined clearly in the lease-to-buy contract—which will be applied towards his down payment on the condo if he takes the option to buy. If he does not take the option—because he cannot make the down payment or changes his mind—you get to keep all the monthly fees. If he paid a $200 monthly fee towards the down payment for a year and still cannot make the down payment, you keep the $2,400—that is 12 months of $200 fees. If he is still interested in buying, you can extend the option for another year if you want to.
>
> Warning: Do not extend the time frame on a lease-to-buy for too long; you may lock yourself into a price that ends up being below average home prices.

What a Rental Agreement Includes

Regardless of which type of rental agreement you decide to use, there are
~~~nts~~ it must include for your own legal protection. You will find a lease and
~~~ment~~ on the Web landing page, www.socrates.com/books/
~~~can~~ use as-is—assuming the one you
~~~~ or delete clauses to suit your purposes.
agreement, it should contain specific
~~ sections:

	Why You Need It
~~al f all ~~~~ldren)	Of course this ensures the lease is legally enforceable, but this section specifically identifies who can live on the property. Any additional occupants may be grounds for eviction.
~~t takes ~~~~ date he or ~~~~ occupancy, ~~~~ lease and ~~~~nant will use ~~~~ residential purposes only.	Ensures lease period, and prohibits tenants from running a business on your property—imagine liability issues if someone were to open a daycare center on your rental property.
Rent terms	Amount of monthly rent, when it is due, how it should be paid (check or credit card AND by mail or in person), who the check should be made out to, whether utilities are included in payment, definition of late payment and any charges or penalties associated with late payment; same for returned checks.	Clarifies payment issues and ensures you are covered legally on issues such as late payments.
Inclusions	Specify what is included in rent, such as any utilities, a parking space or garage and use of common facilities such as a swimming pool.	Anything not included in this section will be paid for separately and/or independently, such as coin-operated laundry on premises or off-site parking.
Alterations and painting	Any alterations the tenant wants to make to the property must be approved in advance by the landlord.	Prohibits major changes to your property without your approval.

Section	What It Is	Why You Need It
Responsibility for maintenance	Specify the tenant's responsibility for keeping the property in good condition.	This is the basis for collecting any security deposit to cover damage, undue wear and tear or extreme mess.
Responsibility for damage	Specify the tenant's responsibility for any damage to the property and any fees or penalties for damages.	Ensures that tenant is responsible, financially or otherwise, for repairing any damage he or she caused.
Insurance	State what is protected by the landlord's insurance policy and note that this does not include the tenant's personal belongings.	Lets tenant know that he or she is responsible for insuring his or her own belongings.
Notice of termination	Note that tenant must give notice of intent to vacate, though this does not release him or her from the terms of the lease.	Reinforces terms of lease.
Subletting	Specify that tenant cannot sublet the property without advance approval from the landlord.	Prohibits a tenant from turning over your property to an unapproved person.
Abandonment	If tenant leaves property without notice, the landlord can collect any rental money owed.	Reinforces terms of lease.
Attorney's and legal services fees	States that if any legal action is required between the tenant and the landlord, then the "winning party" can have the other pay all attorney fees and legal costs.	May help you recover any losses in eviction or other legal action. Of course, if you lose the case, you must pay the tenant's legal costs.
Renter's insurance	States that tenant is responsible for buying renter's insurance to cover personal belongings.	May protect you from liability suits or save you money on insurance if tenant files certain claims with own insurance company.
Disclosures	Signature/initial sentences that confirm tenant has read all disclosures.	Ensures you have shared lead paint disclosure, Megan's Law disclosure, etc. Can also be used if you use an addendum to the agreement that outlines all policies and house rules.
Signatures	All parties—every adult tenant and the landlord—must sign the lease.	Ensures that all parties are liable for breaking any terms of the lease. This is especially important if you rent to roommates.

Your lease—or an addendum to the lease—should also include your official policies or house rules. This ensures that the policies (such as number of pets and noise restrictions) are legally enforceable. Policies are covered in the following chapter, so be sure to examine that information before you finalize your lease.

> **Check Your Legality**
>
> If you deviate from the lease template you use, it is a good idea to run your final draft past an attorney to make sure your additions and changes would hold up in court. Also, check your state and local laws every year or so to make sure your agreement covers any new regulations.

Right of Entry

Your lease should include information on the landlord's right of entry. You have the right to enter the property, but only with certain conditions—and sometimes outlined by state law. Of course, you can enter in a case of emergency, such as if water is pouring through the ceiling of the apartment below, or the smoke detector is beeping and no one is home. Otherwise, you may enter as needed for repairs and maintenance, though you cannot come in just to check on your tenants.

Most state laws require that you provide advance notice to a tenant before entering—typically 24 hours. Your lease should state the terms of your right of entry, including the amount of advance notice you will give.

Rental Agreements and Leases

You will find the following forms on the Web landing page www.socrates.com/books/landlording-handbooks/aspx:

Residential Lease (Form LF310)

Monthly Rental Agreement (Form LF255)

Lease with Purchase Option (Form LF237)

Security Deposits—an Overview

When you sign up a new tenant, you should always collect a security deposit before he or she moves in. This deposit, typically equal to 1 to 2 month's rent, should be held until the tenant moves out. At that time, this money can be used for repairs and cleaning—otherwise it must be returned to the tenant.

In order to gain access to free forms, dictionaries, checklists and updates, readers must register their book purchase at Socrates.com. An eight digit Registration Code is provided on the enclosed CD. See page iv for further details.

Know Your State and Local Laws

When it comes to security deposits, every state has different laws, and even some cities and counties have unique laws. Your local landlord association should be able to familiarize you with applicable laws, or you can check with your state department of housing or real estate agent. Laws specific to security deposits may include:

• Maximum limit allowed on deposit.

• What type of bank account is used for deposit(s).

• Who keeps the interest generated by the account.

• How soon you have to return the deposit after tenant moves out.

Unlike the first and last month's rent, and any fees due at the time of move-in, the security deposit always belongs to the tenant, and should not be spent by the landlord. Even if your state law does not require it, it is a good idea to put all security deposits in a separate, interest-bearing bank account (such as a money market account). This way, you will not accidentally spend the money, plus this helps ensure that it is not counted as income on your taxes. The money will sit there, untouched and accumulating interest, for the duration of the tenant's occupancy. Even if the tenant causes damage to your property or misses a rent payment, the security deposit should not be used until after the tenant moves out.

Setting Up a Separate Account

It is easy to set up a new savings account or money market account specifically for security deposits. Even if you do not have business accounts, your bank can set up a new personal account for you. Talk to the customer service department at the bank where you hold accounts about how to begin.

Getting the Deposit

What is an appropriate amount to ask for when collecting a security deposit? If allowed by your state law, an amount close to 1 1/2 to 2 months rent on the same property is ideal. This ensures that if the tenant uses the deposit as a last month's rent—something that should be prohibited in your lease—you still have some funds left to cover any legal expenses. If you are required to ask for a deposit equaling no more than 1-month's rent, set the amount slightly below your rent. This helps to stop the security deposit as a last month's rent issue; if your tenant pays $700 a month and the security deposit is $675, he or she is less likely to equate the deposit as rent.

Assure your new tenant that you will return the security deposit in full, plus any interest, after he or she moves out. Review any reasons that you would keep all or part of the deposit. (These reasons are outlined below.) This should help soften the blow after turning over hundreds of dollars in addition to rent. Also, give him or her a separate receipt for the deposit money, which will help enforce the idea that you are just holding the money.

One last note: Make sure you have 100 percent of the required deposit before the tenant is allowed to move in—otherwise you may have to fight to get any money owed.

When You Can Keep the Deposit

State laws are very clear about security deposits, so be careful to examine—and document—why you are keeping part or all of any deposit. Here is an overview of the reasons you can and cannot spend a tenant's security deposit:

Security Deposits CAN Be Used for...	Security Deposits CANNOT Be Used for...
Repairing damage to property	Normal wear and tear on floors, walls, etc.
Cleaning a bad mess	Your own time cleaning the property
Missing items	

Note that normal wear and tear is subject to the opinion of a court. Use your best judgment; if a tenant has occupied your property for 5 years, patching nail holes in the walls, a new coat of paint and sanding floors should be expected and the security deposit should not be used.

If you do not return all of a tenant's security deposit, you must indicate how the money you kept was spent. Note that your own time and work is not legally covered in this instance.

Example

If a tenant leaves your property in shambles, you can clean it for free, or you can hire a cleaning service and take the fee out of the security deposit. In that case, you would present your former tenant with a copy of the bill for cleaning to show that part of the deposit went toward preparing his or her former home for the next tenant.

If you are planning to return part or all of the security deposit, hold onto the money for as long as you can under your state's laws. Check for any hidden problems with the property that may appear after your tenant has moved out. Only when you are sure there is no damage should you write a check for the deposit.

To Be Continued...

This chapter has covered some of the essential information and clauses to include in your rental agreement or lease. For complete details on policies you may or may not want to include, turn the page...

10 Pick & Choose Your Policies

Rental policies are your built-in protections. The right policies can manage the behavior of your tenants and ensure your property stays in good shape. Every landlord has their own policies and house rules and you should too.

As mentioned in the previous chapter, you should include any policies in or with your rental agreement to ensure that they are covered by the terms of your lease. This reinforces your tenants' understanding that all policies are official, no matter how minor they may seem; it also gives you more legal standing if you must penalize a tenant who breaks a policy.

Presenting Your Policies

You can include all policies in your lease or create an addendum to the lease. If you prefer the latter, make sure your lease includes a line indicating that the tenant has received and read the policy addendum, and have a space for them to sign or initial this statement.

Consider using an addendum if you have a lot of policies. This allows you to have a shorter rental agreement and should make it easier for tenants to review your policies.

However you decide to include your policies, you should keep them as short and as clear as possible when writing them. Sample policies are outlined below; you can tailor these to be specific to your property.

Various Policies

Consider the following list of policies. You can pick and choose the ones you want to include in your rental agreement—and you may want to have different policies for each property.

Pet Policy

Specify if you do not accept pets of any sort, or if you limit the number and/or type of pets you will allow tenants to keep on your property. Many landlords do not want pets because of the potential damage they can do to floors, carpets and stairs. You can include a policy that leaves the door open, so to speak, to pets, by requiring written permission. That way you can talk to a potential tenant about their pets—whether they are housebroken, declawed, etc.—before making a decision. You can also request a separate pet deposit to be used toward any damages.

> ### Example
>
> "Pets shall not be allowed without the prior written consent of the Lessor. At the time of signing this lease, Lessee shall pay to Lessor, in trust, a deposit of _____ dollars ($_____), to be held and disbursed for pet damages to the premises (if any) as provided by law."

Guest Policy

You should definitely include a policy concerning guests in order to limit the number of people living on your property to those who signed your lease. This type of policy limits the number of guests and the length of time they stay— typically no more than 2 weeks within a 12-month period. Guests who stay longer than the time limit may be considered additional occupants and must leave. Note that state law often dictates how many people may occupy property, and your tenant may be in violation of this.

> ### Example
>
> "Lessee shall not permit any persons, other than those listed on the lease and minor children that are born or adopted into the household during this tenancy, to reside on the premises for more than 14 days of every 12-month period without the prior written approval of Lessor."

Smoking Policy

You can legally require that your property—even a multi-unit building—be smoke-free. This does not mean you can discriminate against smokers when you decide whom to rent to, but you can require that they not smoke indoors. This can make your property more appealing to future tenants, as it will reduce smoke smells that can linger in carpets, draperies and even walls. It can also lower your insurance premiums because the risk of fire will be decreased.

> ### Example
>
> "Lessee agrees that no persons shall smoke cigarettes, cigars or pipes inside the premises."

Illegal Activity Policy

It is obvious that you do not want drug dealers, prostitutes and other criminals working out of your rental property. This can have a direct impact on the reputation of your building, yourself and even your neighborhood. As always, reports of any illegal activity should be handled immediately by the police, but it does not hurt to cover yourself by including a policy prohibiting illegal activity on your property.

> **Example**
>
> "Lessee agrees no resident or guest shall engage in any type of illegal activity on or near the premises. Lessee will not allow the premises to be used for, or to facilitate, illegal activity regardless of whether the individual engaging in such activity is a member of the household. Lessee shall not engage in acts of violence or threats of violence. Lessee agrees that any violation of this policy shall be cause for termination of tenancy."

Noise Policy

To give yourself some leverage when dealing with a noisy tenant, include a policy controlling noise and disturbances in your lease. This can be interpreted to cover everything from loud parties and arguments that lead to police visits, to blaring music or a TV turned up too loud. Repeated offenses can be grounds for eviction.

> **Example**
>
> "Lessee agrees to refrain from making loud noises and disturbances, to keep volume on music, radio and television low at all times so as not to disturb others around them."

Parking Policy

If you offer parking, whether included in your rental agreement or for an extra charge, consider spelling out what that does and does not include.

> **Example**
>
> "Any parking that may be provided is strictly self-park and is at the car owner's risk. Parking fees are for a license to park only. No bailment or bailee custody is intended. Lessor is not responsible for, nor does Lessor assume any liability for damages caused by fire, theft, casualty or any other cause whatsoever with respect to any car or its contents. Snow removal is the responsibility of the car owner. Any tenant who wishes to rent a parking space or garage must sign a Parking Space or Garage Rental Agreement."

Keys/Locks Policy

Keys and locks can become an issue of contention for tenants. A key and lock policy can specify how many sets of keys you will provide at move-in (one or two is sufficient), and that you will change locks between tenants. Tenants are not to change locks.

Another key issue is lockouts. If tenants lock themselves out, your policy should dictate when and how often you will let them back in. It is best to encourage tenants to handle this themselves rather than call you at any hour for lockout service.

> ### Examples
>
> "Keys: Lessee will be given ___ set(s) of key(s) to the premises. If all keys are not returned to the Lessor following termination of lease, Lessee will be charged _____ dollars ($_____)."
>
> "Locks: Lessee agrees not to change locks on any door or mailbox without first obtaining Lessor's written permission. Having obtained written permission, Lessee agrees to pay for changing the locks and to provide Lessor with one duplicate key per lock."
>
> "Lockout: If Lessee becomes locked out of the premises after management's regular stated business hours, Lessee will be required to secure a private locksmith to regain entry at Lessee's sole expense."

Water Bed Policy

If you are concerned about damage to your property from water beds, include a policy prohibiting them. Consider that water beds are very heavy and may increase the strain on your floors; and that if one were to leak it could cause major water damage.

> ### Example
>
> "Lessee agrees not to keep any liquid-filled furniture on the premises without first obtaining Lessor's written permission."

Display of Signs Policy

You want to retain the right to advertise for your next tenant when the time comes. To ensure that your current tenant understands this right, include a policy that states you can and will post signs on the rental property.

> ### Example
>
> "During the last _____ days of this lease, Lessor or his agent shall have the privilege of displaying the usual "For Sale" or "For Rent" or "Vacancy" signs on the demised premises and of showing the property to prospective purchasers or tenants."

House Rules

You can add any policy you like to your rental agreement, as long as it is legal. Consider naming your more minor policies House Rules—which would cover your policies on such topics and responsibilities as garbage removal, regular mail collection or specified window coverings.

How to Enforce Your Policies

While you do not necessarily need all these policies in writing to legally evict a tenant, it will help you when dealing with that tenant. When someone violates a policy—for example, you enter the property to handle a repair and you find the tenant or tenant's guest smoking like a chimney in your designated smoke-free apartment—you can issue them a written reprimand or warning specifying the no-smoking policy that they reviewed and signed when they entered into the rental agreement.

In the above example you probably do not want to evict the person for smoking, and it is likely that a court will not let you. But if the problem persists, you can refuse to renew their lease—or give them 30 days' notice if they are on a month-to-month agreement.

> **Real-Life Experience**
>
> "If I notice an additional occupant, like a live-in girlfriend, I will tell my signed tenant to get that person's name and ID for me, or I will start eviction proceedings."
>
> –Tamera Brake, Independent Landlord, Elkhart, Indiana

No matter what the offense, your first step should be to send a written notice to the tenant, specifying which policy they have violated and providing as many details as possible. (Keep a copy of this and all future communications in case you need to prove justifiable cause of an eviction or nonrenewal.) Let them know the consequences of the violation, which is generally eviction if they continue. Repeated or continuing violations—like a tenant has one dog too many, continues to throw loud parties, or changes the lock on their door and refuses to give you a key—can justify eviction.

If the violation continues or is repeated, send a second, firmer, written notice. If applicable, cite any local or state law that they have broken. Let the tenant know that if the violation is reported again, they will receive a "Notice to Cure or Quit" that will give them a specific time in which to rectify the problem—get rid of the dog, stop hosting parties or give you a key—after which time you will start eviction proceedings. An example of this notice can be found on the Web landing page, www.socrates.com/books/landlording-handbooks/aspx.

For more on evictions, including alternatives for getting tenants to leave and legal steps to follow, read Chapter 17.

Review Your Rental Agreement and Policies

Remember to check your lease or rental agreement over from time to time—especially if you run into problems with a current tenant. See if there are additional policies you should include that might prevent such problems, or stop them from recurring with future tenants. Your lease is a living document that should be updated regularly, both to keep it current with state and local laws and to encompass everything you learn as you go about being a good landlord.

11 Rent

One of the most important decisions you will make as a new landlord is how much rent to charge for your property. If you have bought an existing rental property, this decision will not be required until a tenant's lease is up, but if you are starting from scratch, you need to set a figure before you can advertise and fill your first vacancy.

This Rent Is Too High...

The problem with setting your monthly rent too high is that you can end up increasing the length of time your rental property is vacant—and that can add up to a substantial loss of funds—more than if you were to charge and get a lower rent.

This Rent Is Too Low...

The problem with setting your rent too low is that while you are likely to get a tenant right away, you will basically lose money every month. If your rent is $50 lower than comparable properties on the market, that is $600 a year that you could have put in your bank account. Think how far that money would go towards your landlording costs!

Calculating How Much Rent to Charge

You may feel that you can set the rent at the amount you want, but rent, like most things, is driven by the market. Of course, it is always good to know how much money you are going to make—or lose—but ultimately, the amount of rent you charge will have to adhere to supply and demand. Here are the steps you should take in determining rent:

1. Tally Up All Your Landlording Expenses

This includes your mortgage payment on the property, insurance, utilities, cost of hiring an accountant and/or property management help, plus maintenance and repairs, along with any office expenses you have. Estimate a year's worth of these expenses or base this off of last year's income tax papers.

Divide your annual expenses by 12 to find out how much rent you will need each month to break even. Of course, your rent should be higher than this so that you make a profit—but do not use this figure to set your rent, simply use it as a point of reference to see how successful you will be.

2. Check Your Local Rental Market

What are other landlords charging for comparable properties? The easiest way to research this is to read through your local classified ads for rentals, or to drive around your town or neighborhood looking for For Rent signs and check the prices. Make sure the property you are checking is similar to your own. Not all three-bedroom houses are alike. Note the neighborhood or school district, number of rooms, amenities, etc. to find those closest to what you offer. You may want to call the phone number on the sign or in the ad and speak with the landlord and even go see the property. If this is the case, be honest about your status as a rental owner—and be sure to return the favor some day.

You can also check with your local landlord's association to see if information on comparable rents is available, or to talk to other landlords about their rents. If a similar apartment seems to be priced too high, ask how long it has been on the market.

Remember, you are looking at the rents charged for property that is currently vacant and for rent, not occupied property. There may be a difference between the two, and you are targeting the competition—meaning the apartments or houses that your prospective tenants are comparing with yours.

> ### Real-Life Experience
>
> "Because I am not in town to take care of things, I make the rent a little cheaper because the tenants will have to take a little more responsibility."
>
> –Paul Lorenz, Long-Distance Landlord, Paducah, Kentucky

3. Estimate Your Own Rent

Once you have an idea of how much comparable properties in your area are renting for, price your own rental accordingly. When in doubt, set your rent at the higher end of the scale and see if you get any takers. You will hear comments from prospective tenants if they think your rent is unfair, and if you do not get any nibbles in a week or so, lower the price. Do not negotiate with anyone over your advertised rent—you might be seen as wishy-washy and open to negotiation on everything.

> ### Do-It-Yourself
>
> Even if you end up hiring a property management company to handle your rentals, you should go through these steps. You became a landlord for the additional income, and you will want to make sure you are getting the appropriate amount of rent each month.

Increasing the Value of Your Rental

There are ways to get more rent out of a tight market—or any market for that matter. If you increase the value of your rental property, you can justify charging a higher monthly rent, and you are more likely to get it, too. Here are some ways you can boost the value of the property:

- include parking
- install a washer and/or dryer, or make them available in a multi-unit building
- install infrastructure for cable, satellite TV and/or DSL Internet service
- install a security system
- install air conditioner(s)
- redecorate: sand floors or add new carpet
- add a hot tub, swimming pool or a deck
- allow pets

Some of these steps are quite expensive; it is up to you to determine if the costs of improving your property can justify the increased rents.

Methods of Collecting Rent

There are several ways that you can collect each month's rent from your tenants. You can offer several options if you like, but no matter how you decide to handle this, make sure you tell all new tenants—and put it in writing—how and when you expect their rent. Also, be sure to let them know what name they should make their checks out to.

Your collection options include:

Ask tenants to mail you a check	This is the most common and easiest way to collect rent. You may need to allow an extra day or two for slow mail delivery, but otherwise it should be foolproof.
Ask tenants to drop off their check at your home or office	If you live near your rental property, tenants may like this option—plus, there is no room for the check is in the mail excuse. Make sure you have a secure mailbox or place where they can leave checks if you are not in.
Collect the rent in person each month	Coming to the tenants' homes for the rent is not very common any more. Use this only if you have a tenant with poor payment habits. Bonus: This gives you an excuse to check out the state of your rental property.

Electronic transfer from their bank account to yours	With a signed authorization form from your tenant, you can set up a system where the rent money is automatically transferred from their bank account to yours on the due date each month. This is ideal for both parties—no lag time, no postage, and no late payments—as long as the tenant has enough funds in their account.
Credit card payment	You must set yourself up as a merchant in order to accept credit card payments, and you will be charged a small percentage (one to two percent) of every transaction, but if you have tenants who have trouble paying their rent on time, this may provide a solution.

Rent Receipts

As part of your record keeping and insurance against losing a future lawsuit, give receipts for rent. You can handwrite them from a receipt book (available at office supply stores), or print out a standard form from your computer. If you are collecting the rent in person, hand the receipt over immediately; otherwise you can mail it. This is a good opportunity to communicate with your tenants. Include any information they might need, like upcoming repairs or even neighborhood news like a street cleaning schedule.

> ### One Rent, One Check
>
> If you rent to roommates, they may assume they should each write you a check for their portion of the rent. It is best if you require a single check each month and let them work out the timing and details. That way you are reinforcing the idea that all roommates are responsible for the complete payment and avoid thinking like, "I paid my half—if Brian cannot cover his, that is not my problem."
>
> If the roommates cannot get you one check on time—say, the supplementary checks cannot clear in time—then request that the multiple checks be mailed or turned over in the same envelope. And if you run into problems with late or partial payments, address them with all the roommates rather than singling out the one deadbeat.

Setting and Enforcing Due Dates

No matter when the lease is signed or when the tenant moves in, it is best to require that rent be paid in advance on the first of each month. That means that September's rent is due September 1. Why the first?

- It is very common and tenants should be used to this schedule.

- It is easy to remember.

- If you have multiple rental properties, all rents will come in at the same time, making it easy to keep track of any late payments.

- It should coincide with your mortgage payment.

If the tenant moves in mid-month, you can charge them prorated rent, or 1/30 of their monthly rent for each day until the next month begins.

Be Flexible

If you have a tenant who gets paid on the first of every month and requests extra time for his or her paycheck to clear, consider moving the due date. By offering to change his or her deadline, you will increase the likelihood of being paid on time. You can still keep your late fee structure—just change the dates on the lease to reflect the new date.

When is the rent late? Typically, rent is considered late 10 days after the due date. This is a fair amount of time; no mail delivery, lack of stamps, illness or travel can excuse a check that is 10 days late. Some states require mandatory grace periods, so check with your local landlords association or state department of housing. Note that rent paid within this grace period is still late, and tenants who consistently pay after the first of the month, but within the grace period, can be reported to credit agencies as late payers.

Your lease or rental agreement should include a clause on late payments. This allows you to legally fine any tenant who is officially late with the rent. But the clause must define "late," and must specify the fine. These factors are yours to determine—again, keeping in mind that your state law may limit either.

As for the fine, there are several ways to structure this. Typical late fees are $20 or $25, sometimes higher, or four to six percent of the monthly rent. That should be enough to provide an incentive for the tenant to pay on time. But another way to set late fees is to charge a daily fee so that the tenant has to pay, say, $5 each day until the check is received. This provides the biggest incentive to pay rent if not on time, then as soon as possible.

Example

Your tenant blew all her rent money on a ski trip, and has to wait for her next paycheck before she can pay her February rent. By the time she has the money on February 16, she owes you an additional $5 for those 15 days, or $75. That is a hefty fee compared to the flat late fee of $20 or $25, and she will probably think twice about how she is going to pay for her next vacation.

Review of Late Fees

There are three ways you can structure your late fees.

1. A flat fee for any rent paid 10 days or later after the due date. Typically $20–25.

2. A flat percentage of the rent for any rent paid 10 days or later after the due date. Typically four to six percent.

3. A daily fee, charged for each day the rent is late starting 10 days after the due date. Typically $5 per day.

However you decide to handle late fees, make sure you are fair and consistent. If you charge a late fee one month, make sure you apply the same rules for all future months. If you charge one tenant for a late payment, make sure all tenants are charged for the same offense.

When, Why and How to Increase Rent

As time goes on, you will need to raise your rents. Maybe you need to cover the expenses of improving your property, or simply keep up with rising costs of repairs and services. It makes good business sense to increase your income over time.

The best time to raise rents is when you have tenant turnover. Here is how to handle this:

1. Check with your tenants at least 2 months before their leases are over to see if they plan to renew for another year or move on. Get a commitment from them in writing at least 1 month out.

2. When you know a tenant is considering leaving, go through the steps of checking comparable rents (covered in "Calculating How Much Rent to Charge" above).

3. Estimate how much you can increase rent (if at all).

4. Advertise your upcoming vacancy with the new rent amount.

If you have a tenant who plans to stay on your property and renew the lease, follow these steps—if not every year, at least every 2 years:

1. Go through the process of finding comparable rents to see if an increase is in order.

2. Review your annual expenses, using the previous year's tax forms, to check your profit. You can also use some of this information to justify the rent increase to your tenants.

3. Warn the tenants 2 months in advance that you will be raising the rent. You may not have an exact amount yet, but you can let them know if it will be a cost of living size increase or something more substantial.

4. Be prepared for complaints and threats to move. Handle these professionally, and point out that the cost of everything goes up, and you have to cover your expenses just as the tenant does.

5. One month in advance, let them know what the new rent will be. Give them written notice as well as verbal.

Unless you have inherited a rental property with rents that are too low, or something major has happened in your area or on your property that justifies a major increase (like installing central air conditioning), raise your rent in reasonable increments. That means 10 percent or less each year. If you keep bumping up the amount a little every year or so, you are likely to stay in line with both the rental market and your expenses, and tenants should not complain too much about small increases.

➡ **Real-Life Experience**

"I look at the market to set rents. But I might test it by advertising a property at about five percent higher than the market to see if I can get it. I will lower it if I do not get a lot of response."

–Mark Berlinski, Owner of Multiple Rental Properties, Chicago, Illinois

Rent Control

If your rental property is in California, Maryland, New Jersey, New York, or Washington, D.C., it may be subject to rent control laws, which limit setting and increasing rents. If you rent property in a city or area with rent control, get the most current copy of the Rent Control Ordinance and check all regulations.

If you have a good tenant who always pays on time, takes good care of your property and does not cause any problems, consider giving them a break on rent increases. Consider charging these top-notch tenants a slightly less-than-average rent to encourage them to stay. You do not have to charge the same rent to all your tenants, and can give some a lower increase or none at all if you want to ensure you hang onto them.

If you are using a month-to-month rental agreement instead of a yearlong lease, the steps above still apply. If you are going to raise the rent, do it when it makes sense so it does not appear random to your tenant: Resolve to raise rents only on the first of the year or on the anniversary of the tenant's move-in month.

Remember—You Have Their Last Month's Rent

When you increase the rent for an existing tenant, remember to get the difference from him or her to add to the last month's rent you collected when he or she signed the original lease.

When, Why and How to Lower Rent

It is sad but true—there may come a time when you have to lower the rents you previously set. If the rental market is flooded with property and renters can pick and choose the best home, you may have to bring your price down in order to attract good tenants—but it is likely that other landlords will be doing the same.

You should be able to tell quickly if your rents need to come down, because you will not attract any applicants for your property, let alone tenants. Do your research and see what the market is doing, and talk to other landlords to get a feel for a fluctuating situation. If things are changing fast, this may be a good time to switch from a yearlong lease to a 6-month lease, or even a month-by-month lease, so that you are not locked into a low rent for 12 months.

In Closing

You can see that it is a good idea to stay tuned into what is happening in your local rental market. Keeping an eye on rents, number and types of properties available, and other fluctuations gives you direct input into the perceived value of your rental property. Joining a local landlords association can help you stay informed and may give you more information than you can get on your own. Otherwise, check your classified ads regularly to see what is happening in your area.

Section Five

Dealing with Tenants

12

Should You Hire a Property Management Company?

As mentioned in the first chapter, you can hire out every aspect of landlording from painting and plumbing to showing rentals and screening applicants—or all of the above. As you read the following chapters about dealing with tenants, consider that you do not have to do any of this work; you can hire a property management company to take care of all or part of it. (The same goes for other tasks outlined in this book.)

Obviously, you will pay a price for this service, but there may be instances where the money is worth it. Here are some situations where a landlord might hire a management company to handle some or all of his or her tasks:

- The landlord is renting property in a distant city or state and cannot show the property or respond to tenant complaints.

- The landlord owns multiple properties and cannot manage them all him or herself.

- The landlord is making so much money on rentals that he or she can afford a management company and still make a profit, thus leaving more time to invest in promising properties.

If you do not fall into one of these categories, you probably do not want to spend the money on a management company. However, if some of the duties of landlording are just too hard for you to handle, you might consider finding a company that will take on just those tasks for you.

What a Property Management Company Can Do for You

Let us take a look at what duties a management company can take on for an independent landlord. Keep in mind that most companies will let you pick and choose which tasks you want them to handle.

- advertising your property when new tenants are needed

- showing the property

- screening the applicants

- providing all paperwork, including application and lease

- collecting the rent

- dealing with late payments, partial payments and no payments

- handling all bookkeeping and record-keeping

- maintaining the property

- handling emergency repairs

- enforcing policies and house rules

- any other service you need

It sounds great! Who would not want to turn over these tasks to someone else? But let's look at what it will cost you…

Maintenance Money

Property management firms make most of their money off of maintenance, because they will mark up the service as much as 100 percent. The worse shape your building is in, the more money they will make off of you.

By law, property managers must disclose to their clients how they make money, including any markups. Ask to see this documentation if it is not in the contract.

Price of Outsourcing

Prices and fee structures vary greatly from company to company, but if you were to hire a management company to do it all for you, it would typically cost you seven to 10 percent of your total rental income, with additional fees for showing property because it is so time-consuming. Of course, the percentages and prices will vary depending on what the market is like in the area you rent in.

The bigger your property or the more properties you have, the lower your rate is likely to be. And keep in mind: everything is negotiable in real estate. You can try to talk a company into lowering their price, but be careful—if you are a good negotiator and get them to come down one or two percent, they might spend more time trying to fill another client's vacancy and less time on your vacancies.

Can You Afford It?

Take a look at the expenses you are paying on your rental property. Besides your mortgage payments, add up your insurance, property taxes, income taxes, cost of repairs and improvements, plus any home office expenses you pay to run your landlord business.

Now total up how much money you are making in rent. Subtract your expenses from your rental income and see if you want to pay an additional 10 percent of that rental income to a property management company. Are you still coming out with a decent profit? If so, you can consider passing off some or all of your landlording duties—but keep in mind you will still pay for maintenance costs and all other expenses incurred by the outside company.

If you decide to hire a property management company, make sure you shop around for the best value, because you will find a wide range of services, quality and price.

Tax Break

The fees you pay a property management company are tax-deductible because they are a business expense.

Where to Look for a Management Company

If you are a member of a local landlord association, that group can probably recommend a property manager. Otherwise, you can ask the Institute of Real Estate Management (IREM) for some recommendations. Local chapters of the group are listed on www.irem.org.

Or you can perform a Web search on your own, by typing in property management or rental property management and your town. You can also look in your Yellow Pages under "Real Estate Management."

You can also ask your real estate agent if he or she has a property manager he or she would recommend.

Choosing the Best One

When you are looking for a property management company to handle your rental property and tenants, your main priority should be finding a firm that is ethical and knowledgeable about handling property for independent landlords. Take some time to talk to a representative from each company to get a feel for their trustworthiness and their experience. Ask these questions:

- List out everything you would like them to do and see if they currently handle these tasks. Ask if they will handle only part of the list, such as advertising and showing property.
- What are the costs per task? The company should have a simple fee structure. Study each cost to see if it is worth hiring out for something you can do yourself.
- Do they markup supplies or labor for maintenance and repair work?
- Do they provide 24/7 emergency service?
- How do they communicate with clients? Will you receive a regular report or phone call?
- Do they assign a specific person to one property? This gives you and your tenant a single point of contact.
- Can they provide references of landlords similar to you?

Make sure the company is licensed. In some states, people can get a property manager's license; in others, they should have a real estate license. Also, make sure the company is bonded (insured against employee theft) and insured for liability and worker's compensation.

When you get a list of references from a property management company you are considering, make sure to call every single reference provided.

> **Real-Life Experience**
>
> "Ask each reference about his or her vacancy rates, turnaround time in renting, whether his or her reports come on time and whether the checks come on time."
>
> —Catherine Brouwer, Founder, Blue River Properties, Memphis, Tennessee

> ## Do Not Shop for Price
>
> When you start researching property management companies, you will find that most are within one or two percent of each other in their general fees. Keep in mind that the cheapest one is not necessarily the best one—do not be attracted to a lower price or you could end up losing money. The crucial factor is finding a company that will fill your property fast with good tenants.

A final word of advice on choosing a good property management firm: Look for a company that works for a mix of different landlords; you want a property manager that handles people like you. That means if you are a brand new landlord, you want someone who manages rental property for other new landlords. If you have owned multiple properties for years, look for someone who handles landlords in similar situations. You want a company that has experience dealing with someone in your situation. But be careful: You do not want a company that handles property that is too similar to yours. If you own a multi-unit building, you do not want the company that is filling vacancies in an identical building down the street—all the prospective tenants are likely to end up in those apartments.

> **Real-Life Experience**
>
> "A landlord having his or her first experience with a property manager probably does not have a lot of units. In that case, you should look for a smaller, more personal company. You will not get any attention from a larger company."
>
> —Catherine Brouwer, Founder, Blue River Properties, Memphis, Tennessee

Signing a Contract

If you hire a management company, they will most likely want you to sign an agreement. This document will spell out what they will do for you and how much it will cost. Study it carefully, and if you do not think it is in your best interests, consult an attorney.

Any contract should be cancelable by either party with a 30-day written notice—for any reason. You do not want an agreement that locks you into a year or more with the company.

Doing It Yourself...

If you are just starting out in landlording and are planning to rent a single-family home or small multi-unit building, you are not likely to hire a property manager. It is best to start out that way anyway, so you can learn how to do everything yourself. In that case, read on to learn the nuts and bolts of finding tenants for your rental.

13 Finding Tenants

You are now ready to start your search for the perfect tenants for your new rental property. As long as your property is in move-in condition—meaning completely clean, with everything in good repair, with a tidy exterior—and if you would not be ashamed to take your own mother on a walk-through of the property, then you can start looking for tenants.

Another preparation: Make sure you are ready to show the property. Do you have time to set aside to meet prospects? Do you have the proper applications and paperwork ready to hand out?

If you and your property are ready to start showing immediately, then you can begin the process of seeking a tenant. Your first step is to advertise that you have property to rent. There are several ways to do this, and you should use a combination of methods rather than relying on a single one. You want to get the word out in as many ways as possible, and as cheaply and effectively as possible.

Remember, you are in this for the long haul. Keep track of how you find your best tenants and continue to use those methods. If your newspaper ads have not pulled in anyone in the past 5 years, maybe you can stop using them or try a different paper.

Bare Bones Information...

Anyone who is searching for a home will need to know the following in order to take the step of contacting you for a showing or for more information:

- location—not the exact address, but rather the street name, intersection, commuter train stop or neighborhood;
- number of bedrooms and bathrooms;
- price and whether utilities are included; and
- when it is available.

After they have eliminated properties that do not fit their needs for location, size, price and availability, renters will be interested in these secondary factors:

- parking/garage space
- school district (if they have kids)
- pet policy (if they have pets)
- laundry and amenities
- storage

Word of Mouth

It is free, it is easy and it cannot hurt—and it might find you some excellent tenants! Tell family, friends, friends-of-friends and certainly any current tenants that you have an apartment or house to rent. Tell them the basics (see bare bones box), and ask if they can recommend anyone who is looking.

If no one seems interested in helping you, consider offering a finder's fee to the individual who recommends a tenant. If you are offering this reward to an existing tenant, the finder's fee might be a discount on rent, or a special service like installing a ceiling fan, otherwise, the finder's fee should be cold, hard cash—enough to interest someone without becoming a major expense to you. Maybe $30 or $40.

> **Example**
>
> Tell people, "Do you know of anyone who is looking for an apartment? I have a newly renovated two-bedroom available at the beginning of next month. It is in a two-flat in Bucktown, and the rent is $1,400 a month, but that includes utilities. I am offering $30 to the person who can find me a tenant—after he or she moves in, of course."

Classified Ads

Most renters begin their search for a new home in one of two ways: First, they read through the For Rent section in the newspaper to see what is available, and second, they walk around the area where they want to live and look for signs.

Let's take a look at how to run a classified newspaper ad. Classified ads are those little all-text ads in the paper that are divided into help wanted, homes for rent and sale, items for sale, garage sales, etc. If you are familiar with your town (and its rental market), you should know which newspapers people use most for the classifieds. If you do not, ask around. Long-time residents—especially renters—will certainly know. Of course, cost is a consideration, but if everyone in your entire town uses a particular paper to hunt for rentals, that is the paper you should be in. Once you have pinpointed which newspaper(s) you should advertise in, follow these steps:

1. Call the newspaper office, or check their Web site, to find out how much it costs to run a classified ad. Chances are you will need an ad for more than a week, so find out about package deals where you can buy 3 or 4 weeks or more. The cost will depend on the newspaper's circulation and other factors, but typically publications charge per word or per character for any type of classified ad. So the longer your ad, the more it will cost you.

2. Ask if the paper has an online edition, and if so, if they automatically include their classified ads there. If not, find out additional pricing.

3. Check the paper's deadline for ads. Typically you need to submit an ad for the Sunday paper by the previous Wednesday or Thursday.

4. Start advertising as soon as possible. Remember, you must be ready to show the property as soon as that ad runs, but the sooner you can start, the better off you will be. Either you will have plenty of lead-time or you will find a tenant that much sooner.

5. Write your ad. You want to keep it short, but not so short that no one will see it. Get a copy of the classified section you are advertising in and choose an ad that is three to seven lines long. Count the number of words or characters in the ads so you will have some measure of how long you should write—then check the price of that ad to make sure it is still affordable. Shorten as necessary. You will want to include the bare-bones information mentioned earlier, as well as some other selling points, like the things that might stand out about your rental property, such as: The convenient location. The large size. The heart-shaped Jacuzzi. Mention one or two top features in your ad to draw tenants to the next step: calling you.

6. If your ad runs for more than 2 weeks, consider rewriting it weekly in hopes of getting attention.

Example

Convenient but quiet Bucktown location! 2 bdrm/1 bath on side street but close to transportation, shopping, school. $1400/mo, utilities included. Avail. 9/1. Call 312.555.5555.

Total words: 24; Total characters: 153

Signs on Property

Whether your rental property is on a quiet country lane or a bustling city block, a sign in the yard or on the door is a terrific way to advertise for a new tenant. Why? Well, many people shop for a home by location, whether they want to stay in the same neighborhood or have targeted a specific area as THE place to be. They will notice your sign as they walk the sidewalks or drive by, and take note of your property.

➡ This is effective in hot neighborhoods where schools are good or the hip people live, and equally good in out-of-the-way neighborhoods and streets.

> **Real-Life Experience**
>
> "If you have a nice apartment in a nonestablished neighborhood, signs work really well. People who do not know the neighborhood may make an appointment to see your apartment, but they do not show up because they do not like the neighborhood or it is too far from transportation. But people who already work or live in the neighborhood will not do that."
>
> –Mark Berlinski, Owner of Multiple Rental Properties, Chicago, Illinois

Make sure your sign is neat, easy to see from the street (at least the For Rent headline), and aligned neatly, whether taped to the door of a multi-unit building or posted on the yard in front of a house.

What should you include on your sign? Mainly the same information you have in your classified ad, but you do not have to count characters because signs are free. Also, you can skip any description of the exterior of the property since anyone reading your sign can see it themselves. You might also include a line requesting interested parties to call, NOT knock on the door and bother the current tenants.

Example—Sign Taped to Door

FOR RENT—available Sept. 1

Spacious 2 bedroom apartment with 1 bath, living room, dining room, eat-in kitchen. Hardwood floors throughout.

Street parking available. Close to #33 bus line and interstate on-ramp; walk to shopping and Elmwood High School.

$1400/mo, utilities included. Pets OK. Landlord off premises—call 312.555.5555.

(It is a good idea to have tags cut into the bottom of your sign or take-away flyers with your phone number.)

Example—Sign on Lawn

FOR RENT—available Sept. 1

2 bedroom apartment with 1 bath

$1400/mo, utilities included.

Pets OK.

Landlord off premises—call 312.555.5555.

There is less information on the lawn sign because you want it to be readable at a glance, as people are walking or driving by.

Flyers and Handouts

Similar to posting a sign on your rental property, but a bit more proactive, handing out flyers in the same neighborhood increases your chances of catching people's attention. Print out or photocopy a notice on 8 1/2" x 11" paper. Use colored paper to draw attention, and consider printing two half-sheet flyers on a page and then cutting them down to make 8 1/2" x 5 1/2" flyers. You can also include a photo if you have a good one.

However you design your flyer, you need to distribute them in either the neighborhood where your property is, and/or the neighborhood where you feel your ideal tenants might be residing. You can:

- Stick one under every car's windshield wiper in the area.

- Slide one under every screen door.

- Ask local businesses if you can tape one up in their window.

- Stand on a street corner and hand them out.

- Give a handful to family members and/or friends and ask them to distribute them.

Any way you spread the word, you will draw attention to your property. Neighbors who do not see your sign will still get the message—and may become your next tenants.

Example
Your flyer can have the same text you use on your sign.

Notices on Bulletin Boards

Another way that renters look for their next dream home is checking the bulletin boards at their local grocery store or coffee shop. Post a card with details of your rental on any bulletin board in your neighborhood and beyond. Maybe your workplace has a board. Put up a notice there (if you do not mind renting to a co-worker), or check your church, your kids' school and any community buildings for boards as well.

If you have neat handwriting, write up the description. (Some grocery stores want everyone to use the card provided so you will have to write it out.) Otherwise, post a copy of your flyer or print up descriptive index card-sized sheets on your computer. Again, colored text and/or paper will help draw attention, and providing tagged cut-outs with your phone number may increase your response. Use a large For Rent headline since your card will be posted with all sorts of notices, from used motorboats for sale to free kittens. You want prospective tenants to easily see your card on the board and recognize what you are selling.

> ## Example
>
> FOR RENT:
>
> 2 BDRM BUCKTOWN APARTMENT
>
> Spacious 2 bedroom, 1 bath apartment with living room, dining room, eat-in kitchen and hardwood floors throughout.
>
> Street parking available. Close to #33 bus line and interstate on-ramp; can walk to shopping and Elmwood High School.
>
> $1400/month, utilities included. Pets OK. Call 312.555.5555.

Rental Listing Booklets

There are national, regional and local publications that exist solely to advertise rental properties—particularly for major metropolitan areas. These free guides— *Apartment Guide* and *For Rent* are two of the nationals—are available in supermarkets and other places of business. They are mostly used by large rental companies, but do offer ad space to "the little guy."

Check your area for a local version by contacting your local landlord association or browse area convenience stores. Next, find out if advertising in the guide is cost-effective. Generally, advertising in these guides is more expensive than running classified ads in the newspapers, but depending on your area, it may be worthwhile to try it.

Listing with a Rental Agent

There are plenty of companies and agents out there who are willing to take on the responsibility of marketing your property and finding you a tenant. Many real estate agents will handle rentals as a side job. Keep in mind that either you pay them for the service or the tenant does. That said, here are some pros and cons of working with a rental agent:

Pros	Cons
They will do all the work—including making the decisions on how and where to advertise.	They may spend a lot of your money on advertising if your contract does not specify what costs are included in their rental service.
They are likely to find higher-end tenants—especially if the tenant is paying the agency's fee.	If you pay the fee, it could cost you the equivalent of 1 month's rent.
Rental agents and agencies are a good way to open your marketing to people who are relocating to your town or neighborhood.	These relocators may not be likely to rent long-term.
You do not have to pay until they find you a tenant.	They may take a while to find a tenant— and meanwhile, you are losing money!

Target Good Tenants

Whichever means you use to market your rental property, keep your eye on your target market: responsible, financially stable, long-term tenants. You want to position your property to appeal to these people by stressing the quality of the property, its cleanliness and its upkeep.

Price also has a lot to do with who you attract. If you accidentally undervalue your property and offer an unusually low rent, you may attract people who cannot afford the real price, which you will eventually want to charge once you wise up. But do not be afraid to slightly overvalue the property to see if you can get a nibble from a good tenant. (There is more on pricing rents in Chapter 11.)

And finally, where you advertise helps to target who you are advertising to. All of the above advice that involves letting locals know about your property should be taken with a grain of salt if your property is in a declining neighborhood. You might do better to target slightly wealthier communities.

Do Not Discriminate

It is illegal for you as a landlord to discriminate against any particular group or person when making a decision to rent. The 1988 Federal Fair Housing Act ensures that landlords cannot discriminate based on race, color, national origin or ancestry, religion, sex, familial status or physical disability. (Complete details on the act are in Chapter 16 on choosing your tenants.)

Be careful that you do not include any hint of discrimination in your advertising. A good way to ensure that you do not do this is to avoid describing the type of tenant you are looking for, or you could get into legal trouble. Examples:

- Do not include "no children, please" in your classified ad.

- Do not suggest that your one-bedroom is great for singles.

- Do not point out that your rental house is a quick drive to the church or steps from the synagogue.

What Is Next?

Your advertising is in place. You have the word-of-mouth grapevine humming with news of your rental, your classified ads are placed, your signs are up, your flyers have been distributed and posted on bulletin boards. What happens next?

If your advertising works and your timing is good, then your phone will start ringing off the hook. Your job then is to begin the screening process and nudge all promising callers to come and see your property for themselves, which is the topic of the next chapter.

14 Showing the Property

Remember how you got your rental property perfectly clean and ready to show before you started advertising? Well, make sure it is still in good shape, because the showing is about to begin!

Clear Your Schedule

Most landlords would agree that taking calls from prospective tenants and showing the property is the most time-consuming aspect of the business. So when you start to advertise a vacancy, clear your schedule. Set aside time to talk to callers, whether they end up scheduling an appointment or not; plus travel time to the property if you do not live on the premises; plus waiting-around time while you sit there waiting for latecomers and no-shows.

Another piece of advice: Keep your phone handy.

Man the Phones

If you do a good job with your advertising, you should start getting phone calls within a day or two. If you do a great job, if the rental market is tight, or if your property is simply outstanding, you are going to get a lot of calls.

If you find that a.) you are overwhelmed with the quantity of phone calls you are getting, or b.) most callers want to know simple facts like if you allow dogs or if utilities are included in the rent, then you should consider screening initial calls with your answering machine or voice mail. Here is how it works:

1. Record a greeting message that includes basic information about your property. Tell callers more than you did in your ad or flyer and be sure to address any questions you have already heard.

2. Callers who have three Great Danes will hang up when they hear no dogs on your message, saving you both time.

3. Return any phone messages as promptly as possible. Callers are probably working their way down a list of possible properties, and you want to reach them before they are on their way to becoming someone else's tenant.

Example

"Hello, this is Bob. If you are calling about the house for rent, please listen carefully. It is a three-bedroom house on Swing St., and has a living room, dining room, eat-in kitchen, one and a half baths and a full basement. There is a two-car garage and a back deck. The rent is $1,500 a month plus all utilities except water. No pets are allowed. Leave a message if you are interested and I will call you back within 2 business days. Thanks for calling."

When you answer the phone in person (or when you return a prospect's call) be ready to talk about the property and answer questions. If you are in a noisy environment, negotiating heavy traffic, or in the middle of an important meeting, do not answer your phone. Listen to the message and return the call as soon as you are in a more appropriate place and can give the prospect your full attention. You want to sound competent and professional, not scattered and untrustworthy.

At Your Fingertips

The entire time period that you are advertising a rental property, make sure you have these items at your fingertip every time you answer the phone:

- A cheat sheet on the property—especially if you are showing more than one place or this is your first time showing this property.

- Directions to the rental from north, south, east and west, including public transportation, so you are ready to tell them how to meet you there for the showing.

- Your personal calendar so you can make an appointment without creating a conflict.

Full-Time Worker, Part-Time Landlord

If you have a job that prevents you from taking calls for your landlording business during the day, here is how to handle this flood of phone calls: Record a greeting saying you are unable to take their call right now, but will return the call after 5 p.m.—or whatever is appropriate. That way your tenants or possible tenants will not be frustrated at not hearing back from you all day.

Once you are on the phone with the tenant, give him or her a chance to ask questions about the property first. This can save the both of you valuable time. (See Man the Phones, p. 111.) Also, use this as an opportunity to point out some more good features and sell, sell, sell.

If your answers do not send them packing, then it is your turn. This first phone conversation is actually your first chance to screen your possible tenants. Find out who would be moving in (A family? Roommates? A football team?), where they live now and when their current lease is up and their financial state. The most diplomatic way to handle the financial question is to tell them what you will require up front.

Example

"As my ad says, the rent is $1,500 a month, and I require the first and last month in advance, plus a $1,000 security deposit. If you end up taking the place, would you be able to have that money by the first of October?"

Take notes on your conversation so you will keep all your prospects straight.

If the tenant is still interested after this exchange, ask if she wants to see the place. If she hesitates, do not press the subject. You are likely to end up standing around waiting and she will never show. Instead, ask if she has any other questions or concerns. If not, and she still does not want to meet, suggest that she call you back when she is ready.

Landlord Q&A

Here are some questions you should be prepared to answer about your rental property:

Do you allow pets?

Is the property nonsmoking?

How much is the pet deposit?

Are utilities included?

What are the average utility bills?

Is there parking?

Is it close to public transportation?

Does the property have a washer and dryer? How much does it cost?

Is there a dishwasher?

How many square feet is the apartment/house?

When is the rent due?

Can I get cable/satellite there?

Can I get Internet access?

When can I move in? Can I move in early?

Tenant Q&A

Here are some questions you should ask interested prospects before you arrange to meet in person:

When are you looking to move? What date?

How many people would be moving in? Do you have any roommates?

The rent is $1,500 a month. Is that in your price range?

Where are you living now? Why are you moving?

Do you have any pets?

Do you or your roommates/family members smoke?

Schedule the Showings

If the caller wants to see the property, consult your calendar and schedule a time that works for the both of you. Typically this will be in the evening or during the weekend.

> **Note**
>
> Your property will look best in daylight. If possible, try to schedule the appointment at least half an hour before sundown.

Ask for the caller's phone number in case you have to reschedule. (Do not actually reschedule. This is a tactic to ensure that he or she feels obligated to actually show up for the appointment.)

Also, be specific about where you will meet. Will you be inside the property, or waiting outside? Let them know so he or she will feel more confident about the meeting.

> **Note**
>
> This first phone call is when you will set the tone for the landlord-tenant relationship. Try to strike a balance between firm and friendly, professional and relaxed. Treat it like a job interview—but you are both the interviewer and the one being interviewed.

Showing the Property

When it is time to meet the prospect at your rental property, come ready for action. You should have:

- your notes from the phone conversation so you remember who this person is;
- several copies of the rental application;
- pencils or pens;
- copies of your policies to review with very interested people; and
- your cell phone.

Then, follow these steps for each showing:

1. Show up a bit early if you can. This puts you in a slight position of power, and may give you more time to scope out the prospect(s) as they arrive. Also, if the property is vacant, you can do a quick walk-through to make sure it is clean and ready to show.

2. When the prospect(s) show up, welcome them and introduce yourself. (Keep in mind that they probably did not take notes on the phone call and may not remember your name.)

3. Briefly show them around the outside of the property first, then lead them inside.

4. It is a good idea to walk them through all the rooms once and point out features such as good water pressure, new windows, any storage, kitchen appliances, plenty of electrical outlets, etc. Be sure to mention any work done in the past year.

5. Once the guided tour is over—and it should be brief—ask if they have any questions for you. If not, suggest they take more time to look around and make yourself scarce. Go examine the outside hall for cobwebs or check your voice mail messages in the room they are least likely to examine in detail.

6. Once they have had time to examine everything they are interested in, offer an open-ended question, such as, "So…what do you think?" This allows time for more questions, an easy out, or even a "We'll take it!"

7. Gauge their reaction to the property, and if they seem interested, offer them an application.

8. If they take it, ask for a photo ID to verify their name, address and any other information you will need. This is probably the last time you will see them in person before you check their credit and references and you want to make sure you are checking out the right people!

9. If they are interested enough to take an application, this is the time to go over any restrictive policies they should know about. Mention limitations on pets, smoking, number of occupants, etc. Any of these may be an instant disqualifier. If no red flags are raised by your rules, give them a list of all your policies along with the application so they can read it over.

10. Explain that you will perform a credit check and check references once they turn in the application, and also what money is due to seal the agreement. Make sure they understand how much money they will need and what date they will need it—most people need a little advance warning to come up with that much money.

If a prospect is very interested in the property, consider asking for a deposit and completed application on the spot. Of course, you will still thoroughly check his references and credit, but the deposit ensures that you will not rent to anyone else while his application is in process. And, for the record: This process should only take a couple of days. Check out his credit, etc. immediately. If for some reason he does not pass your examination, return his deposit with an explanation. If he decides he does not want to rent from you, you get to keep the deposit.

If a prospect tries to negotiate rent or rental terms, stand firm. It is best to stick to the pricing terms and policies you originally set. Once you start negotiating terms, you are on a slippery slope to less rent and potentially more work for you.

Safety Issues

Keep in mind that when you are showing your rental property, you are making arrangements to meet strangers you know nothing about (who knows if what they tell you over the phone is true?) all by yourself in an empty house or apartment. It does not hurt to take precautions to protect yourself.

Basic Safety Measures

1. If a prospect were to commit a crime, they would most likely rob you. Do not carry valuables to showings. That includes cash, expensive jewelry, fur or leather coats. And if your property is empty, do not keep anything of value in it.
2. Tell a family member or friend the time of each appointment and who you are meeting. Give the prospect's name and phone number.

Taking a Little More Care

1. Check the person's name and number before you meet her. Call her back at the number she gave you to confirm that she can be reached there.
2. If you are nervous about meeting strangers alone, bring a friend along. But keep in mind that your prospective tenant may be nervous about her own safety!
3. Alternatively, call a designated friend on your cell phone as soon as you see the prospect approach. Tell him you will call him back—within earshot of the prospect.

If You Are Really Nervous

1. Ask to see the person's photo ID when you meet him to make sure he is who he says he is. THEN call your designated friend and give him the person's name.
2. Carry a noise-making panic button or whistle.

It is up to you to gauge how careful you should be. Determining factors include where your property is located, how remote it is and how physically vulnerable you are.

Should You Hold an Open House?

Hosting an open house, where you let any interested party traipse through your property during a Saturday or Sunday afternoon, can be a big time saver if you have a lot of prospects and little time. But your open house should be by invitation only. Do not post a sign for all to see; instead, qualify who will be there when you start taking those initial calls.

Open houses can be effective, and many prospects prefer them to individual showings.

Note

When you have scheduled a lot of showings, be prepared to get stood up. A sizeable percentage of prospects just do not show up. Maybe they already found another place, maybe they checked out the exterior of your rental and did not like it, or maybe they just could not muster the energy to look at one more place on their list. Because of the high percentage of no-shows, you should encourage any initial callers who are not 100 percent certain of the neighborhood, the rent or the size of the property, to drive by or walk by the property and take a look. They may call you back and ask for an appointment—and actually show up for it!

Stop the Showing

When can you stop the process of advertising, taking calls, scheduling and showing your property? Only after you have 100 percent of the rents and the deposits you require—that means the checks have cleared and the money is in the bank. Until then, keep up the good work!

15 Screening Tenants

There are a lot of things you will not know about your tenants until they have lived in your rental property. They may be slobs or amateur tuba players or nudists—a background check is not likely to turn up habits like these. But performing a thorough check of each applicant's employment, finances and references can save you a world of grief.

Just imagine how you would handle a situation where your tenant is living in your property and cannot or will not pay the rent. Could you still cover your mortgage and other expenses? How would you handle the stress? By taking the steps in this chapter and checking your applicant's history before the both of you sign the lease sealing your relationship, you can greatly reduce the chances of this situation happening to you.

> **Timing**
>
> Once you have the completed application in hand, get to work! That applicant—and maybe others—will want to hear from you as soon as possible. As you will see from the information in this chapter, checking someone's background takes less than a day, so try to complete all your checks within 2 or 3 days. That means making any initial phone calls right away, in case it take a day for someone to return your call.

Your Rental Application

You will find a Rental Credit Application form on the Web landing page, www. socrates.com/books/landlording-handbook.aspx along with a separate Tenant Reference Check Form and a Banking Information Form. You can use these forms and revise them to suit your personal needs or you can create your own. However you decide to handle the form, your rental application should include the following fields:

Identification
Complete name of applicant
Date of birth
Social Security number
Current address
Home, work and mobile phone numbers
Emergency contact information
Move-In Information
Number of people to live in rental property
Number of pets to live in rental property
Have you ever filed for bankruptcy?
Have you ever been served an eviction notice or asked to vacate?
Have you ever refused to pay rent?
How did you find out about this property?
Rental History
Length of time at current address
Name and phone number of landlord
Prior address (at least one)
Prior landlord's name and phone number
Employment Information
Name and address of employer
Contact name and phone
Length of employment
Financial Information
Bank name, address and phone number
Checking account number
Savings account number
Personal References
Names, relationships and phone numbers for three personal references

Only by checking all these areas—as well as performing a credit check—will you know if a prospective tenant can afford your rent, will care for your property and will stay out of trouble. Later in this chapter, you will learn how to check all the facts.

> **Note**
>
> Every adult who plans to live in your rental property should complete an application, and you should thoroughly check each applicant's background. That includes both spouses in a family or each roommate in a group. If they are signing the lease, they need to give you their information.

Who Are You?

All the hard work of screening your applicants needs to be based in reality. Are the applicants who they say they are? Ask for a photo ID and compare their face to that in the picture. Do this for each adult you are screening. Ask for their ID when you hand over the blank application form or when they return the completed form to you. If they forgot their ID, tell them you cannot process the application until you see identification.

Think this is too cautious? Imagine how easy it would be to cover up your terrible credit by giving a landlord the name and Social Security number of your sister the pediatrician, who has never made a late payment in her life.

Signed Consent

It is important that people understand that you will be examining their finances and other extremely personal information. You would think that by providing all the contact numbers for their employer(s), bank(s) and personal references, etc. that they would understand this. But they may not realize you will be contacting everyone directly, and that you will perform a credit check on them. To keep everything legal, you should have them sign a statement saying they agree to let you check the information they provide, and to let you perform a credit check. You can provide a separate form, or include this statement on your application, if there is room. Above the signature line, add:

I authorize the verification of the information I have included on this form, as well as verification of my credit history, as they relate to my tenancy and to future rent collections.

Check Them Out

Now you have a completed rental application and verified the identities of all adults who will sign your lease. Your first step is to review the application and make sure that all fields are filled in and legible. If any of the information is missing, give the prospect a call and ask them for it. Either they will provide the information or you will discover that it is no accident they did not provide a phone number for their current employer.

Some of your work will be making phone calls to speak with references, and some will be Internet-based. You may end up sending some letters or faxes requesting information as well.

Keep It Confidential

Your applicants are trusting you with some vital and valuable information. If their name and Social Security number were to fall into the wrong hands, they would be subject to the nightmare of identity theft—and spend months, if not years, trying to clean up that credit history after the thieves ruin their reputation. Keep all applications, accepted or rejected, in a safe place. When you are ready to get rid of them, shred them before you throw them away.

Note

If you belong to a local landlord association, find out if they can help with credit checks, employment and financial verification. They may offer these services, or your membership may get you a discount on a company that can handle everything for you. This will not include phone calls, but may cover all the Web-based research described below.

Here are the checks you should perform. Remember, do not skip any of these steps. Your goal is to cover all the bases to ensure an applicant has a perfect record.

Rental History

The only way you can verify a person's rental history is to check with his or her current and previous landlords. But first you should verify the landlords themselves. Look them up in the phone book first. A rental company should be listed in the Yellow Pages, but even an individual landlord (such as you) may have a listing in either the Yellow Pages or the white pages. If so, check to see if the address listed matches that on your form. You can also try finding references to them on the Internet by going to www.google.com and typing in the entire name in quotation marks and the name of the town they live in. If they have advertised rental properties on the Internet (including online newspapers), they are likely to show up.

Once you have done your best to verify that both landlords are genuine, give each a call to find out what he or she thinks of your prospective tenant. Now, there are two reasons you may not get much information from these sources.

1. Landlords can be sued for slander if they badmouth their tenants to you. Yes, even if they call someone financially irresponsible or a dog-kicker in a one-on-one phone conversation with you—that is slander.

2. A current landlord may be eager to get rid of a deadbeat tenant, and so will tell you he or she is no trouble at all, hoping the tenant will finally leave his or her property and come live in yours.

There is not much you can do to get around these two information-blockers, but you can verify the length of time the tenant has lived there, and that he or she paid the rent (maybe). If the tenant has lived there for more than 2 years that is a good sign. Another good question to ask your fellow landlord is, "Would you rent to them again?" If the landlord cannot reveal details for fear of being slapped with a lawsuit, he or she can still answer this with a resounding "no."

Finally, verify that the applicant has no history of evictions. If your local landlord association cannot help with this, you may need to contract with a private service. You can search the Internet for eviction search to find hundreds of companies that specialize in this; others combine eviction searches with credit checks, criminal background checks and other services. Prices vary but should not be more than $10 for each search (on eviction only) and some companies require that you pay a one-time setup fee.

How Do You Choose a Trustworthy Screening Company?

One way to check the authenticity of one of these search firms is through the Better Business Bureau. Get the complete company name and address (if possible) off the search firm's Web site, then visit www.bbb.org and enter the information. A company in good standing should have a Better Business Bureau listing with good customer comments.

Note

If you belong to a local landlord association, find out if members share their personal information on current and previous tenants who pay late or not at all.

Employment Information

As you did with the applicant's landlord references, check the authenticity of her employer. If there is anything that makes you suspicious about either the company or the contact that the applicant gave you, call them up and ask to speak to someone in the Human Resources department. This should ensure a more professional call than if you speak with the applicant's direct supervisor or anyone else they listed.

Ask the employer to verify the information on the form: occupation and length of employment and, if they will tell you, the applicant's salary. You are not likely to get more information than that out of an employer, but if you feel you have an informal or chatty person on the line, you might dig for more information.

If the applicant says that she is self-employed, you should check her income. Because cash flow can be uneven for self-employed people, the best way to do this is to ask for copies of her income tax forms for the past 2 years, as well as 3 to 6 months of bank statements. Check her income to see if it is comparable to the annual salary needed to pay your rent. Be sure to look at the big picture. Some independent contractors may be paid $10,000 one month and nothing the next. They should still be able to pay the rent on time!

If the applicant notes that she is unemployed, do not write her off yet. First check her bank accounts. If she has a lot of money in her accounts, you could consider her. For example, you might request 6 months' rent in advance. If she does not have the funds to support herself for more than 3 months, or if she lied about her employment on the application, keep looking for a tenant.

If the tenant lists other sources of income such as alimony payments, Social Security or sales commissions, ask for substantial records to back up the information.

Financial Information

Banks have a certain way of doing things. But you can start by calling the phone number the tenant provides for his or her bank (or look them up in the phone book) and explain what you are looking for. The bank will probably want your request in writing, and may provide their own form. Depending on your location and circumstances, you can ask to come in and fill out the form on-site (make sure you have the application with you), fax it or mail it in.

The bank will verify the current amount in each account. They may request a copy of the application or form with the applicant's signed authorization statement.

Personal References

It does not hurt to call each of the references an applicant provides. While it is highly unlikely that people would provide a reference who does not speak highly of them, calling each of these people may give you some reassurance. Another good reason to call: To make sure the applicant gave you real names and phone numbers of references. If you cannot reach a reference because he or she does not exist or the number is disconnected, something is fishy. On the other hand, if you have three solid references, you have three points of contact if your tenant turns out to be a nonpayer, does a disappearing act or gets in trouble with the law.

Credit Report

There are several easy ways to get someone's credit report; it is up to you to choose the least expensive and best way for you. As mentioned earlier, your landlord association may be able to do this for you. There are also a number of local agencies that will handle this service. Most services go through one of the top three national credit reporting agencies, which do not deal directly with independent landlords. The big three are:

Equifax	Experian	TransUnion
www.equifax.com	www.experian.com	www.tuc.com
800.685.1111	888.397.3742	800.888.4213
PO Box 740241	PO Box 2002	PO Box 1000
Atlanta, GA 30374	Allen, TX 75013	Chester, PA 19022

Here is a breakdown of your options for getting a credit report:

Company	Cost	Time	Other Factors
Local credit bureau	Subscription fee plus $30 to $40 charge per person you have checked.	Within half a day.	You will need to fax in the application so the bureau can check that the applicant has given permission for the check. This is your best option if you do not have Internet access or prefer not to use the Web.
Web-based credit reporting agency	Online service including credit check, criminal background check and eviction search typically costs $10 to $20 per search.	Some searches can be done instantly while you are still online. Others—typically less expensive—can be done within 1 day.	Be sure the online service you are dealing with is reputable. Read their Web site carefully and check them out with the Better Business Bureau.
Ask applicant to order his or her own report from one of three national agencies	Free for you; may cost the applicant a small fee but no more than the typical screening fee charged by landlords.	Your applicant may be able to find a free trial offer and pay nothing; otherwise he or she can order a report from any of the three major agencies for $9.	Make sure you see the complete and real report. Know what a credit report from each of these agencies look like.

> ## Your Responsibility Regarding Bad Credit
>
> If the applicant's credit report turns up something negative and you reject him as a result, you have to notify him of the bad report—that is the law. The Fair Credit Reporting Act requires you to provide notice to the person, including the name, address and phone number of the reporting credit agency (one of the three national agencies listed above), a statement that the agency that supplied the report did not make the decision to reject him, and a notice of the person's right to dispute the accuracy or completeness of the information on his credit report, as well as his right to a free report from the agency within 60 days.

Criminal Background Check

Many credit bureaus and online services will include a criminal background check in their general tenant search. If this is included and does not cost much, go ahead and check it. Otherwise, consider skipping it. Here is why: Most states do not require landlords to check the criminal background of applicants, and some states will not allow landlords access to this information. If you can get access to the records, which will include any convictions and sometimes arrests, keep in mind that generally state records are not up-to-date, comprehensive or reliable.

Reasons You Can Legally Turn Down a Prospective Tenant

- lied or misled on rental application

- incomplete application

- excessive debt

- poor rental history

- poor payment history

- criminal history

- landlord or personal reference(s) did not recommend them

- income/finances indicates he or she cannot afford the rent

What to Do with the Data

Once you have collected all the information on the applicant's finances and credit, what do you do? Many sources will suggest that your rent should not exceed a certain percentage of your income—usually 25 or 30 percent. But other factors can throw off this equation. It is better to look at your applicants on a case by case basis. Here is an example:

1. Take out your calculator and go over the person's income and credit history.

2. Estimate his or her monthly income after taxes (including any extras like alimony or Social Security).

3. Subtract any existing monthly payments such as car payments or student loans.

4. Check the remaining amount. Is there enough money to pay your rent and still cover living expenses?

5. Remember if you are renting to a couple or to roommates, it is best to divide the rent among them when you make your calculations.

Factors that might influence your decision include the amount of savings the person has in the bank and the number of late payments for credit cards, car loans, etc. that show up on the credit report.

Who Pays for the Background Check

As you can see, no matter how you go about checking the information on the form, it is going to cost you various fees. You may consider these a cost of doing business, but it is okay to pass those costs on to the applicant as long as they are reasonable. Decide which services you are going to use to check credit, eviction history, etc. and calculate how much each tenant screening will cost. It is not ethical (or legal) to charge for your own time checking references. Try to keep the screening fee as low as possible, and ask for it at the time the applicant turns in the completed application form.

Last Word: Acting as a Reference

After completing your background check on all your applicants, consider that you will one day be asked to give a reference for your tenants. Most likely, other landlords will call and ask you the same questions you have been asking. But you may also be asked to act as a reference for a tenant when he or she is applying for a new job. In either case, consider the liability issues raised in the section on rental history. If your tenant is not good about paying or caring for the property, be careful in how much information you give or how you phrase it. Keep in mind that even comments made in a one-on-one phone call can be regarded as slander.

16 Choosing the Best Tenants

Now that you have shown your rental property, received several applications, and thoroughly checked employment, finances, credit and backgrounds for all applicants, what is next? How do you decide who you will rent to—or more importantly, who you should not rent to? Some decisions may be obvious, but others are tougher. Let's start with the reasons you absolutely must reject someone.

An applicant should be immediately rejected if:

1. She refuses to provide a piece of required information such as employment history or a current or previous landlord.

2. You discover she has lied about any aspect of her background.

3. She does not have sufficient proven income to pay the rent.

All other reasons are up to you to decide, based on your values, instincts and experience.

Warning Signs

What about the gray areas of a background check or credit history? Here are some warning signs to watch out for:

Credit History Shows Late Payments

If their credit report reveals many late payments on credit cards, car loans, etc., you can probably expect your rent to be late as well. But check the frequency of the late payments, and the most recent history. If the problem does not appear in the past 6 months, it may not be a problem any more.

Credit History Shows a Lot of Debt

Is the applicant carrying thousands of dollars in credit card debt? Do not condemn him for the debt—this situation is very common.

But consider that he has a lot of monthly payments to make. Check his income and bank balances to make sure he can afford his debt and your rent.

Bank Records Show Low Bank Balance

A low or non-existent savings account coupled with a low balance in a checking account may mean the applicant is living month-to-month on her paychecks. Of course, she could also have all her money stashed in mutual funds, but her income should clarify that possibility. If you think your applicant has no financial cushion, consider dropping her from your A list.

Tenancy Check Shows Applicant Moved Around a Lot

An applicant who has previously rented the same property for more than a year could be a good tenant. One who has rented the same place for many years—or has stayed in each of his past two rentals for several years each—is ideal. Take a careful look at someone who has lived a year or less in his current and past homes. Of course, there may be a good explanation for his moves, but that type of history warrants a careful conversation with the landlords—and perhaps the applicant as well.

Criminal Background Check Reveals Past Convictions

If a criminal background check turns up a past arrest or conviction, it is not an immediate reason to discount the applicant. Factors to consider here: Did the person mention her criminal record to you first, or wait for you to find out about it? Mentioning it first shows that she is honest about it and more likely to be a safe tenant. What was her crime, how many convictions did she have and how long ago was the last conviction? You can consider giving a one-time offender a chance, but someone with multiple convictions would be a definite no.

Choosing the Best

Now you are down to the applicants who passed your background check with flying colors. Any one of them is a good tenant on paper, so how do you choose among them?

➡ **Real-Life Experience**

"The two toughest things about being a landlord are finding the right property and making sure you have good tenants."

—Mark Berlinski, Owner of Multiple Rental Properties, Chicago, Illinois

The fairest method would be to take the one who was first to apply. If you made any promises, or accepted a deposit from anyone, you should go with that choice, or you had better have a good explanation ready.

If you did not take any deposits or make any promises regarding priority, then the choice is up to you. You can go with your gut instinct on someone, or pick the person with the highest bank balance or income. But when you are making the decision, be careful not to discriminate.

The Fair Housing Act

You must be very careful when rejecting an applicant, because if any discrimination is suspected, you may end up facing an expensive lawsuit. The Fair Housing Act, passed by Congress in 1968 and amended in 1988, protects people from discrimination from landlords and property managers.

In general, the FHA applies to all sorts of housing, public and private, including single-family homes, apartments, condominiums, mobile homes and others. However, the Act includes some exemptions. For example, it does not apply to a single-family house sold or rented by a private owner without the use of a real estate agent, provided that among other conditions, the owner does not own more than three single-family houses at any one time. The FHA also does not apply to rooms or units in a dwelling containing living quarters occupied, or intended to be occupied, by no more than four families living independently of each other, if the owner occupies one of the living quarters.

The Department of Housing and Urban Development states:

> "Title VIII of the Civil Rights Act of 1968 (Fair Housing Act), as amended, prohibits discrimination in the sale, rental, and financing of dwellings, and in other housing-related transactions, based on race, color, national origin, religion, sex, familial status (including children under the age of 18 living with parents of legal custodians, pregnant women, and people securing custody of children under the age of 18), and handicap (disability)."

Note that physical disabilities referenced in this act include chronic alcoholism, AIDS or AIDS-related complex, hearing or visual impairment, chronic mental illness and mental retardation.

You can see that the Fair Housing Act covers much more than racial discrimination. It means that you cannot reject an applicant because you do not want young children tearing up your property. It also means you cannot pass over the unmarried couple who applied because you do not approve of their living together. So carefully consider why you are choosing one applicant over another, and make sure you are making a fair and legal decision.

Because their rights are protected by the Fair Housing Act, it is a good idea to tell applicants why you are not renting to them. If they do not have a problem with credit or other background checks, this is where the first-come, first-served method may come in handy.

When No Pets Does Not Mean No Pets

If you have a no pets policy, you must make an exception for someone with a guide dog or other animal that assists him. If an applicant mentions that he needs such an animal, check to see if he has a medical prescription for a companion animal.

Keep a Paper Trail

Because of the risk of a discrimination lawsuit, it is good practice to keep records of all applications and rejections for at least 3 years. If you have all the paperwork (including her original application, your notes from phone calls and meetings, and a copy of your written notice of denial) that proves that you turned down someone based on her bad credit history and not her marital status, you will be in a much better position to field any accusations.

How to Notify the Chosen Applicant

Once you have chosen which applicant you want, call that person and let him know the good news. During the call, you should cover the following:

1. Remind him of the amount of rent and security deposit you will require immediately.

2. Review your major policies (no pets, number of occupants etc.) that might be deterrents to his moving in.

3. Set up a time to meet so he can sign your rental agreement or lease.

Only after you have the signed lease and 100 percent of the required rent and security deposit are in hand—and that includes a cleared check—should you begin letting the other applicants know that the property is rented.

How to Turn Someone Down

Because of the discrimination issues mentioned above, it is best to send a written notification to those applicants who did not make the cut. It would be nice to also give them a call as soon as you can and let them know your decision. Do not tell them anything not included in your written notice; this just gives them more time to look for another place to rent.

Your written notification can be the Notice of Denial Form which can be found on the Web landing page, www.socrates.com/books/landlording-handbook.aspx. If you prefer to create your own notice, it should include the following:

• the date you send the notice;

• the applicant's name and address; and

• the legal reason you have decided not to rent to him or her.

That is all—keep it short and sweet. And keep a copy of the notice for your records.

Consider Accepting a Co-signer

Once in a while you will come across a prospective tenant who asks if you will accept her if she provides a co-signer. Maybe the person is too young to have a credit history, or maybe her credit history is checkered.

If you consider accepting a co-signer on your lease, it must be with the following conditions:

1. The co-signer has to fill out your standard application and pay any fee you would normally charge.

2. The co-signer is screened with the exact methods and standards used for tenant screening, including credit check, employment, finances—the works.

3. After reviewing the co-signer's bank accounts and income, you need to verify that this person can afford to cover both his or her own living expenses and your rent, in the event that the tenant cannot.

If the tenant, the co-signer and you all agree to these conditions, it should be a safe arrangement as long as you have a lease that will stand up in court. Your tenant lacks a sound background, but you have a legally responsible co-signer who is personally responsible for covering any rental payments the tenant cannot make, so this arrangement is as solid as any lease with a regular tenant.

Make It Official

You have made your choice and the applicant (or applicants) is ready to sign on the dotted line. But before you ask him to sign your rental agreement, you should go over a few things in person with him. Ask the person to meet you for 15 minutes or half an hour to review the lease and sign it. You can meet at the rental property if it is empty, at your home office or somewhere public like a coffee shop.

Sit down and review all your policies and house rules with the applicant. Make sure he understands each of the points clearly and ask if he has any questions. It is crucial that you do this before he signs—imagine if you have a tenant signed up and you hear the awful words, "What do you mean, you do not accept pets?"

You can use your own judgment on how many of your policies you want to review; if you have a lot of them, you may end up sounding like the world's toughest landlord. If that is the case, have your policies ready in writing and give them to the applicant to read through. You should definitely mention the most important policies, which include:

- number of occupants
- pet policy—how many; what kind of animal
- smoking
- payment of rent

In addition to reviewing your policies and house rules, this meeting is the time to review any disclosures you must legally make to a new tenant. This includes:

Lead Paint Disclosure

If your property was built before 1978, federal law requires that you notify tenants of possible problems with lead paint. This includes providing them with any information about lead-based paint and/or lead-based paint hazards in your property; any available evaluation reports; and a copy of the Environmental Protection Agency's (EPA's) pamphlet, "Protect Your Family from Lead in Your Home." Complete information on this topic is available in Socrates' Lead Paint Disclosure form, and a disclosure form and a copy of the EPA's pamphlet is available on the Web landing page www.socrates.com/books/landlording-handbook.aspx.

Megan's Law Disclosure

The 1996 federal Megan's Law requires that a list of registered sex offenders be made available to the public. Some states have their own Megan's Law, which may require that law enforcement actively notify the public of the presence of registered sex offenders. While it is not specifically required that landlords provide information on known sex offenders to their tenants, you can cover all bases by letting your new tenants know that they can obtain a list of registered sex offenders from your local law enforcement agency.

Once you have reviewed some or all of your rental policies—and given the applicant a written list of policies to review—and made all disclosures you are legally required to make, ask if he or she has any questions. Take time to provide as much information as you can—this is a good chance to get to know him or her a little bit better, and to start building a good relationship.

Once all questions have been answered, it is time to seal the deal. Have the applicant sign two copies of the rental agreement or lease and let him or her take one. Collect the rents and deposits you have requested and make plans for a move-in date and for turning over a set of keys—which will be after his or her check has cleared, of course.

When you leave the meeting, both parties should be clear on what happens next, and when the next contact will be. And your first stop should be the bank, to deposit that check as soon as possible.

17 How to Keep Good Tenants & Cope with Bad Ones

Once you have tenants living in your rental property, it will not take long for you to determine if they are an asset or a liability. The most obvious thing you will watch for is if they pay their rent on time, but there are other traits to good tenants (and bad ones) that will determine how much you will want to try to entice them to stay at the end of their lease. Remember, showing your property can be the most time-consuming aspect of landlording, and if you can avoid that process, along with the expense of advertising every year, it is worth your while to court a good tenant to stay on for years and years.

First let us take a look at what constitutes a good tenant.

Definition of a Good Tenant

A good tenant is, first and foremost, someone who pays the total amount of her rent promptly every month. After all, you are in this business to get rental money. But there is more to the ideal tenant than responsible payments. You want someone who:

- Takes good care of your property, whether she is fulfilling her obligations to mow the lawn or she makes sure to call you about maintenance issues before they get out of hand.
- The neighbors never complain about. You do not receive phone calls about loud parties, cars parked where they should not be or police visits at 3 a.m.
- Abides by your house rules and policies.
- Is interested and able to stay in your property for more than a year.

What You Can Do for Them

If you have tenants who fit all or most of the descriptions above, you want to hang on to them! That means making them happy and giving them reason to continue living in your property when their current lease expires. They are making your life pleasant, and here are some ways you can return the favor:

- Keep their home in good repair. Respond to any complaints and, if you do not hear from them, check in to see if anything needs fixing or updating. (Within reason, of course—stopping a dripping faucet is in order; replacing the bathroom vanity is not.)

- Do not raise the rent too much. When you talk to them about renewing their lease, a cost-of-living increase is OK, but do not drive away good tenants by trying to get more out of them. Save the big increases for when you switch tenants. Think of the money and effort you are saving by not advertising, showing and screening!

- Get rid of bad tenants. If you have some noisy tenants living in the same building, do your best to bump them out at renewal time and assure your model tenants that things should be quieter.

- Generally keep your property nice. Do your job: Keep the exterior of the building looking good and the inside running smoothly.

- Respect their privacy and rights. Leave your good tenants alone unless they call you. Checking in every quarter or so is fine. And be sure to follow the law on letting them know when you need to enter their home.

- Do not neglect the long-term tenant. If you typically paint the interior of an apartment between tenants every year or so, offer to paint the apartment of someone who is staying for their second or third year. The same goes for updating appliances, replacing windows and sanding floors or installing new carpeting.

Definition of a Difficult Tenant

In spite of your careful and thorough background checks, you may end up with a difficult tenant. Of course, the worst-case scenario is a tenant who pays his or her rent late, bounces checks, makes partial payments or simply does not pay at all. This is a serious problem, and may lead to serious action and even eviction, which is covered later in this chapter.

Hopefully, you will not have to deal with such a tenant. But other difficulties may arise, such as tenants who:

- Are over-demanding and request unrealistic amounts of work and effort on your part, such as repainting an apartment every 6 months.

- Damage your property, either by accident or on purpose.

- Draw complaints from neighbors about noise and disturbances.

What You Can Do about Difficult Tenants

Not all of these bad tenant traits should lead to trying to get rid of them. You can train people to become better tenants either by working with them or penalizing them. Here are some examples:

Over-Demanding Tenant

When dealing with a tenant who calls you at all hours wanting immediate attention and repairs—be firm and focused. Do not jump to respond to every phone call. Instead, assure him that you will fix his problem the next time you are at the property, and do so in batch repairs. If the repairs he is requesting are too minor to consider, tell him so. Explain what your responsibilities are and what his are. A tenant like this can end up being an ideal tenant, because he can be meticulous in caring for your property. Other tips for dealing with over-demanding tenants:

- Set business hours for taking calls, along with an emergency number for overflowing toilets, etc. Do not answer your landlord line after hours, though you can check messages to see what the person is calling about.

- Stick to your responsibilities as outlined in your rental agreement and policies. Point out the sections that cover repairs and maintenance to your tenant.

- If he asks you to make repairs or improvements not outlined in the agreement or policies, offer to have the work done if he will cover the cost.

- Offer to teach him how to handle a recurring minor problem such as a running toilet or loose doorknobs.

Property Damage

If a tenant damages your property, she is responsible for the cost of repairs. This should be clearly stated in your lease or rental agreement. You can ask her to have the damage fixed—or do it herself—and check to make sure everything is done to your satisfaction; or you can handle the repairs and present her with a bill. Of course, you have her security deposit, but spending that (or reserving it) before she moves out would leave you with no coverage for future damage.

> **Note**
>
> If the damage is a safety hazard, like a broken lock on an outer door or a shattered window, have the repair made immediately and then present her with a bill.

Disturbances

As a landlord, you are not legally responsible for any complaints about loud parties or music or domestic disturbances. If another tenant or a neighbor calls you about a noisy party late at night, advise him or her to call the police. But if the problem persists, ask the person complaining to send you a letter about the problem and start a file of written documentation, so you can substantiate the problem if necessary.

If there is a recurring problem, send the problem tenant a note with a firm warning about breaking your house rules for noise, disturbance, etc. Mention dates and times so that he or she knows you are aware of what is going on. Remind him or her that excessive noise, violence and complaints from neighbors are all grounds for eviction.

Late Payer

If a tenant is ever late with his rent payment, call him up immediately—a day or two after his payment is due—and ask him for it. Find out why it is late, and make a note of it for your records. In your conversation with the tenant, make it clear that the rent is due on time, with no exceptions. You want to ensure that he is not putting you at the bottom of his list of monthly bills, but rather at the top. Each time you talk to someone about a late payment (or a partial one), you are working to enforce good payment habits.

Hopefully it will not happen again—but if it does, call him again. Be firm and businesslike and remind him of his obligation, and that the lease requires that he pay his rent on time. Charge him a late fee if your lease includes provisions for this. And, beginning with the second late payment, send him a written notice of late payment. Keep adding to that paper trail, because you may need it in the future!

Check Bouncer

If a tenant's rent check does not clear, ask him or her for a cashier's check or a money order for the rent immediately. If this happens a second time, tell him or her you cannot accept a personal check for rent any more, but will require a cashier's check or money order each month—on time.

Handling Evictions

If you are stuck with a really terrible tenant—one who is not paying her rent, for example, then you need to get rid of her, no matter how many months are left on her lease. When you start thinking about eviction, first consider other options. Evictions can be messy and unpleasant as well as costly. Chances are that neither you nor your tenant wants to go through one.

Legal Reasons to Evict

Can you terminate a lease and ask a tenant to move out immediately? Yes—if it is for a legal reason. Here are some causes for eviction that will stand up in court, as long as you have good records and a solid lease or policy statement.

- Failure to pay rent

- Late payment of rent more than once

- Repeated violation of a significant policy or house rule included in the lease

- Serious damage to your property

- Engaged in serious criminal activity on the premises, such as drug dealing

At this point, you can approach the problem tenant with some alternatives. Remember, your goal is to get her out of your property as quickly and painlessly as possible. Let her know you are willing to evict her—this should come as no surprise to her, since you should have been sending her warning notices and/or talking to her. Then offer one of these alternatives:

Negotiate a Voluntary Move-Out

Agree that she can walk away from some or all of her unpaid rent if she evacuates by a certain date. Get the terms in writing and have both parties sign it. You keep her security deposit, and in return agree not to report her bad credit to a credit bureau or landlord's association.

Cut a Deal

If you really want that tenant out, offer to pay for a moving van or even movers if she will leave. Or offer to hold her belongings in storage for a set time if she vacates immediately. If she is broke, this gives her the option to go live with friends or family for a while until she gets back on her feet—and you can rent your property to someone who pays!

Come up with your own deal. If you have a tenant who is not paying you rent, it is worth taking a loss to get her out of your property so you can start earning income again.

Things You Cannot Do

You want those tenants out of your rental house, and you want them out now. Do not lose your head—you do not want to do anything illegal. Here is a short list of things you cannot do to get rid of tenants:

- Lock them out—or in
- Pile their belongings in the street outside
- Turn off their utilities—even if they are in your name
- Threaten or intimidate them

Actions like these are dangerous, and illegal in almost every state. And regardless of state law, you may be sued for everything from compensation for tenants' belongings to costs of their temporary housing.

How to Legally Evict Someone

If you have tried everything and failed, it is time to start the eviction process. If this is your first time going through the process, you should hire an attorney to make sure you are doing everything correctly.

Here Are the General Steps to Follow:

1. Serve the tenant with a Notice to Pay Rent or Quit—in writing, of course. A notice is included on the Web landing page www.socrates. com/books/landlording-handbook.aspx. This notice gives the tenant a short time (usually 3 or 5 days) to either pay the entire amount of rent he owes or get out. Most problems end here—if the tenant cannot pay, he will leave. If he does neither, then you start the legal eviction process. (If the problem is not rent but, say, too many occupants, you would serve a Notice to Cure or Quit. In this case, the tenant must solve the problem within the time frame by getting rid of the additional occupants.)

2. If the tenant pays the rent owed during the specified time, you must accept it. If he wants to pay after the time limit is up, do not accept any partial payments or the eviction process may be considered nullified.

3. File Unlawful Detainer, or UD, action papers. (This is where your attorney comes in.)

4. Appear, when called, in court and get a judgment to collect the rent and an eviction.

5. Have the court serve your tenant with final eviction papers, including the date of eviction.

6. Have your local law enforcement agency evict the tenant on that date and give you possession of the property.

7. Change the locks on the property immediately to ensure the tenant cannot come back, and begin preparing it for your next tenant.

If the eviction is uncontested by the tenant, this process should take between 1 and 2 months. There are specific timelines for each step outlined above; that is one reason that it is a good idea to have your lawyer handle this for you.

Real-Life Experience

"When you have to evict someone, find an attorney who only does evictions. He or she will be faster and have the ability to recover all your money. He or she will cost more, but it is worth it because he or she can get the tenant out faster."

—Catherine Brouwer, Founder, Blue River Properties, Memphis, Tennessee

Check State Laws

Another reason to hire an attorney: Every state has its own detailed process for evictions, and some cities and towns also have eviction laws. While the steps above are true across the board, the timing, forms and other details should follow your state law.

Getting Your Money Back

If the court has ordered the tenant to pay you the rent they owe and you have not received a dime, you can hire a collection agency to help you get the money. An agency will charge you a hefty percentage of the funds they recover—as much as one-third or even one-half—but it is a simple way to get something out of that tenant.

Some credit bureaus will handle this task, or you can look up collection agencies in the Yellow Pages or in an Internet search.

If you are a lucky landlord, and if you are careful in screening and selecting applicants, you will only need the beginning of this chapter—the part on keeping good tenants. But if you remember only one thing from the previous pages, it should be to keep careful and complete records. You do not have to be an unscrupulous landlord to be sued; good record-keeping can help keep you out of trouble if a tenant should ever decide to take you to court for any reason.

Section ■ Six

Your Responsibilities

18 Before & During Move-In

Before your new tenant moves in, you want your rental property to be in the best shape possible. Not only will this make you look like the great landlord that you are, but having everything in working order will save you untold time and effort after he or she moves in, and is sure to cut down on phone calls about plumbing problems or missing window screens.

Make Sure Your Property Is Tenant-Ready

Of course, when you prepared your rental property to show to prospective tenants, you made sure it was clean, freshly painted, and everything was in fine working order. But before your tenant moves in, you want to double-check the state of the property and see if it is truly in move-in condition.

Here is a checklist to follow after the lease is signed and before your tenant moves in:

- Are the ceilings and walls smooth and free of cracks and nail holes?
- Is the interior freshly painted?
- Is the carpet clean or are the floors in good condition?
- Do the windows all open smoothly? Does each window have a screen and storm window?
- If you provide window coverings, are they in good condition? Are they clean?
- Do the doors open and close smoothly? Do the latches shut? Hinges squeak? Doorknobs wobble?
- Do the faucets leak? Is the cabinet under the sink dry? Do all sink and tub drains drain quickly and completely? Does the toilet flush without running or overflowing?
- Is the heating/air conditioning unit(s) in good working order? Has the furnace filter been changed?

- Are the smoke detectors placed according to your local or state laws? Are they in working order? Are the batteries new?

- Do all the electrical outlets work? Do all the lights and light switches work?

- Do the appliances all work? Is the stove complete with all racks and broiler pan?

- Are all furnishings you provide with the property still present and still in good condition?

- Is the property clean and free of the previous tenants' belongings— including the storage area?

Take some time to perform your own check of the property, and take care of any necessary repairs, including decorating and cleaning, before you contact your new tenant and schedule a walk-through.

How Clean Is Clean?

When you are cleaning up your property in preparation for a new tenant, do not go overboard. The place should be free of trash, vacuumed and/or swept, but not necessarily spotless. As long as you pay special attention to the bathroom and kitchen, the new tenant can take care of scrubbing floors or baseboards and washing windows if he or she wishes.

A Word about Locks

As a security measure, you should always change all outside locks when you change tenants. You do not want the tenants who are moving out to have access to the property—let alone anyone they have given copies of their keys to, such as their out-of-town guests, their dog sitter, their cleaning lady, etc. Make sure your new tenants start out with locks that only they (and you) have keys for.

If you do not want to buy new locks each time, you can remove the locks and take them to a locksmith to have them rekeyed. This is less expensive than purchasing brand new locks each time you get new tenants. If you rent multiple properties, you can buy one or two extra locks and rotate all locks among your properties as tenants come and go. Just keep track of your keys if you do this!

Consider your tenants' safety and invest in some good, strong outside doors and locks. All exterior doors should be metal or solid wood with a single- or double-cylinder deadbolt lock. If a door swings outward, ensure you have nonremovable pin hinges. Also, consider installing a peephole in outside doors so your tenants do not have to open the door to see who is calling.

Your ideal deadbolt lock:

- Should have a hardened steel bolt that is at least 1" long;

- Includes a strike (the plate in the door jamb) held with screws that are long enough to engage the structural stud behind the door frame; and

- Has a box strike, which surrounds the bolt.

> **Note**
>
> Your state may have laws that dictate what type of door locks and window locks you should install, so check with your local landlord association or state housing office to make sure you are in compliance.

Schedule a Premove Meeting

Once you are confident that the property is in good shape, schedule a meeting with your tenant to look it over and review some important information. The meeting will probably take about an hour. If possible, try to avoid meeting on his or her move-in date, because he or she will be preoccupied with the move.

When you meet with your new tenant, remember that this is another chance to set the tone for your landlord relationship. You can be friendly and enthusiastic, but let him or her know that you are not a pushover. Be firm on your requirements, such as getting all money upfront, so that he or she understands this is a business relationship.

Here are the items on your agenda for this premove meeting:

1. If you have not already agreed to a move-in date, do it now. Be flexible on this if you can, but do not budge on one issue: If you do not have 100 percent of the required rent and deposits, do not allow the tenant to move anything in yet.

2. Collect any money she owes you at this meeting. It is best if you can get all funds beforehand, but that is not always possible. If she still owes you the first or last month's rent or any required deposit at the time of your meeting, ask her to bring a certified check for the total amount due. If she brings a personal check, you can call her bank to verify that she has funds to cover the check. Otherwise, do not turn over the keys until you ensure the money is available!

3. If you are renting a condominium or co-op unit, you and the tenant should review the association rules for moving in—such as reserving the freight elevator in advance or using the back entry rather than the front. Also, be sure to turn over any documentation on the association's general rules and regulations, which your tenants are required to follow.

4. You should have reviewed your policies and house rules when the tenant signed the lease, but go over everything again. With the tenant "on location," the reasons for some of your policies, such as noise restrictions, may be clearer.

5. Recommend that the tenant buy renter's insurance to cover the loss of her belongings due to fire or theft. Explain what your insurance covers, and what would be covered by her insurance. It is a good idea to provide phone numbers of some major insurance companies at this meeting so she can get started on finding a carrier as soon as possible.

6. Remind the tenant she is responsible for some or all of her utilities. First-time renters may not realize that they have to set up accounts for electricity, phone and gas. You may want to provide phone numbers for each local utility they must contact.

7. Review any disclosures you must make. This includes a lead paint disclosure, radon gas disclosure and others. (See below for more on this.)

8. Perform a walk-through and fill out the Move-In Inspection Sheet together.

9. Give the tenant copies of keys to the property—one set per adult tenant. Point out that the locks were changed after the previous tenant left.

The Walk-Through

The walk-through is when you and the tenant examine the property and document its condition in writing. Both parties sign off on the documentation, which is then used as a reference point when the tenant moves out. Any damage done to the property during his or her tenancy would then be charged to his or her security deposit. The walk-through is also an opportunity for the tenant to point out any necessary repairs and to learn more about his or her new home.

A Move-In Inspection form can be found on the Web landing page, www.socrates. com/books/landlording-handbook.aspx. It includes a check-off list for each room in the rental property, noting the condition of walls and ceilings, floors and floor coverings, appliances, windows, fixtures, etc. The checklist states that everything is clean and without damage unless otherwise noted. As you and the tenant walk through the property, if either party sees any damage, it should be noted on the appropriate form. For example, if a window screen is missing, you should note exactly which window it is and determine whether action will be taken (a new screen provided within the month) or not. Be precise in recording any damage so that when the tenant moves out, you will both understand which problems existed before move-in. Have the tenant initial each room or sheet as you go, and then sign off on the document when you are finished.

The walk-through is also a good time to review features in the property and educate the tenant on any appliances. You might want to complete the Move-In Inspection form first, then cover this. Your tenant should know the following before he or she moves in:

- How to operate each appliance, including kitchen appliances and laundry, and the thermostat or other heating elements.

- How and where to shut off the water, gas and electricity. This can be very important in an emergency!

- Where the smoke detectors and fire extinguishers are located and how to operate the extinguishers (if you provide any).

- If you are renting a single-family home, give the tenant a brief lesson on operating the furnace, water heater and sump pump, if applicable.

- If the property has chronic problems or unique features, explain them to the tenant. Example: In a vintage condo building, the pipes may be old. Let the tenant know that products like Drano® and Liquid-Plumr® will ruin the pipes and that bleach or Alka Seltzer® should be used for clogged drains.

If you are renting a furnished or partially furnished rental property, you should also review a complete list of the contents and have the tenant sign off on that document as well.

Carpet Cares

Most landlords will agree that one of the most disputed items on move-out is the condition of the carpeting. Be precise in describing the age and wear and tear on the carpet before the tenant moves in. Note any stains, worn spots or tears.

What to Do If the Tenant Cannot Meet with You

If your new tenant is unable to meet with you before he moves in, perform the walk-through by yourself and fill out the Move-In Inspection form according to what you see. After the tenant moves in, set up a time to meet with him and go over policies, disclosures, etc. Review the sheet with him and ask him to sign or initial it at that time. If he has caused any damage during move-in, note it on the form and ask him to initial. If he simply cannot (or would not) meet with you, you can correspond by mail.

Disclosures

Federal, state and local laws require that landlords inform tenants of certain dangers in a rental property. You only need to make these disclosures if the dangers are present in the property you are renting, or if you suspect they may be present. Otherwise, you can skip this section.

Asbestos

There are no federal laws on disclosing the presence of asbestos-containing materials in rental property, but you may be subject to state or local laws. Asbestos can be found in some types of insulation and other building materials, and is not harmful unless those materials are disturbed. Products that contain asbestos are not labeled, and the only way to find out if your property contains such products is to hire a professional testing firm, which is very expensive.

Check your state and local regulations to find out your responsibility on finding asbestos and/or alerting tenants to its presence.

Lead Paint

If your property is an older building, it may contain lead-based paint, which, when it deteriorates, can cause serious health hazards. Federal law requires that all landlords renting properties built before 1978 provide specific information to tenants. This information includes:

1. All available records and reports concerning lead-based paint and/ or lead-based paint hazards.

2. A lead warning statement.

3. A copy of the pamphlet provided by the Environmental Protection Agency, "Protect Your Family from Lead in Your Home."

Electronic versions of the warning statement and the pamphlet are included on the Web landing page www.socrates.com/books/landlording-handbook.aspx. Complete information on lead-based paint disclosures is available in "Lead Paint Disclosure" from Socrates.com.

Radon

Like asbestos, there is no federal requirement for disclosing the presence of radon gas to tenants. Radon is a naturally occurring, cancer-causing gas typically found in basements of tightly sealed buildings. Unlike with asbestos, it is easy and inexpensive to test for the presence of radon gas. You can purchase a test kit at a hardware store—just make sure it meets the standards of your state law. More information on radon gas is available from the EPA at www.epa.gov/radon.

Sexual Offenders

Some states require landlords to inform all tenants of the availability of information on known sex offenders in the area. You do not have to provide more than instructions on how to get this information, which is available through local law enforcement agencies. Contact your local police department or sheriff's office for specific information.

Last-Minute Landlord Tasks

In addition to changing the locks, remember these two last-minute duties:

1. If the utilities for the rental property are in your name, contact the utility companies and request that they be turned off. The telephone can be turned off immediately, but electricity and heat (if it is winter) should be left on until the day after the move-in date. You can request a specific turn-off date. Your tenants will be responsible for paying their own utilities from that day forward.

2. Change the name posted on the tenant's mailbox and/or doorbell. This is a minor task but the tenant will appreciate seeing his or her name up when he or she moves in. If you are renting to a couple, make sure you know which name(s) they want included.

When Tenants Move Out

When your tenants move out at the end of their lease, you can check over the condition of the property yourself, using the Move-In Inspection form. The tenant does not need to be present, but make sure to document any damage you find. Provide the tenant with a copy of the form and any notations if you end up keeping part or all of the security deposit.

Sprucing Up an Occupied Rental

If you are renting for the first time, or if you have a vacancy, you have a unique opportunity to get that vacant property in ship-shape condition for the next occupant. Take advantage of that opportunity and do as much as you can afford, from sanding hardwood floors to installing new window coverings or light fixtures. You may not have a vacancy period again, so you want to do work and add improvements that will last for several years.

In a tight rental market, you would not have any time between tenants—one person may be moving out the same day that the next is moving in. A lack of down time between tenants is a good thing for your bank account, but makes tasks like painting the interior more complicated. In a situation like this, you will have to work around the occupants. If you have been diligent in your maintenance and repairs, the property should be in good working order and will only need cosmetic work.

Schedule any work that needs to be done as soon as possible after the new tenant moves in. (Do not ask the tenants who are leaving to paint or do repairs that they would not get to enjoy.) Check with your new tenants to find days and times that are convenient, and try to batch up as much of the work as possible for 1 to 2 days. Be sure to address any repairs or improvements that came up during the walk-through, and update the Move-in Inspection form to reflect the work you have done.

Once Your Tenants Are Home

Once your new tenants have settled into their place, check in with them to see if they have any questions or problems. You should have taken care of any repairs noted during the walk-through, but other things may have come up since they moved in. Remember, your goal is to have everything in perfect working order at the beginning of their tenancy, so that you would not have to make as many repairs throughout the year. But anything can go wrong, and that is why the next chapter deals with tenant complaints.

Discounts on Other Socrates Products

In addition to a variety of free forms and checklists, you will find special offers on a variety of Socrates products. Visit www.socrates. com/books/landlording-handbook.aspx for more information.

19 Dealing with Complaints

Once you have your tenants selected, screened and moved in, you can sit back and relax, right? Well, that is almost true—except for the phone calls you will get asking you to come over and fix everything from a running toilet to a cold stove. Assuming you are an excellent landlord who keeps your rental property and everything in it in top condition, you should be able to manage these calls fairly easily.

The title of this chapter refers to tenant complaints, but that is not really fair. When tenants call to let you know the furnace stopped working or water is dripping from the bathroom ceiling, they are doing you a favor. You need to keep your property in good condition for the sake of your investment, as well as the sake of your tenants. You want to encourage them to let you know when something goes wrong, and you want to respond as quickly and efficiently as possible. Responding to complaints results in a well-kept property, a reputation as a good landlord, and happy tenants—all good things. It can also keep you out of legal trouble, because you are required by law to provide a rental property that is livable and in good working order.

Take Advantage of a Complaint

Responding to a tenant's request to repair something in his or her home gives you a chance to get inside and see if he or she is taking care of your property. With some tenants, this may be a rare opportunity and you should make the most of it. If he or she is home when you enter, ask if there are any other problems you should take a look at. Scope out the place to see if it is clean or if there is obvious damage—or pets that are not allowed to live there!

First, let us take a look at the logistics of how you receive and respond to complaints. As with every aspect of landlording, you should have a set system for this.

Managing Tenant Calls

You should determine a process for receiving calls from tenants before you get the first renter in the door, and let each tenant know that process before he or she moves in. You must decide the following:

The Means Through Which You Will Communicate

Tenants will undoubtedly need to reach you by phone, especially in an emergency. Which number do you want them to use? If you have a cell phone, consider using that as your landlord line, but make sure you carry it everywhere and have it turned on when you are charging it. For nonemergency complaints and communications, consider suggesting that tenants e-mail you. This will cut down on the number of phone calls you get. But again, make sure you check your e-mail regularly. Reply to let them know you have received their message, and let them know the next steps. E-mail is an excellent tool because it has a built-in paper trail, which will help your record-keeping.

How You Will Handle Emergency/Late Night Calls

You must let your tenants know how to reach you in an emergency. An emergency may be a major plumbing problem, heating failure or other breakdown that may make their home uninhabitable. It may be that they are locked out with no place to go on a cold winter's night. If your cell phone can be used as an emergency number, stick with that. Just make sure it is near your bed all night, and that the ring tone will wake you up from a sound sleep. Otherwise, you might have to give out your home phone number.

If you have a tenant who abuses the emergency number—calling at 11 p.m. with a minor complaint, make it clear immediately that he or she has acted inappropriately. Some tenants honestly may not know the difference between an emergency and a repair that can wait, so be careful how you respond. The next section deals with emergency calls in more detail.

Time Frames for Types of Complaints

As a do-it-yourself landlord, you are probably at your rental property regularly. As you will see in the next chapter, you should have a regular maintenance schedule for cleaning and yard work. So if a tenant contacts you with a minor problem, such as a dripping faucet, let him or her know that you will stop in on the next day you are scheduled to be on-site—and, of course, let him or her know what day and time that will be. If the problem is more immediate, such as a broken window that may pose a security or safety risk, respond the next day if possible.

Record-Keeping for Calls

You should keep a record of all tenant complaints. Noting each point of contact and your response will help you monitor several things: costs of repairs per rental property, which you can use for your tax return; a time estimate for maintenance and repairs, which shows how much time you put into landlording; and a tenant record so you can monitor problems with a specific property or person. The easiest way to keep records is in a computer spreadsheet program like Microsoft®

Excel. Depending on the amount of complaints you get, you can set up a spreadsheet for each property, or a master spreadsheet for all properties. Set up columns with the property address, the tenant and the problem(s). Then you can sort by any of the above to find patterns.

Here is an example:

Property	Tenant	Date	Contact	Problem	Response	Outcome
123 Main St., Unit 3	Joe Renter	10/3/04	Called at 11 p.m.	Refrigerator stopped working	Called Steve's Fridges for repairman	New regulator; fixed under warranty
123 Main St., Unit 3	Joe Renter	2/5/04	Called at 5:30 p.m.	Refrigerator not working	Called Steve's Fridges for repairman	Replaced regulator; under warranty
123 Main St., Unit 3	Joe Renter	3/28/04	Called at 3:45 p.m.	Refrigerator out again	Called Steve's Fridges for repairman	Replaced refrigerator; under warranty

This example deals with a problem that could be handled by an outside repairman under warranty; imagine if the issue was not a refrigerator but the ceiling fan you installed yourself, or a doorbell that is on the fritz. Tracking problems can reveal when it is time to hire outside help (like a professional electrician) or buy a new appliance or fixture.

Information, Please

Each time a tenant contacts you about a problem, get as much information as you can. Find out exactly what is wrong so you will have a good idea what tools are needed and how major the work might be.

Also, remember to get the tenant's permission to enter the premises to do the work!

Emergencies: Be Prepared

Eventually, you are going to get a phone call from a tenant in the middle of the night about a problem that would not wait until morning. It is best if you are ready to respond. Do your research now and have phone numbers handy for the following:

- a plumber
- an electrician
- a board-up service for broken windows
- the gas company
- upstairs and downstairs neighbors in your rental building (in case of leaks between units)

Tell your tenant what to do to stop or slow the problem, such as turning off the water. Give him or her clear directions, then act yourself by making a phone call for outside help or heading to your rental property to handle the matters in person.

The important thing is to have a plan in place, so that you are not scrambling around trying to think of what to do at 3:00 a.m.

Types of Complaints

Depending on what type of tenant you have, you may receive complaints about a variety of issues. Be prepared to respond to any of the following:

Complaints about Lack of Maintenance or Cleanliness

A tenant may feel you are not doing a good enough job at taking care of the property—particularly in a multi-unit building, when you will be responsible for keeping common areas such as hallways clean. If you get calls like this, consider yourself lucky—you have a tenant who cares about the property and is likely to take good care of his or her own rental unit. Check the appearance, inside and out, of the property and see if the complaints are warranted. Maybe you need to schedule cleaning or lawn care more frequently. If you think the property looks nice, let the tenant know that his or her expectations are too high. Make sure he or she understands your schedule—once a week for cleaning and yard work, for example.

Complaints about Necessary Repairs

These are the calls you want to get. A quick repair to a leaking pipe under the kitchen sink can save you hundreds of dollars later, if it were to go unreported. You will have to gauge the urgency of these calls as you get to know your property and your tenants, but it is best to respond to every call or e-mail to check the problem for yourself.

Legal Notification That You Are Coming in

Remember, you must give your tenants notice that you plan to enter their premises. If you have scheduled work to be done, whether you do it yourself or hire an outside contractor, you must give your tenants a formal Notice of Intent to Enter Premises. They cannot prohibit you from entering, but you must give them this advance notice.

If the situation is an emergency and you do not have enough time to give them written notice, get their verbal permission over the phone. In a true emergency, such as smoke pouring out of their windows or water pouring out of their bathroom floor, you do not need to give them notice.

Calls That Tenants Are Locked out

You should have set rules for how you deal with lockouts, and those rules should be included in your lease or your policies. Your tenants know that you have a set of keys to their home, and they may call you at any time if they are locked out. You want to discourage this—particularly those calls that come late at night—so a fee structure is in order. For example, you might charge $20 or $25 for lockout service performed Monday through Friday from 8 a.m. to 9 p.m., and $40 or $50 for lockout service at any other time.

It is a good idea to have a spare key to the tenant's front door(s)—in addition to your own, that is—in case he or she has lost his or her keys.

Complaints about Noise or Neighbors

If a tenant calls you about a problem with her neighbor, or vice versa, direct her to call the police (if appropriate). Whether the trouble is between two of your tenants, or a tenant and a non-tenant, you want to know about it—so encourage her to call you and let you know about any problems. Then document the call in case the problem recurs. But also ask that she call the police if the problem is excessive noise or disturbance or suspected criminal activity. Any of the above is grounds for eviction, and it may come to that if the problem persists—but you do not want to mediate between neighbors. That is the job of the police.

Dealing with Persistent Complainers

Despite the advice in this chapter that a complaining tenant is a good tenant who can help you keep your property in excellent shape, you may end up with a renter who drives you crazy with constant phone calls and unrealistic expectations of your responsibilities. If you have a tenant who you believe is asking too much—whether it is a request for a new paint job 6 months after you just painted the place, or complaints about a chipped countertop you have no intention of replacing—it is time to take a stand. You can do this by following these steps:

1. Put your foot down. Let him know that you are not going to respond to every call. Make it clear what constitutes a complaint-worthy problem—you can even give him a written list of specific problems you will respond to.

2. Request all future communications in writing. This will cut back on the number of phone calls you receive, and, if you are lucky, slow down the complaints. When you receive a letter or e-mail, respond in writing letting him know if you will or will not address the problem. Be straightforward and businesslike in tone. If your answer is no, be specific about why you would not do anything.

3. If all else fails and he continues to press for unnecessary work, ask if he a.) wants to do the work himself or b.) is willing to pay you an hourly rate to do the work.

4. If this does not work, ask if he would be more comfortable living somewhere else and consider a mutual agreement to break his lease. At least you will be rid of him!

After the Call

This chapter has covered how to receive tenant complaints, how quickly to respond, how to record each contact and what you might expect to hear. Read on to learn more about the nuts and bolts of responding—how to handle maintenance and repairs on your rental property.

Handling Maintenance & Repair

This chapter covers both the general maintenance work on your property and the repairs that your tenants will request. Both are ongoing chores for the do-it-yourself landlord.

It makes sense to keep your property in the best possible shape: Well-kept property has a greater value, and may allow you to raise your rents and keep good tenants in place longer. It also prevents "erosion" through problems that go unfixed, such as a leaking roof that can result in thousands of dollars in interior wall and ceiling repair.

In order to keep your rental property looking good and running smoothly, you should have a checklist of tasks to perform on a regular basis.

Make a Master Maintenance Plan

When you start out as a landlord, you should create a maintenance plan with a detailed schedule to help you stay on top of issues with your rental property. Such a plan will keep you on track, ensure that you are on-site at the property regularly—which is desirable so you can keep an eye on things—and alert you to any potential problems that need attention. You can tweak your maintenance plan as time goes by based on your experience. Maybe you will find that you need to clean more frequently or stop by less often. It all depends on the state of your property, how harsh the weather conditions are in your area and how sloppy your tenants are.

To create a maintenance plan, break down necessary chores into time frames—typically weekly, biweekly (every 2 weeks), monthly, quarterly and annually. You should perform these chores regardless of whether you have tenants or a vacant property.

Here is an example of a maintenance plan for a multi-unit building:

Weekly or biweekly tasks	• Clean stairways and foyers • Check common areas for burnt out light bulbs • Mow lawn and/or rake leaves; pick up trash
Monthly tasks	• Clean laundry facilities and collect money from machines • Clean basements • Pick up trash in parking lot or garage
Quarterly tasks	• Inspect common areas and exterior for damage, or any wear and tear • Change filters in furnace and/or air conditioner • Check hardware/locks on common doors
Twice-a-year tasks	• Change batteries in smoke detectors, carbon monoxide detectors and radon detectors in common areas and tenant homes • Clean outside windows • Trim bushes and trees, fertilize lawn and plants • Inspect roof and clean gutters
Annual tasks	• Service furnace, water heater and air conditioning units • Have carpets in hallway/stairs professionally cleaned • Rod out sewer lines

How to Schedule Twice-a-Year Tasks

A good way to keep track of tasks that you need to complete twice a year is to schedule them around daylight-saving time. When it is time to set your clock back or forward an hour, that is the time to change batteries in smoke detectors and take care of other biannual chores.

In addition to your regular maintenance tasks, you will have to take care of certain things as they come up. These include:

Repairs in Common Areas

As you go about caring for your property, you will check for problems such as dry rot, loose railings or stair steps, broken windows, peeling paint, etc., and get those taken care of as soon as possible—especially if they pose threats to tenant safety.

Snow Removal and Salting of Sidewalks and Driveways

You have to take care of this as soon as possible, both for the convenience of your tenants and to avoid liability if someone should slip and fall on your icy sidewalk. If you do not have the time to be on-call all winter for shoveling or snowblowing, hire a professional service. They are more reliable than a tenant or neighbor, and will get the job done fast, even on a weekend morning. After you contract with them, check their work during the first few snowfalls to see how fast they respond, and ask your tenants to report to you on whether they are satisfied with the service.

Repairs Inside Your Tenants' Homes

When a tenant calls about a problem, you must respond. If it is a toilet that keeps running or a stove burner that would not light, you can schedule a repair during your next maintenance call—say, when you are due to mow the lawn. If it is more urgent, you will have to respond right away.

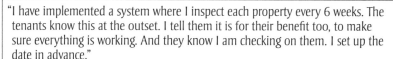

Real-Life Experience
"I have implemented a system where I inspect each property every 6 weeks. The tenants know this at the outset. I tell them it is for their benefit too, to make sure everything is working. And they know I am checking on them. I set up the date in advance." –Tamera Brake, Independent Landlord, Elkhart, Indiana

Maintaining a Single-Family Home

When you rent a house to tenants, you can generally assume that they are willing and able to take on some of the maintenance work and repairs themselves. Just be clear when you rent to them what your expectations are on this subject. If lawn care and snow removal are to be their responsibilities, note that in your lease or in your policies. And if your tenant is responsible for maintaining the lawn, all that is left for you to do is answer any repair calls you get and perform an occasional inspection of the exterior. (Remember, you cannot check the interior without advance notice to the tenant—and you should have a reason such as changing the furnace filter.)

Making Repairs

As a working landlord, you should be able to make minor repairs yourself, even if you are unable to handle everything. Some people are handier around the house than others, but if you are starting from scratch, you should learn how to make the following repairs:

Plumbing Repairs	Hardware Repairs
Stop a faucet from leaking	Tighten a loose doorknob
Stop a toilet from running	Take off and install a deadbolt lock (for rekeying locks)
Unclog a stopped-up drain	Replace an outlet or GFI
Cosmetic Repairs	**Exterior Repairs**
Patch nail holes in wall	Cleaning gutters
Touch up paint, interior and exterior	Caulking windows
Hang window shades or blinds	

There is no shame in calling in professional help for serious repairs or fixing appliances. But if you can handle the little stuff that comes up, you will save a lot of money and effort.

You can educate yourself on these repair skills from reading a good how-to book, or by hiring someone to teach you in person (or trade services with them). Web sites such as these can help, too:

> www.allabouthome.com
> www.naturalhandyman.com
> www.homeinspectorlocator.com
> www.thefunplace.com/house/home

No Water!

You must give your tenants advance notice if one or more utilities must be shut off during maintenance or repairs. Post a notice or slip a note under their door if the water, electricity or heat will be turned off. Let them know when and for approximately how long.

Save on Supplies

Set up an account with hardware stores and suppliers to get trade discounts on fixtures, equipment, tools and maintenance supplies.

What If You Do Not Make a Repair?

If you do not respond when a tenant requests a repair, then your state law may allow the tenant to take care of the problem him or herself and make you foot the bill. Here is how this works: The tenant must inform you of the problem and give you a reasonable amount of time to take care of it. If you do not do anything about the problem, the tenant can either do the repair work or hire outside help (e.g., a plumber or electrician) to do the work and deduct the cost from his or her next rent payment.

There are several reasons why you do not want this to happen: If the tenant is not handy, and tries to fix a leaky kitchen sink, you may end up with a worse plumbing problem and extensive water damage. Or if he or she decides to call a plumber, you have no control over which plumber he or she calls or how expensive the repair might be. Whether or not your state law supports this action, it is best to respond to calls for repair yourself and ensure that you control who is fixing problems at your rental property. Keep in mind that your tenants may be familiar with this law, so be sure to either make the repair or let them know exactly why the repair is unnecessary.

Uninhabitable Property Is Unrentable Property

If a problem is so severe that your rental property is uninhabitable for a while—such as lack of heat in cold weather, or lack of water—your tenants must find another place to stay until you can get the problem fixed. Do not charge rent for the days that they must live elsewhere; you cannot ask your tenants to pay to live in a property that is unlivable!

Working with Contractors

You may decide that you need help handling all maintenance and repairs on your rental property. Consider whether you have the time, the skills and the tools to handle all the necessary tasks. Maybe you can handle the cleaning and lawn care, but have to call in skilled labor for everything else. Or maybe you have the skills to fix problems with plumbing, hardware, etc. but cannot devote time each week for property upkeep. You can hire out any or all maintenance tasks depending on your needs—there are many resources available, from property management firms to independent contractors, to cleaning services. But keep in mind that, especially with skilled labor, you should know enough to tell if the person or people you hire are doing a good job.

For skilled contractors such as plumbers and electricians, you should have some recommended sources ready to call when you need them. You can ask members of your local landlord association for recommendations, or talk to employees at the hardware store or even your neighbors. Call each contractor and introduce yourself, and ask for another reference or two. Find out if they will handle emergency calls—say, a flooded basement in the middle of the night. Get information on their hourly rate or other pricing information. Then, after checking out their references, keep their numbers on hand.

For help with general maintenance, you can also get recommendations from your local landlord association. If you do not belong to an association, find rental properties that are comparable to yours and call up the landlords. Ask if they know of and would recommend any maintenance help. Once you have found a maintenance company or individual, screen them. These workers will have access to your property and you want to make sure they are ethical, insured and bonded.

When you are looking for help with maintenance, draw up a detailed list of the work you want done—including a schedule—and ask each company or individual to quote a price. When you compare their quotes, make sure that each contractor has included the same work and schedule.

Some contractors may want you to sign a contract locking you into a year of service; avoid this until you are sure you trust the company and are satisfied with their work.

> **Note**
>
> You should note that if you use contracted help—such as a maintenance person who handles all regular maintenance duties—the IRS may view that contractor as your employee, even if you have not officially hired him or her and do not pay his or her employment taxes. To clearly qualify as a contractor, your maintenance help must provide services to other landlords or companies, and they must provide their own equipment and tools. If the IRS deems your maintenance help is an employee, then you will be responsible for paying retroactive employment taxes! So be careful to hire a company or person who has other landlord clients and supplies their own

Hiring Employees

Another option for getting help with maintenance and repairs is to hire one or more employees. This is a big step, and requires a lot of paperwork—for taxes and insurance—as well as a lot of expense. But if you own several rental properties or one huge building, it might make sense to hire some permanent help. Landlords can generally hire contractors to handle the manual labor of repairs and maintenance; you are most likely to need help managing the property or properties. In fact, some states may require an on-site manager at a large multi-unit building or complex.

Bringing on full- or part-time help generates more work and expense for you. You will have to handle payroll and taxes, work schedule and assigning tasks and generally overseeing your employees. It is much easier to hire contractors—and you pay only for the work you require. So take a close look at your need for a permanent employee, and make sure you are prepared to deal with your new role as manager/employer.

Maintain Your Calm

As you begin to follow your maintenance plan, remember that the work, time and energy you put into maintaining your building are all part of the investment you are making in your rental property—and your financial future. Every window you wash or lock you change is a step toward maintaining or increasing the value of your property. Every time you vacuum the hallway or fertilize the lawn, you are ensuring that you attract and keep reliable, paying tenants. And every trip you make to unclog a tenant's drain or replace his or her blown fuse enhances your reputation as a good landlord. Performing these maintenance and repair tasks is called sweat equity because you are helping to build your own equity—in your property, your rental income and your landlord business.

21 Communicating with Your Tenants

An often-overlooked aspect of good landlording—like keeping the lines of communication with your tenants open—can benefit everyone. Staying in touch with your tenants helps ensure that you stay informed about the state of your property, and it sends the message that you care about their satisfaction with their home. Communicating with tenants is especially important with those renters you never hear from—you want to ensure that your quiet tenants are not overlooked.

This chapter will look at how and why you should stay in contact with your tenants, including ways to strengthen your relationship as a good landlord and good tenant.

Legal Reasons to Communicate

Every landlord has to contact their tenants on occasion, because state and local laws dictate instances where notification is required. Here are some examples of communications:

- notice of intent to enter premises
- advance notice of utility shut-off
- notification of late rent payment or violation of policy
- notice that the lease expiration date is approaching

All of the above are formal written notices, and should be mailed or delivered to the tenant. They constitute the bare minimum of landlord communications. The following are some ideas on how to build on these communications to position yourself as a thoughtful, professional landlord.

Additional Reasons to Communicate

You would be surprised at what else you need to communicate to your tenants. Here are some other opportunities to share information with your tenants:

1. Notify them when you have work scheduled—either in their home or on the property in general. If you are having improvements made to the property, this keeps them informed that the value of their home is increasing. This makes you look good and gives you leverage when it is time to raise rent. It also prepares them for any noise, dust or inconvenience. Be sure to provide dates for the work and let them know how it might impact them.

2. If you or a contractor has made a recent repair in a tenant's home, follow up with a phone call or e-mail to find out if the problem has been 100 percent fixed. If an outside contractor handled the work, ask if the work was done neatly and completely.

3. Keep your tenants informed of building or neighborhood news that might impact them. This could include sharing a schedule for garbage pick-up, street cleaning, information revealed at the latest block club or city council meeting, news of any recent break-ins or other criminal activity, or even an invitation to take part in a block party or neighborhood rummage sale.

4. Advertise any impending vacancies you have on the property or a nearby property, and ask your tenants for recommendations. Consider offering a finder's fee, which may be a discount on rent or a special service like installing a ceiling fan.

5. If a tenant has recently violated a policy—such as playing his or her stereo too loud late at night—send a reminder to all tenants reminding them that they have agreed to follow your policies. Make this a friendly, straightforward note—not a scolding or accusatory notice.

6. If 6 months have passed and you have not received any complaints from a tenant regarding repairs, be proactive. Schedule a doorknob-tightening Saturday and ask if he or she wants you to come over for no more than half an hour to check doorknobs, oil hinges and perform other minor maintenance. This is a good way to check the interior of your rental property while you maintain it. While you are there, ask about any problems with plumbing, heat, etc.

7. Send holiday cards to all your tenants thanking them for their business.

Sharing information on your property and the surrounding neighborhood can help make your tenants feel they have an investment in their home, which in turn will lead them to take better care of your property and heighten their desire to stay put when their current lease runs out.

Your Timing

You want to keep in contact with your tenants, but you do not want to overwhelm them with messages, notes and reminders. However you choose to contact them—through a written notice slipped under their front door, an e-mail or a phone call—limit your additional communications to approximately once every 6 to 8 weeks. Of course, if something comes up and you have to give notice of intent to enter premises, for example, do not try to fit that into your communications schedule.

If your maintenance schedule calls for monthly tasks, try to leave a written communication every 2 months. You can slip a note under tenants' doors or post it in the common hallway.

Your Tone

While your official notices should be formal and businesslike, your additional written communications should be more relaxed. Try to match the tone you would use for an informal business letter or e-mail. Do not try to be funny or warm and endearing—remember, you still need to maintain your landlord-like distance in case you have to deal with tenant problems. But you can write a note that is straightforward and informal without going overboard on friendliness. You might want to start with one of these phrases:

- "I thought you would like to know…"
- "Good things are coming to 123 Main St. apartments this winter…"
- "I would like to remind all tenants…"
- "You may have noticed that we experienced some heating problems last week…."

Means of Communication

There are several ways to communicate with your tenants. You might want to mix it up and use all of the suggestions here, or consider asking each tenant outright how he or she prefers to be contacted. Typically, phone calls should be reserved for last-minute notification of repairs or permission to enter his or her home. Your tenant communications should be less intrusive. Here are some examples:

Visit Your Property

If you are handling your own maintenance and repairs, you will be on-site at your rental property every week or two. Keep an eye out for tenants and take some time to chat with them if you can. Ask about a recent repair, or if the temperature in their home is comfortable. Note: Cleaning the laundry facilities on a weekend morning is an excellent opportunity to catch someone with some extra time while he or she is waiting for his or her clothes to dry.

Written Letters or Notices

You can mail written communications, post them in the common hallway of a multi-unit building or slip them under each tenant's front door. However you deliver the message, it should be brief and informal. Consider having some landlord letterhead printed and using a sheet each time you write or print your message. This places your contact information in front of your tenants with each communication.

E-mail

Collect your tenants' e-mail addresses when they move in, and you will have the perfect way to communicate informally with them. Writing a quick e-mail is a great way to share information, and can be less formal than presenting a hardcopy notice. It also helps steer tenants toward contacting you via e-mail rather than phone for non-emergencies.

Newsletters

If you manage a large building, you might consider putting out a quarterly newsletter with information on the property or the neighborhood. This is a little extra work, but it can position you as a professional property manager. You can distribute a short hardcopy newsletter, or an electronic version, which is cheaper. It does not have to be longer than one or two 8 1/2" x 11" pages, and can contain all the information you would normally include in your bimonthly notices or e-mails.

Tenant Surveys

If you are curious about how you are doing as a landlord and what you can do to improve your property and your services, consider asking your tenants to fill out a brief, annual satisfaction survey. Ask no more than five to seven multiple choice or yes/no questions. This greatly increases your chances of getting responses back. Your tenants are not likely to take the time to write long answers, so write a survey they can answer quickly. Include information on what improvements they would like to see to their home and how responsive they think you are to their requests. You can send out your survey in hard copy or electronic form.

The Message You Are NOT Sending

By communicating so often with your tenants, you are positioning yourself as a partner of sorts—one who wants to keep them informed about their home and neighborhood. What you do not want to communicate is that you are their buddy who will do anything they ask. That is why it is important to strike the right tone in your communications and not come across as overly friendly or eager to please.

You need to have a clear understanding of what is a reasonable tenant request, and respond only to those requests. If a tenant becomes over-demanding or unreasonable, you need to put your foot down. (See Chapter 17 for more on dealing with over-demanding tenants.) But keep those communications coming! You can still keep tenants informed and engaged without promising them extra benefits.

One last thing regarding the message you do not want to send: By posting or sending communications, you do not want to encourage tenants to contact you each time. Avoid including a "contact me for more information" line unless absolutely necessary. When providing information about upcoming work, include all the information to avoid having tenants calling you with questions.

Putting Pen to Paper

If you are not comfortable composing messages, get some help. Ask a friend or family member who is a good writer to edit your first draft, or write you a starting draft. Then you can work from that. With short, simple messages, it should be easy to tell the tenants what they need to know without causing writer's block!

Consider Hosting a Web Site

If you own a large apartment building or multiple rental properties, consider hosting important information for your tenants and prospects on your own company Web site. You can use the site to make the following information available:

- your current policies and house rules
- your maintenance schedule
- information on upcoming vacancies
- announcements about building and neighborhood news

You can then use your Web site to post information on all vacancies as part of your marketing mix, along with classified ads, signs, flyers and other means.

22 Why You Have Insurance

Many of your responsibilities as a landlord are enforced by local, state and even federal laws. If you slack off on keeping your property in good shape, you could be sued if a tenant or his or her guest is injured as a result of your negligence. Your failure to take care of a requested repair could get you slapped with a lawsuit. Chapter 7 covered the importance of liability insurance for landlords. Here, we will take a closer look at your legal responsibilities—and why performing them can go a long way towards keeping you out of court.

Landlord Responsibility #1: Tenant Safety

In most states, landlords hold at least minimal responsibility for protecting their tenants from theft, assault and other criminal activity—whether criminal acts are committed by other tenants or by strangers. Basically, you are responsible for taking basic preventive measures against criminal acts on your property. If you take these steps you will increase both the safety of your tenants and their belongings, and protect yourself against a lawsuit:

- Provide a safe and secure environment, with strong exterior doors, sturdy, working locks on doors and windows, and bright lighting in exterior areas. Make sure that you meet any state and local security laws regarding locks and lighting.

- Install security measures including adequate lighting in common areas, elevators and parking lots or garages. Ask your insurance company or local police station for advice on how to secure your property.

- Conduct regular inspections of your property to check for security problems such as burnt out light bulbs or doors that do not latch-shut automatically.

- Follow up immediately on tenant complaints and calls regarding suspicious activities or security problems. Make any necessary repairs or improvements, and do not hesitate to call the police (or ask the tenant to call the police) regarding suspicious activities.

- Keep your tenants informed about criminal activity in the neighborhood. Block clubs and other neighborhood organizations usually know and share information on break-ins, attacks, vandalism and other crimes. Read the police blotter in your local newspaper, and talk to your neighbors to find out what is happening in your immediate area.

If one of your tenants is suspected of drug dealing, you must do everything in your power to get rid of that person. If you notice a lot of people coming and going from your property, or if neighbors complain of drug deals, contact the police immediately and let them know your suspicions.

You cannot evict someone based on suspicion alone, but if the suspected party violates your policy on noise and disruption, or number of occupants allowed, you have good reason to begin eviction proceedings. It is essential that you act as decisively as you can; the drug dealer or his or her customers may end up harming other tenants; your property values (and reputation) can plummet; and you may even have your property confiscated by the government due to the drug dealing.

Landlord Responsibility #2: Repairs and Maintenance

Did you know that landlords in most states have a legal obligation to maintain their property? That is right, you are required to provide rentals that meet certain standards, which may include available heat, water and electricity, adequate weatherproofing, and sanitary and structurally sound housing. Your local building codes will also set standards you must follow regarding ventilation and electrical wiring.

Right of Entry

You are also responsible for providing tenants with advance notice of your intent to enter their home to make a repair or show the property. Most states require that you give at least 24-hours' notice unless there is an emergency, which requires immediate entry.

If for some reason you do not meet these standards—say, by not responding to a tenant's complaint that the heat has stopped working—the tenant may have the right to respond by:

- Withholding rent until the problem is fixed.
- Paying less rent.
- Making any necessary repairs or hiring outside help to do so and then deducting the cost from his or her rent.
- Moving out and breaking his or her lease.
- Contacting your local building inspector, who can require that you make the repairs.

The tenant's actions and the repercussions for the landlord are dictated by state and local laws. In addition to these actions—or instead of them—the tenant may also sue for a partial refund of rent and even for damages resulting from inconvenience, discomfort and emotional distress caused by the problem.

Delegating Repairs Does Not Delegate Liability

Say you work out an agreement with your tenant that he or she will take care of all maintenance and repairs on the single-family home he or she rents, in exchange for reduced rent. If he or she fails to make necessary repairs or do a poor job, you are still responsible for providing habitable property and can be held liable.

Landlord Responsibility #3: Tenant or Guest Injury

If a tenant or his or her visitor becomes injured on your property, are you liable? Technically, you will only be found responsible if the tenant can prove that you were negligent—say, by not repairing a loose railing on the back porch that was reported to you last week. In order to prove negligence, your tenant must prove that:

- You had control over the problem that caused the injury.

- You could have foreseen the accident.

- You did not take reasonable steps to prevent the accident.

- It was reasonable to expect you to fix the problem, given expense and level of difficulty.

- The person was genuinely hurt, and his or her injury was probably caused by the unfixed problem.

Example

If the tenant falls through the back porch railing because it was loose, you may be held liable if your tenant can prove that:

- It was your responsibility to maintain the porch railings—an obvious fact, since the porch is a common area.

- An accident of this type was foreseeable—you were informed that the railing was loose, and you know that the railing must be weight bearing in order to be safe.

- You failed to take reasonable measures to maintain the property—in this case, the porch railing.

- Repairing the railing would have been relatively easy and inexpensive.

- The probable result of a loose railing is a serious injury.

- The injury was caused by the loose railing and the tenant was genuinely injured by falling off the porch.

In a case like this, your tenant may file a personal injury lawsuit against you, asking for funds to cover his or her medical bills, lost wages, pain and other physical suffering, permanent physical disability and even emotional distress.

Your landlord's liability insurance will cover your legal fees in this instance, but not the settlement costs. Keep in mind that many cases like this are settled out of court for less money than initially requested.

Your best bet is to prevent these accidents from happening—or ensure that you have a record of keeping property in good repair. Checking your property thoroughly, asking tenants to report problems promptly, and making repairs in a timely manner are all the best insurances against personal injury lawsuits.

Landlord Responsibility #4: Environmental Hazards

You may be held liable for any tenant health problems arising from exposure to environmental hazards on your property. This can include symptoms and sickness resulting from asbestos, lead-based paint, radon gas and other toxins.

However, as long as you make the proper and complete disclosures about these hazards to new tenants—covered in Chapter 18—you should be protected against lawsuits. If you fail to make a disclosure that applies to your property, you could be in big trouble. For example, if you rent a property that was built before 1978 and you fail to comply with federal regulations regarding lead-based paint disclosure, you could be fined up to $10,000 for each violation. And if one of your tenants sues you for lead poisoning, you could be forced to pay as much as three times what the tenant requests in damages.

Mold

A new environmental hazard in rental properties is mold. No matter how clean your property appears, it could be harboring mold behind the walls. Mold occurs in poorly ventilated, moist areas such as behind a bathtub, and can typically be cleaned—if you can reach it—with chlorine bleach. A bad mold problem can cause respiratory problems.

The Latest Landlord Responsibility: Your Tenant's Dog

Recent lawsuits have found landlords to be liable for dog attacks that the landlord could have prevented. If one of your tenants has a dog that you know has a history of biting people or acting dangerous, and you have the opportunity to prevent another attack and do not act on that opportunity, you may be held responsible if that dog attacks someone on your property.

Example
Your tenant's dog tried to maul the plumber who was supposed to fix a leak. You know of the attack—which was scary enough for the plumber to refuse to enter the premises—but figure it is your tenant's problem, not yours. When the same dog is in the backyard and bites another tenant, you can be held liable because you did not require the owner to get rid of the dog, muzzle it or contain it in a specified area.

Lawsuits like this may also apply to adjoining property under certain circumstances.

What Are Tenants Liable for?

If landlords can be found responsible for everything from a tenant falling off the porch to a dog biting the mailman, what are tenants responsible for? Your tenants are responsible for only a fraction of what you, the landlord, can be held liable for. And keep in mind, liability is not set in stone; any judge in any courtroom can rule in favor of a tenant (or other party) over you. Life is not fair, and landlords are often seen as at fault even when they are hardworking, honest people.

That said, you can expect that your tenants will be held responsible for the following:

- Following the terms of their lease, including timely payment of rent and adherence to your policies. Of course, if a tenant moves in a water bed that is expressly forbidden in your policies, do not expect a judge to throw the book at him or her. An illegal number of occupants, however, may be grounds for eviction.

- Keeping property clean and in good shape. Yes, tenants are typically required by state or local law to maintain some semblance of cleanliness in your property.

Avoiding Litigation

As mentioned earlier, your best defense against any of these types of lawsuits is to take excellent care of your property—and make sure you have proof to back it up! Keep records and receipts for all repairs, inspections, etc. so that you can show you have acted diligently over time to prevent accidents, injuries and health hazards. You may not be able to fend off every injury to tenants or their guests, but you can go a long way towards persuading a judge or jury that you have taken all possible measures to ensure the safety of everyone on your property.

And remember to ensure you are covered by adequate liability insurance!

Section ■ Seven

Selling the Property

23 When Should You Sell?

Why would you want to unload your rental property? Well, you should certainly plan to sell if landlording is not working out for you. Or if you are in this venture for the short-term and can sell and walk away with a tidy profit. You might be offered so much money for a property that it makes sense to take the money and run. But unless Donald Trump needs your land for his next multi-billion dollar venture, take a hard look at the math. Does the money you will make from the sale match your profits for the period of time you plan to rent the property? Does it make sense to take that money and invest in a new rental property and start over?

Even if the real estate market in your area has recently declined, you still have a chance of netting quite a bit of cash by selling if you have owned the property long enough or made a large enough down payment. So if you have accumulated a lot of debt as a landlord, you have a chance to turn your losing business venture into a winning transaction.

Temporary Problems

Most financial problems with rental properties are relatively short-lived. If you can afford to supplement your expenses from your paycheck or other income and ride out a long, tenantless vacancy, or pay off expensive emergency repairs, you can find yourself back in calmer waters.

> **Note**
>
> Most high-priced rental properties take time to break even or generate a profit. It is perfectly acceptable to put your money into a property and wait for it to make money—if you can afford to do so.

Keep in mind that real estate is an ever-changing business. Rents and property values change over time and a negative cash flow situation can correct itself.

There are ways to inject cash into your landlord business to keep it afloat. If you need a lot of cash fast, you can refinance the property or take out a home-equity loan—or even a second mortgage—rather than sell. This assumes that you are continuing to earn equity, as well as something in rental income. That adds up to financial security, a stable investment and can potentially float your retirement.

Insurmountable Problems

But what if refinancing your rental property is not going to get rid of your problems? Generally, landlords are forced to sell for two reasons: They are losing too much money or they hate being a landlord. Specifically, any of the following situations calls for selling your rental property:

Financial Reasons to Sell	Personal Reasons to Sell
Your property and landlording expenses are too high and your income is too low.	You cannot handle the workload of being a landlord, and cannot afford to hire someone else to help you.
You run into expensive repairs that you cannot afford.	You find you do not like being a landlord and want out.
You cannot get paying tenants and thus do not have the rental income you need.	The stress of the extra work and responsibility is affecting your health, sleep, marriage and/or peace of mind.
You over-renovated the property, causing a negative cash flow.	You cannot get good paying tenants and spend a lot of time and energy on penalties, threats and evictions.
You lost your job or the income source needed to finance your landlording venture.	
You have to pay for a large insurance loss for which you were not covered.	

You Will Know by Your Cash Flow

How do you know when it is time to sell your property and move on? The trick is to keep a close eye on your cash flow. You had to get a lot of financial information together in order to buy the property, and you inherited a lot of the building's information at the closing. Use this as a starting point to create a budget that shows income and expenses. If you perform a quarterly review of your budget, you should have an ongoing sense of how the property is doing.

If you are sticking to your budget and not overspending, and you are still losing money each quarter, take a hard look at the numbers. Are there ways you can cut expenses without losing tenants? Can you refinance the property and lower your monthly mortgage payment? Are there ways you can increase your rent when the current lease is up? If the answer to all of these questions is no, and you cannot afford to keep the property, it may be time to sell.

How to Sell Your Rental Property

Once you have determined that you are involved in a losing business venture that is not going to turn around, you should act immediately before you get mired in debt. And your first step should be contacting a real estate agent.

Hire a Specialist

For the best price and fastest turnaround in selling your rental property, be sure to hire a realtor who specializes in selling your type of property in your area.

A real estate agent can help you in a number of ways: he or she can make suggestions on easy, inexpensive ways to make the property more saleable, help you determine a fair and profitable selling price, and will guide you through the selling process. Of course, he or she also shows the property to interested buyers. For all this, a real estate agent will take a small percentage of the purchase price—typically five to seven percent. It is definitely worth paying an agent when you are anxious to sell, because your property will sell faster.

A property that is listed with a licensed real estate agency will be advertised on one or more Multiple Listing Services (MLSs), which is something an individual seller cannot do. It is safe to say that every buyer who uses a realtor will rely on MLS listings to find properties to view. Ask your realtor to list your property in the MLS as soon as possible.

Ask your agent to prepare a Comparable Market Analysis (CMA), which estimates your property's value. The details in the CMA will help you determine your selling price. Plus, you and your agent will have a basis for negotiating the final deal.

➡ Real-Life Experience

"When a duplex appreciates, you have twice the market for selling because it can be sold to an owner or a landlord. You will get broader appeal if it can be owner-occupied; these buyers are not looking at returns, they are looking at a home."

—Catherine Brouwer, Founder, Blue River Properties, Memphis, Tennessee

---

Doing It Yourself

If you decide to save some money and sell the property yourself, without the aid of a real estate agent, you will need to follow these steps:

- Advertise the property as For Sale—put a sign in the yard or on the front door; buy listings in your local classified ads and real estate sections of newspapers; tell your friends, family and acquaintances that you are selling.

- Show the property—make appointments to show the property to all interested buyers. This is even more time-consuming than showing to a prospective tenant, because the buyer will want a lot more information.

- Negotiate the price—you need to determine your asking price and then negotiate directly with the buyer or with his or her agent until you have an agreement on price.

- Close the deal—acting without a real estate agent, you will rely on your attorney to guide you through the closing.

This sounds easy, but it is not. It is difficult and time-consuming. Unless you have experience selling property and know the ropes, you are better off hiring an expert who can find a buyer quickly and ensure that you get the best price.

Turn Your Rental into Your Home

If you are renting a single-family home or a condominium, does it make sense for you to stop renting and live there yourself? Take a look at the value of your own home compared to your rental property. If your living situation allows, you should keep the property that has the most equity.

If you get more than one offer, handle them separately; do not counter more than one offer at a time. If you do, you might end up in the uncomfortable position of having to back away from a negotiation—or, worse yet, of having accepted more than one offer. So once you are in negotiation with one party, reject all other offers or ask them to wait and see if negotiations fall through.

If you suspect the buyer may not have adequate financing to purchase your property, you can ask his or her permission to contact his or her lender. Find out if he or she has been pre-approved for a mortgage that is large enough to cover your property. If you still have several buyers to choose from, remember: If you need to sell the property fast, you want the buyer who can close the fastest.

Look for the Best Terms

Look beyond price when you are negotiating and choosing a buyer. Someone who offers a lower price to take your property as is can save you a bundle in making repairs and improvements.

Hidden Costs of Selling Your Property

As with buying your property, you will find that when you sell you have to pay various fees, taxes and other expenses when you close the deal. Sellers typically do not pay as much as buyers in this situation, but you may be expected to hand over a check at closing for some of the following:

- your real estate agent's commission
- attorney's fees and any other professional fees
- sellers' taxes
- your share of the year's property taxes and/or your share of any condo assessment
- surveys, inspections, certifications, etc. that sellers pay for in your area

Ask your real estate agent for an estimate of your seller closing costs.

How to Turn over Your Tenants

If you sell your rental property while your tenants are under contract with your current rental agreement, they—and the new owner—will still be bound by the terms of that agreement. You cannot kick out tenants in the middle of a yearlong lease just because you have sold the property, and neither can the new owner. Your tenants will be protected by that lease until the date it expires, which means their rent cannot change, nor can the policies they agreed to regarding pets, number of occupants—whatever you have included.

Once you have accepted an offer from a buyer and have the deposit, you should start sharing information on the property and your tenants. See Chapter 6 for details on what that buyer will need.

For a smooth transition, you should alert your tenants that you are selling the property as soon as you are sure the sale will go through. Let them know that the new owner would like to contact them for information and, when the sale is final and you have a closing date, send a letter letting them know the details and introducing their new landlord. You might even arrange to send a joint letter with the new owner.

As soon as the closing is complete and you have turned over all keys, deposits and paperwork, you are no longer their landlord. The new owner must take responsibility for the remainder of any leases or rental agreements.

Tax Term Glossary

Use this brief glossary to help you through the following section.

Basis–The basis of property you buy is usually the cost, unless you inherited the property or received it as a gift. The adjusted basis is your original cost plus certain additions such as selling expenses, and minus certain deductions, such as depreciation and casualty losses.

Exchange–A transfer of property for other property or services, as opposed to a sale of property.

Fair Market Value–The price at which the property would change hands between a buyer and a seller when both parties have reasonable knowledge of all the necessary facts and neither is forced to buy or sell.

Paying Taxes on Your Sale

Once the closing is over and you are counting your money—and counting yourself lucky to be rid of a cash drain—do not shut the books just yet. You will still have to deal with taxes on the sale. Specifically, you will have to pay capital gains tax or regular income tax if you made money on the sale, or you can deduct a capital loss if you lost money.

Here is a closer look at the different tax scenarios of selling a rental property:

Capital Gains

When you sell a property you have owned for more than 1 year, it is considered a long-term investment, and you will pay capital gains on the amount of the selling price minus your selling costs and your adjusted basis in the property. The tax on this amount is calculated at capital gains rates, which are lower than regular income tax rates.

Generally, capital gains on sales of rental property are taxed at a maximum of 15 percent of your net profit. Your net profit is your profit on the sale minus the cost of purchasing the property and the cost of selling of the investment, as well as expenses for maintenance or upkeep that you have not deducted. Note that any gains due to depreciation that you have already claimed are taxed at 25 percent. (To put this in perspective, your ordinary income can be taxed at rates up to 35 percent.)

When you sell a property you have owned 1 year or less, that is considered a short-term investment, and you would typically pay your marginal (or top) tax rate on the net profit.

If you have been depreciating your property on your taxes each year, you will pay more tax when you sell. That is because when you sell, the depreciated price is considered your cost basis.

Short-Term or Long-Term?

To determine how long you have owned your rental property, start counting on the day following the date you acquired the property. If you closed on September 1, then start counting your ownership from September 2.

Capital Loss

If you lose money on the sale, you may get a tax break in the form of a capital loss. Keep in mind that a paper loss—a decrease in the property's value below its purchase price—does not necessarily qualify. The loss must be calculated on the sale or exchange of the property.

If your capital losses are higher than your capital gains, the difference is subtracted from other income on your tax return, up to $3,000 per year, or $1,500 if you are married filing separately. If you have more than $3,000 in capital losses, you may be able to carry over the deduction to the next year.

You will report your capital gains and losses on Schedule D: Capital Gains and Losses, which can be found on the Web landing page, www.socrates.com/books/landlording-handbook.aspx.

If you sell a property that was used as your personal home and as a rental, such as a duplex, then you must figure the gain or loss on the property twice—once for the percentage of the property that is a rental and once for the percentage that is your home. Gain or loss on the rental property should be figured separately; any gain on your home is a capital gain—you cannot deduct a loss on your personal residence. If you sell your home at a loss, the IRS considers that a nondeductible personal loss.

Like-Kind Exchange

If you buy another property after selling your rental, you can avoid paying capital gains tax altogether. Do this by using a 1031 tax-free exchange, or "Like-Kind Exchange." Here is how it works: You sell your investment property and purchase another property that costs the same or more than your sales price on the first property, all within a specific time frame. The IRS allows you to defer any capital gains until you sell the new property.

Note

If you arrange a like-kind exchange with a family member—your spouse, parent, child or sibling—and either person disposes of the property within 2 years, the IRS disqualifies the original like-kind exchange.

If you want to take advantage of a 1031 tax-free exchange, your first step—before selling or buying—should be to hire an attorney who specializes in real estate, and consult a tax accountant for details and deadlines regarding this exchange.

The Worst-Case Scenario

If you find yourself in debt and unable to continue to keep up with your expenses, you may be forced to back out of your mortgage. This means either contacting your lender and working out an agreement for lower payments, or hiring an attorney and going through foreclosure, which is the legal process by which your lender can take repossession of the property.

If you have to foreclose and your property value is less than the amount you owe on your mortgage, you will owe your lender the difference.

Example

At the time of foreclosure, you owe $476,000 on your original mortgage. Your lender assessed the property and determines its value at only $450,000. They will repossess the property and you will owe them the difference—$26,000.

Taxes and Foreclosures

The IRS treats foreclosure or repossession as a sale or exchange. You must declare a gain or loss from the property.

Foreclosure can seriously hurt your credit history and your ability to get a mortgage in the future. The good news is that because your lender wants to avoid foreclosing on your property, they will work with you to help you find an alternative. Here are some possibilities:

Mortgage Modification

If you can make your current monthly payment, but cannot afford the past due amount, your lender might agree to a mortgage modification. For example, they can add the past due amount into your remaining loan. Your lender also has the ability to lower your payments (and extend the length of your loan).

Selling

If you simply cannot afford the mortgage anymore, your lender might agree to postpone foreclosure for a specific amount of time in order for you to attempt to sell the property. Then you can pay off the mortgage in full or as much as possible. If you sell at a loss, you will still owe the remaining amount on the mortgage.

Deed in Lieu of Foreclosure

If you cannot sell the property or do not have enough time to find a buyer, the lender may allow you to give your property back to them—and forgive the debt. This has negative impact on your credit, but not as much as a foreclosure.

Last Word on Selling

If you are considering selling your rental property, review your reasons for doing so. If the property is profitable—or promises to be in the near future—you are likely to be better off hanging onto it. If you need quick cash, you can refinance, take out a home equity loan or get a second mortgage on it and you will still have the long-term investment of the property for security.

But if the property is causing you to lose money continually and you do not see a way to change that cash flow to a positive, you are probably right to sell it. Ideally you will make a profit on the sale or reap a huge tax benefit.

Continue Your Landlording Education

The information in this book should be enough to get your landlording business successfully up and running. From now on, you are sure to learn as you go—both from your own experience and from any mistakes and from information you pick up along the way.

Ongoing Resources

As for your continuing education, there are dozens and dozens of books, Web sites and even classes on owning and managing a rental property. Since you have already read this book, you have a good grounding on what your landlording responsibilities and workload will be. Here are some suggestions to fill in the gaps as you continue your education:

Stay Up-to-Date

To ensure that you keep up with changing laws, rules and trends regarding rental properties, Socrates has set up a special Web landing page at www.socrates.com/books/landlording-handbook/aspx for latest information and updates on being a Landlord.

Learn Your State Laws Regarding Landlords and Tenants

You can access a list of laws by state at www.landlord.com/legalmain.htm. Check this site—or ask your local housing agency—to find out your obligations on security deposits, disclosures and much more.

Join a Local Landlords' Association

Learn from the experiences of other landlords—and use them to get references for contractors, real estate agents and even tenants. An association is an excellent source of information on everything from the current rental market to how to perform a complicated repair. Search for an association near you at www.realestateassociaitons.com/index.html or www.landlord.com/assoc_main.htm.

Chapter 24

Keep an Eye on the Classified Ads

Even if you have a tenant who is only 2 months into his or her yearlong lease, you should be checking the For Rent ads in your local newspaper. It pays to have an idea of how many properties are for rent, the amount of rent being asked for and how long those properties are advertised. You want to have a big picture of the rental market so you will know if it will be tough or easy to get another tenant if necessary, and how much rent you can charge. The rental market can change constantly, so make this an ongoing research project.

Do not get complacent about keeping an eye on legal issues, your local rental market or trends in landlording (such as new tenant scams)—there will always be something new to surprise you in this field. With the help of the Socrates landlording Web landing page and the resources listed above, you will be prepared to face new challenges with your rental property and tenants.

The End

Thus ends the lesson in landlording. With your newfound knowledge, your skills, some hard work and a little luck, you should be able to translate your rental property into the foundation of your financial security.

Good luck with your landlording business!

Section Eight

Appendices

Managing Risk & Limiting Personal Liability as a Landlord

The possibility of losing some or all of their hard-earned real estate investments is something most landlords do not want to even consider. Unfortunately, the possibility of this happening is real, and it can happen in unforeseen ways. As a landlord, you face countless risks associated with property management and maintenance. Damage from lightening, fire, water, wind and hail—not to mention personal injury claims from a tenant or even from visitors to your buildings—cost building owners and managers hundreds of millions of dollars each year.

How do you manage these risks without spending huge sums annually? How do you ensure that your own personal finances and property are protected? How do you ensure that you and your family or heirs are protected from unexpected losses? Managing these risks and balancing the cost benefit equation requires you to take action on several fronts.

First, incorporate, as discussed in Chapter 8, as your principal means of asset protection in the event of a lawsuit. The proper incorporation plan will keep personal assets (home, cars, savings and investments) free from any claim should your rental properties experience unreasonable and unexpected claims. The added tax benefits of incorporation discussed in Chapter 8 are an added bonus.

Second, establish a well-defined and cost-effective risk management program by:

- purchasing a variety of insurance plans to reduce the risk of loss for specific perils;

- transferring some risks to a third party (e.g., your tenant) by insisting that each tenant carry renter's insurance or sign Tenant Self Insured Responsibility form. For more information and help on renter's insurance, visit www.socrates.com/books/landlording-handbook.aspx to learn about the Minotaur Insurance Renter's insurance Program for Landlords;

- retaining some risks through higher deductible levels on your insurance policies to reduce premiums; and

- practicing good loss reduction strategies—keeping the building in good repair and leasing to quality tenants.

Four Types of Insurance Coverage Landlords Should Carry

At a minimum, residential rental property owners should carry the following four types of insurance coverage:

1. **Property and Casualty Insurance.** A "P&C" policy, as it is called in the trade, in its most basic form will provide you with protection against damage to the property from events as diverse as civil commotion, glass breakage and vandalism to lightening, fire, smoke or damage resulting from a car running into your building. P&C insurance will also provide protection against lost income if a unit is uninhabitable due to a peril covered under your policy.

2. **General Liability Insurance.** This kind of coverage insures you against claims by third parties (for example tenants or visitors) for negligence, damage caused to the property of a tenant or visitor to your property, injury to someone on the premises or damage or harm to a third party who may be working on your property. Falling on a slippery stair and physical harm to a visitor or tenant due to a faulty handrail are examples of the kinds of risks managed by a general liability insurance policy.

3. **Flood Insurance and/or Water Damage Insurance.** As the name implies, this coverage protects against any sort of water damage except sewer back-up. Such insurance takes in a considerable range: accidental damage as a result of malfunctioning plumbing, heating, refrigeration or air conditioning systems, as well as water damage caused by nature, such as rain or snow. Normally, this sort of coverage is in addition or an endorsement to a basic property insurance policy.

   A provision in most property insurance policies excludes water damage caused by floods. Often people in areas susceptible to floods (or to hurricanes) must rely on federal government backed insurance programs to cover this sort of risk.

4. **Umbrella Liability Insurance.** For most businesses, and landlording should be treated as a business, this is coverage beyond that which a basic liability insurance policy provides and comes into force after the basic policy has paid the maximum it will pay. In other words, this is insurance against an unexpected, even catastrophic, loss; a basic policy is only sufficient for basic needs and losses.

What Your Insurance Coverage Should Protect You against as a Landlord

Depending on whether or not you have employees, your property and casualty and general liability insurance coverage should include:

1. A Dwelling Policy that will protect your property against:

    • riot, civil commotion, vandalism, theft, glass breakage;

    • lightening, wind, hail, volcanic eruption;

    • fire, smoke and explosion; and

    • damage from impact of an automobile/truck or airplane.

2. Liability for tenant and guest injuries.

3. Crime policy and a fidelity bond to protect against employee and other burglary and theft.

4. Loss of rental income.

    Beyond the mandatory workmen's compensation insurance required of all employers, additional coverages to consider if you have employees include:

    • libel and slander by employees against tenants;

    • discrimination lawsuits filed by disgruntled employees; and

    • allegations of fraud, misrepresentation and other intentional acts by employees.

Require Everyone Working on Your Property Be Insured and Bonded

To reduce general liability insurance premiums, you should require a certificate of insurance from any contractor or repairman working on your rental properties. The certificate of insurance will give you proof that these contractors have adequate levels of liability insurance and are up-to-date on their workmen's compensation insurance. If they do not have adequate insurance, any damages become your liability and will increase both your risk exposure and insurance premiums.

As added insurance that your contractors will complete a job, require a surety bond that will allow you to hire another contractor to complete the work at the surety bonding company's expense should your contractor leave your job unfinished.

Require All Tenants Carry Renter's Insurance Coverage or Sign Self Insured Responsibility Form

As part of your risk management program, use your Socrates lease rental agreement to require tenants to provide proof of renter's insurance coverage prior to taking possession and occupying the premises. Should you decide not to require renter's insurance, you and your tenants may initial the decline option to opt out of this requirement. Minotaur Insurance Agency provides easy access to a basic renter's insurance policy that is backed by an A.M. Best 'A' rated national insurance underwriter and accepts all applicants. Most renter's insurance policies provide coverage against everything from fire and theft to personal property and personal liability coverage for injuries and damages caused by tenant neglect. In essence, this provides an extra layer of liability protection for you as a landlord—

at no cost to you! An added benefit is the natural inclination of tenants to take greater care of your property when they are required to explicitly take responsibility for their actions.

Four Ways to Reduce Risks and Limit Personal Liability

Here are four ways to reduce your risks and limit your personal liability as a landlord:

1. Maintain adequate property and casualty and general liability insurance coverage on your rental property.

2. Use the Socrates Incorporation Kit to form a separate business entity to hold the title to your rental property, with a separate corporation for each property to provide maximum protection. Talk to your accountant or lawyer to ensure you maintain a separate identity for the company in practice by not comingling funds and to learn about other easy-to-avoid traps.

3. Practice risk management techniques that reduce your risks and personal liability as a landlord such as requiring scheduled maintenance and inspections.

4. Use the tools like those available on www.socrates.com/books/landlording-handbook.aspx to screen prospective tenants for credit history, criminal background, eviction history and other determining factors to ensure you only accept high quality tenants.

Questions Frequently Asked by Landlords

General

Who determines my responsibilities as a landlord?

The landlord and tenant each have duties and responsibilities toward each other as well as duties to the property. Some of the duties are set out in the rental agreement. For example, the amount of rent the tenant must pay is a duty included in the agreement. Other duties can be found in federal and state laws—such as prohibiting discrimination in renting properties. State laws may require landlords to make specific repairs. A wide range of contract provisions and legal regulations cover your obligations as both a landlord and tenant.

Advertising

What should be included in an advertisement when I have an available property?

A well written advertisement can save you time and money in the long run. Be specific in your description of the premises and provide the amount of monthly rent required so only those who can afford it respond to the ad. If a security deposit and first and last month's rent are required, include that in your ad as well. By making clear exactly what you are offering and requiring, you stand a better chance of getting a suitable tenant and avoiding possible problems in the future. For example, if you state in your ad that references from previous landlords are required, you automatically exclude applicants who are unable to supply such references.

What issues do I face when placing an advertisement?

Your advertisement should not and cannot in any way be considered discriminatory. Attempting to exclude applicants through advertising on the basis of race, ethnicity, national origin, gender, religion or disability violates the Fair Housing Act. Local ordinances and regulations usually re-emphasize these restrictions and may even broaden them. For example, the city of San Francisco prohibits discrimination in housing based on sexual orientation.

> **Tip**
>
> Age discrimination laws prohibit discriminating against people over 40 years old in housing. Including terms like students, recent graduates, college-aged, etc. that tend to exclude older individuals violates the law. Of course, by posting a rental notice at a college or university, you are most likely to get student applicants.

What should I ask for when seeking new tenants?

Nearly all landlords require prospective tenants to complete a rental application. The application requires information about the applicant's:

• income	• credit
• employment	• rental history
• Social Security number	• references

The application should also contain details about the property (for example, 2 bedroom, 2 bath apartment) as well as statements concerning:

- the amount of the application fee, if any;
- the amount of the security deposit;
- length of the tenancy;
- what notice is required for terminating the rental agreement; and
- the applicant's consent to a background and credit check.

Although the application form is not a substitute for the actual lease agreement, including such basic information helps the tenant understand the fundamental terms of the lease he or she may be signing later.

Can I charge an application fee?

An application fee may be required to cover the landlord's cost for credit and background checks. This fee should be less than $100; it will not be refunded if the application is rejected or the applicant decides not to rent the property (you should make the applicant aware of this provision by either telling him or her or including it on the application).

Application deposits are becoming more common. This fee is an advance security deposit and shows that the applicant is serious about renting the property. If the applicant ends up renting the property, it is applied toward the security deposit.

> **Tip**
>
> Ask questions of prospective tenants from a prepared list. It is important to ask each of the applicants the same questions to avoid accusations of discrimination. Do not ask questions about age, ethnicity, sexual orientation, disabilities or religion.

Can I rent to a minor?

No. Minors cannot enter into real estate contracts. If you do rent to a minor, the minor has the right to disaffirm the lease agreement, making it void and unenforceable. A minor can occupy the premises; however, an adult must sign the lease agreement. For example, college students typically have an arrangement where the parent signs the lease and the student lives in the apartment.

Can I ask about religious affiliation or marital status on the rental application?

No. If it applies to your rental property, the Fair Housing Act prohibits questions concerning race, color, national origin, religion, sex, handicap and/or familial status.

Background Check

How do I check a tenant's banking history?

Banks are unlikely to discuss specific details of a tenant's account; however they will generally confirm whether the applicant has an account and if it is in good standing.

Tip
If the applicant has written you a check for the application fee, you may call the bank, ask for the accounting department, tell them the account number and amount of the check, and ask if the check will clear.

I pulled the credit history for a rental applicant and checked with previous landlords. The applicant's history showed some late payments, but I primarily denied the application based on his or her rental history. Is he or she entitled to an Adverse Action Notice?

Yes. Although your decision not to rent to the applicant was not based on his or her credit history, since it was part of what you looked at in deciding whether to approve the application, you must provide a notice.

If my property manager uses a consumer reporting agency to verify rental applications, am I, as the landlord, still responsible for notifying applicants of an adverse action?

Yes. Although you are using a reference-checking agency, any information you receive from them based on a consumer report that results in your decision not to rent, increase a security deposit, etc. triggers an Adverse Action Notice. You must comply with the FCRA even though you did not actually view the credit report.

If the property manager did not use a consumer reporting agency, you are not required to provide an Adverse Action Notice. Your obligation to notify an applicant is triggered only when you use a report from a consumer-reporting agency to make your decision.

> **Tip**
>
> If you are a landlord and do not want to be subject to FCRA requirements, you or your employees should verify the application on your own. Although the consumer-reporting agency provides information you cannot obtain, you can still verify employment, income, check criminal history and talk to previous landlords about the prospective tenant.

Can an applicant I did not rent to and failed to give an Adverse Action Notice to sue me?

Yes. If you used a consumer-reporting agency to make your decision not to rent and failed to give an Adverse Action Notice you can be sued. The FCRA allows the applicant to sue you in federal court for compensatory damages, punitive damages (if the violations are deliberate), and attorney's fees. If you simply made an isolated mistake and you normally send out Adverse Action Notices, you are not liable to the applicant and the lawsuit will be dismissed.

Landlords want and need to know whether a prospective tenant can pay the rent. The applicant's employer may be contacted to verify employment and salary.

Discrimination and Fair Housing

Who must comply with the Fair Housing Act?

It is illegal to discriminate against prospective tenants. The U.S. Department of Housing and Urban Development (HUD) enforces federal laws and regulations prohibiting discrimination in buying, selling and renting housing properties. The Fair Housing Act prohibits any kind of discrimination in renting based on race, ethnicity, national origin, gender, religion or disability. If you own more than three rental units or use a leasing agent, you must comply with federal laws prohibiting discrimination in housing. Additionally, many cities have passed their own anti-discrimination ordinances with which you will have to comply. For example, in some locations, discrimination is prohibited on the basis of sexual orientation, although there is no such prohibition in federal civil rights laws.

> **Tip**
>
> The HUD Web site www.hud.gov has information on compliance with federal anti-discrimination laws for landlords, tenants, and prospective tenants who believe they have been a victim of discrimination.

Can I reject applicants if they have children under 18 years of age?

Landlords cannot reject an applicant because there will be children under 18 years of age in the household. The Fair Housing Act requires that children under the age of 18 living with parents or legal custodians, pregnant women, and people with custody of children under the age of 18 may not be denied housing.

However, properties that meet the definition of senior housing can deny housing to families with children. That is because senior housing is exempt from age discrimination prohibitions. These properties can also deny housing to people over 40 years of age who would normally be protected under age discrimination laws where the property:

- is occupied solely by persons who are 62 or older;
- houses at least one person who is 55 or older in at least 80 percent of the occupied units; and
- is specifically designed for and occupied by elderly persons under a federal, state or local government program.

Tip

If you are a landlord, whether you are regularly renting properties or not, keep organized files on each applicant. If a complaint is ever filed against you, the agency investigating the claim will ask about your basis for rejecting an applicant. You must be able to show that the applicant was rejected for a nondiscriminatory reason, such as a poor credit rating. Always avoid making personal remarks about any of your applicants in your notes.

My mother's large home has been divided into four separate apartments. Does she have to rent to anyone who applies?

No. As long as your mother continues to live in the house, she can refuse to rent to whomever she chooses. The Fair Housing Act does not apply to owner-occupied buildings with four or less units.

I own several duplexes and have instructed my rental agents to give people of my religion a rent reduction. Am I discriminating?

Yes. The Fair Housing Act prohibits a landlord from offering different rental terms or deals to prospective tenants based on their race, color, national origin, religion, sex, handicap and/or familial status.

Because of a job transfer, I need to rent my home for a year and I do not want to rent to anyone with children. Am I breaking any laws?

No. The Fair Housing Act does not apply to single-family home rentals where a real estate broker is not involved. As long as you handle the transaction yourself, you can refuse to rent to families with children (or anyone else) without violating the Fair Housing Act.

Lease Agreements and Policies

What are the basics I need to keep in mind about leases?

The lease agreement is the contract between the tenant and the landlord that sets out the duties and rights of each party. For example, the tenant has the duty to pay the rent on time and the landlord has the right to enter the premises for repair. Typically, tenants renting units in apartment complexes sign a standard lease form used by landlords in that state. A condominium complex owner or homeowner who is leasing will probably use a different form. A private landlord may use his or her own form or the standard form.

Some states have adopted the Uniform Residential Landlord and Tenant Act (URLTA), which covers many issues in lease agreements, as well as tenant rights and landlord remedies in lease disputes. A lease agreement may incorporate URLTA's provisions. For example, if the lease agreement states that return of security deposits is governed by URLTA, the landlord must follow those requirements.

Lease agreements that are less than a year in length do not have to be written. An oral agreement between the landlord and tenant is binding in these circumstances. In this situation, state law, rather than a written agreement, covers the duties and responsibilities of the landlord and tenant. Oral lease agreements are not recommended.

> **Tip**
>
> Always get a copy of the lease agreement after it is completed and signed by all the parties.

Do I need a written lease agreement if I am renting from a good friend?

It depends. Without a written agreement, certain laws covering the rental and leasing of property apply, rather than the terms you and your friend agreed to. Many states have laws that favor the tenant. For example, without an agreement, the law provides that you are in a month-to-month lease. The advantage is that you can move out with a month's notice. The disadvantage is your friend only has to give you a month's notice to end the lease.

Are there limits on how I can structure my leases?

Like any contract, a lease agreement can contain almost any terms to which the parties agree. Leases are typically written to favor the landlord and not the tenant. The tenant has the option to reject the lease and find another rental property if he or she does not like the terms of the lease. However, some leases can go so far beyond simply favoring the landlord as to make them patently unfair to the tenant. If this happens the entire lease is considered void because of its unconscionable lease terms. An elaborately lopsided lease provision favoring one party (usually the landlord) is unconscionable or unreasonable.

In order to better protect tenants from unconscionable provisions, the URLTA prohibits provisions in a lease agreement that require the tenant to:

- agree to waive or forego rights or remedies under the URLTA;
- authorize a person other than the landlord to obtain a judgment against the tenant on a dispute arising out of the rental agreement;
- agree to pay the landlord's attorneys fees in a dispute; and
- agree to limit the landlord's liability for injuries or damages the tenant suffers through the fault of the landlord.

Example

In New York State, courts have found the following provisions in lease agreements to be unconscionable.

- A clause prohibiting the tenant from asserting a defense in any proceeding the landlord brings against him or her.

- A clause raising the rent if the tenant brings a legal action against the landlord.

- A singles only clause that would allow the tenant to be evicted if he or she married or had a girlfriend/boyfriend move in.

- A clause prohibiting animals without the landlord's written consent and allowing the landlord to evict the tenant, when the landlord assured the tenants an animal would be allowed in order to induce the tenant to sign the lease.

Many states have not adopted URLTA. However, recently courts are ruling in the renter's favor in lease disputes based on unconscionable terms.

If part of a lease is considered unfair, will the entire lease be ruled unacceptable?

If a court determines that certain provisions are unconscionable, the entire lease may be unenforceable, since the landlord has a superior position to the tenant because:

- renters are not familiar with the carefully drafted legal terms in lengthy printed lease forms;

- the lease is usually carefully drafted and designed solely for the landlord's protection;

- the terms of the printed contract are usually non-negotiable;

- in most cases, the tenant is not represented by an attorney;

- the landlord not only possesses superior knowledge but also offers a scarce commodity; and

- the landlord is often assisted by expert legal counsel.

Can I change my mind about enforcing provisions of a lease?

A landlord cannot enforce a lease provision if he or she has previously chosen not to enforce it. The landlord's previous nonaction waives the provision. For example, if there is a rule against pets in the lease agreement and the landlord knows that the tenant has a pet when the tenant renews the lease, the landlord cannot later insist that the tenant comply with the rule.

> ### Example
>
> If your monthly rent has increased, but your landlord continues to accept the original amount (say by cashing your check), he or she cannot terminate the lease for your failure to pay rent. The landlord's continued acceptance of the original amount means he or she has waived the right to terminate the lease on the basis of nonpayment.

Policies and Practices

What are my rights as a landlord in terms of tenants' use of my property?

The landlord has the right to restrict the tenant's use of the premises. The typical lease agreement requires that the landlord must approve any modification, addition or change to the property. Additionally, the landlord may prohibit visual clutter such as flags, signs, outdoor decorations, plants, lights and additional items that can be seen by others.

Lease agreements also contain provisions concerning the behavior of tenants and their visitors, the landlord's treatment of the tenant's premises and the tenant's use of facilities.

There are usually a variety of rules concerning parking, mail, trash disposal and the like, which may not be incorporated directly in the lease, but will be set forth in a separate document, often referred to as house rules. The rules are still part of the lease (by reference), although they are not written into it. You should always ask for a copy of the house rules so you can avoid breaking them, and thereby inadvertently violating your lease.

What is the best way to control use of an apartment's facilities?

Tenants typically have the right to use swimming pools, tennis courts, exercise rooms, and party rooms under the terms of the lease agreement. However, the landlord has the right to control the time and manner of the tenant's use. For example, swimming pools are usually open during certain hours of the day only. The tenant's use of exercise equipment may be limited to an hour or two per day to give other tenants the chance to use the equipment. Tenants can reserve party rooms upon request, but may have to put up a deposit and sign a cleaning agreement.

What kind of policies should I have in place in order to protect myself and my property?

Standard lease forms commonly used by landlords prohibit a variety of conduct, including:

- behaving in a loud or obnoxious manner;
- disturbing or threatening the rights, comfort, health and safety of other residents and property employees;
- engaging in or threatening violence;
- disrupting business operations;
- possessing or displaying a weapon in a common area;
- tampering with electric and cable connections;
- storing gas appliances in closets;
- heating the unit with a portable cooking stove;
- using windows for entry and exit;
- drug possession and manufacture; and
- making libelous or slanderous allegations against the property owner and employees.

Not all bad behavior will automatically result in termination of the lease agreement. Some limitations on conduct set out in the lease may require the tenant to:

- dispose of trash every week in the dumpster;
- use passageways for exit and entry only;
- use non-glass containers at the pool;
- not cook on balconies or patios; and
- not operate a business on the premises, such as a daycare.

While violating rules which merely limit behavior may not result in immediate termination of the lease, repeating lesser offenses can eventually lead to eviction.

All limits on tenant behavior should also apply to the tenants' visitors and guests. Make it clear that unruly conduct by a visitor or guest will result in possible termination of the tenant host's rental agreement.

Can I enter an apartment whenever I think I need to do so?

Although the tenant has a right to privacy, the landlord typically has a right of entry to make repairs to the premises under the lease agreement. Some state laws allow landlords to enter to make health and safety inspections for dangers that present a hazard to the building and other tenants. However, in nearly all cases, the tenant must have notice that the landlord plans to enter or has entered the premises.

In California, for example, a landlord must give the tenant 24 hours notice and even then may only enter the premises:

- to make necessary or agreed-upon repairs;
- to show the apartment to prospective tenants, buyers, mortgage holders, repair persons and contractors;
- when the tenant has moved prior to the expiration of the rental term;
- when the landlord has a court order authorizing entry; and
- in case of an emergency that threatens injury or property damage if not corrected immediately.

What rights do landlord's have in regards to pets?

Landlords typically have strict pet policies. Standard lease forms usually prohibit animals of all kinds, including mammals, reptiles, birds, fish, rodents and insects. A tenant must get the landlord's consent in order to have a pet on the premises. An animal or pet deposit is almost always required.

Are there any limitations to my pet policies in my buildings?

Landlords can create as many restrictions as they want when allowing pets on the property, including:

- limiting the number of pets allowed;
- requiring proof of rabies and distemper vaccinations;
- requiring proof of registration with the local municipality;
- creating leash and collar rules;
- restricting the presence of animals in common areas; and
- requiring spaying and neutering of pets, and declawing of cats.

Exotic animals are routinely prohibited on properties where other pets might be allowed. For example, large snakes are usually not allowed under the lease agreement. Also, many landlords will prohibit vicious, poisonous or venomous pets, and certain dog breeds from the property.

However, service animals or assistance animals are excepted by a variety of local and federal laws, and cannot be barred from the property. They may still have to abide by certain rules, such as having appropriate vaccinations and being registered with the municipality, but they cannot be barred.

Tip
In some lease agreements, landlords may reserve the right to ask for verification that the dog is a service animal. Tenants should have a copy of the dog's service certification readily available for the landlord to keep in their file.

Apartment Subletting

As a landlord, I am confused about subleases and assignments. What are they?

A "sublease" or "sublet" is a transfer of the tenant's right to occupy the rented premises to someone else. The sublease can cover all or a part of the rental property, such as the second story only of a town home. The tenant remains obligated under the lease agreement for rent if the sublessee fails to pay. Under a sublease, the tenant has the right to reoccupy the premises, taking it back from the person to whom he or she subleased. For example, the tenant with a 6-month lease who must leave the country for 4 months can sublease his or her apartment to a friend (now called the "sublessee"). If the tenant returns before he or she expected, he or she can retake the premises and require the friend to move out.

An "assignment" is similar to a sublease. However, in the example above, if the tenant assigned his or her lease to a friend, the tenant cannot retake the premises. The lease assignment results in the friend stepping in the shoes of the original tenant. The friend is now the tenant under the terms of the original lease.

Subleases and assignments are commonly prohibited in a lease agreement. Standard lease forms usually allow subletting only when the landlord agrees in writing. However, a tenant does have a right to sublease or assign his or her lease, if there is nothing in the lease agreement or a law that prohibits it. Generally, laws require the prior consent of the landlord if the tenant wants to assign or sublet his or her lease.

Subsidized Housing

What is Section 8 housing?

Section 8 housing is low-income housing. However, there are two very different programs. One Section 8 program distributes rental vouchers to households that cover a portion of their rent. The family gets to choose where it wants to live and use the voucher to pay for part of the rent.

The second Section 8 program concerns the housing development itself. The entire development is Section 8 housing and any person or family qualified to live there pays a reduced rent. They do not receive a voucher. Instead, federal funds are paid to the housing development to cover the portion of the rent the occupants do not pay.

Can a Section 8 housing development reject a qualified applicant?

Yes. Applicants with a history of drug use and drug-related criminal activity can be rejected. Also, applicants with a poor credit rating do not have to be allowed to rent. A prospective tenant with no credit history cannot be rejected on that basis.

An applicant can never be rejected on the basis of race, color, religion, sex, familial status, national origin, disability and age. A single parent household or a family receiving welfare benefits cannot be rejected merely for their status.

Other than low-income families, is anyone else entitled to receive Section 8 rental vouchers?

Yes. Elderly and disabled individuals can obtain vouchers so that they may rent decent housing.

Does a private landlord have to rent to a tenant with a Section 8 voucher?

No. Only landlords who participate in the program (including companies that own and operate apartment complexes) are required to take tenants with vouchers.

A landlord cannot prohibit a Section 8 tenant from keeping a pet. However, he or she can require a pet deposit and exclude "dangerous" animals from the property.

Can a landlord evict a Section 8 tenant?

Yes, for good cause. Good cause includes failure to pay the rent, criminal activity and repeated behavior that seriously affects the health and welfare of other tenants.

Section 8 tenants have certain rights if a landlord attempts to evict them. The tenant can contest the notice of eviction by requesting a hearing with the local housing authority.

Move-In Deposits and Advances

It is the rare landlord that does not require a tenant provide some amount of money for a security deposit to insure the tenant does not damage the property. Additionally, a landlord may ask for first and last month's rent. Both amounts are due at the time the tenant signs the lease agreement.

Who determines the amount of advance rent?

The requirement for advance rent is part of the lease agreement. At the end of the lease, the advance payments are returned to the tenant or applied to the last month's rent. If the tenant breaks the lease, the agreement typically allows the landlord to keep the advance rent money.

Am I required to put it in an interest bearing account?

That depends on whether state or local law requires it. Generally, a landlord must keep advance rentals and security deposits in a separate noninterest bearing account.

Is there a limit to how much advance rent a landlord can require?

Some laws limit the amount to a certain percentage of one month's rent. For instance, a law may prohibit the landlord from collecting more than 150 percent of a month's rent as an advance rental payment.

How do I explain the difference between a security deposit and rent?

The difference between rent and a security deposit is that the landlord keeps rent and returns security deposits. The difference is important because laws require the landlord to handle security deposits in a certain manner.

Landlords typically require tenants to pay a security deposit to insure that the tenant will comply with certain provisions of the lease concerning damage to the premises and clean-up at the end of the lease. If the tenant complies, the deposit must be returned at the end of the lease.

A deposit that can be withheld for late rent or nonpayment of rent is considered to *not* be just a security deposit. In such situations, the security deposit is also advance rent, and the landlord does not have to return the money if the lease is broken.

Is there a maximum amount a landlord can demand for a security deposit?

Some states have laws setting a limit on the amount of security deposits, while others have no limit. As an example, California law requires security deposits to equal no more than 2 months rent on unfurnished rentals.

But remember, security deposits are different from advance rent. So although the California law has a limit on security deposits, it permits a landlord to demand 6 months rent in advance where a lease is 6 months or longer.

Is there a limit to the amount a landlord can require for a pet deposit?

No. Generally, pet deposits (if pets are allowed) are at the discretion of the landlord. Obviously, an exorbitant deposit will keep away pet owners, and some landlords keep the deposit high for this very reason. You can attempt to negotiate a lower deposit. Also, it might help to provide references from a former landlord concerning your pet's behavior.

Laws in some states place a limit on the total amount of all advance fees and deposits that a landlord can collect for a pet deposit. For example, California law limits all fees and deposits, including pet deposits, to 2 month's rent in an unfurnished apartment.

> A service animal must be allowed to reside with the disabled tenant; however, the pet deposit can remain the same for the disabled tenant as for a nondisabled tenant. However, if there is a "no pet" policy, then the pet deposit should be nominal since the law requires the landlord to accept the service animal.

What can I do if the tenant does not pay rent on time?

Leases typically allow the landlord to accelerate the rent when the tenant is in default. Failure to pay rent is a default—a provision of the lease has been broken. The landlord now has the right to demand all the rent due for the remainder of the lease. If you have a $500 per month apartment and fail to pay the rent on time with 4 months left on the lease, the landlord can demand $2,000.

Lockout and Liens

Can I lock a problem tenant out of the apartment?

Landlords may change the locks on the tenant's rental unit for nonpayment of rent. Laws permit lockouts if the landlord follows certain procedures. Most often, the landlord must:

- notify the tenant in advance that the locks are going to be changed;
- leave a notice telling the tenant where the new keys may be accessed; and
- make the new keys accessible 24 hours a day.

The tenant can still occupy the premises; however, he or she does not have possession of a key. Obviously, the inconvenience to the tenant is the landlord's bargaining chip to get the tenant to pay the rent he or she owes.

What are my rights as a landlord?

> Laws require the landlord's lien to be printed in large bold-faced letters in the lease. If it is not, it may not be enforceable against the tenant.

The law allows a landlord to take possession of a tenant's property and sell it to cover rent in certain situations. The landlord has the ability to take the property because he or she has a landlord's lien. The lien is a provision in the lease that makes all of the tenant's property subject to sale if the rent is not paid. Since the landlord's lien is part of the lease agreement, a court order is not necessary.

Some property is exempt from the landlord's lien and cannot be taken and sold for rent. Depending on the law of the state where the landlord is attempting to enforce his or her lien, he or she may not take:

- clothing
- tools, apparatus, and books of a trade or profession
- schoolbooks
- a family library
- family portraits and pictures
- furniture
- beds and bedding
- kitchen furniture and utensils
- food
- medicine and medical supplies
- a motor vehicle
- agricultural implements
- children's toys not commonly used by adults
- goods that the landlord knows are owned by a person other than the tenant or an occupant
- goods that the landlord knows are subject to another creditor's lien

> ### Seizure of Property
>
> The lien authorizes the landlord to take possession of the tenant's property only if he or she can do so peacefully. He or she may not break down the door, threaten the tenant or be disruptive when seizing the property. The landlord is prohibited from breaching the peace to enforce the lien.
>
> ### Notice of Seizure
>
> The landlord must leave a notice with the tenant that the property has been taken for nonpayment of rent along with an itemized list of the property.

What notice must I give a tenant about seizure for back rent?

The notice must state:

- the amount of past-due rent;
- the name, address, and telephone number of the person the tenant may contact regarding the amount owed;
- and that the property will be promptly returned when the past due rent is paid in full; and
- the fee for packing, removing, and/or storing the property (this fee must be part of the lease agreement or the landlord is not entitled to collect).

Sale of Tenant's Property

If the lease provides that the tenant's property may be sold for past-due rent, the landlord may go forward with a sale. However, the tenant must be notified of the date and time of the sale before it takes place. Laws typically require 30 days notice. The property is auctioned off to the highest bidder. After the past-due rent is paid, any remaining money must be sent to the tenant.

> When a tenant *abandons* the property, the landlord may remove all of the items in the unit. Under this situation, the landlord does not need a court order or a specific provision in the lease authorizing the removal and sale of the tenant's property.

Changes in Rental Amounts

My costs keep going up. Can I increase the rent to cover these costs?

Unless authorized by law, rent cannot change during the lease period. Of course, no tenant would oppose a rent decrease unless services were decreased as well. In rent-controlled apartments, laws may allow a rent increase if the landlord spends money on capital improvements, such as building a deck on the building's roof.

Landlord's Duties

As a landlord, what must I do to maintain my property without violating the law?

Under housing codes, residential rental properties must have, at a minimum:

- safe heating—a heating system that is in good working order and provides an adequate supply of heat to the property
- natural (or artificial) lighting that will allow normal indoor activities
- adequate ventilation
- satisfactory facilities for preparing and cooking food
- a sink with hot and cold running (and sanitary) water
- a flush toilet
- facilities for bathing
- a private entrance so that the tenant does not have to go through another property to get to the premises
- a means of escape from fire
- a working smoke alarm

Are there laws other than housing codes that I am required to follow?

Yes. The term housing codes typically refers to a number of regulations concerning rental properties. There are federal laws regarding the removal of lead paint and asbestos. Additionally, your landlord must follow certain city codes. Building codes cover the dwelling's electrical, plumbing and structural framework. Health codes concerning pests, rodents, garbage and other issues of cleanliness also apply to rental units. Finally, fire codes exist to ensure that smoke alarms, fire exits, extinguishers and alarms are present and working on the property.

What exactly constitutes a housing code violation?

Violations vary from city to city, but typically one exists if your apartment has:

- dilapidated stairs, railings, balconies or decks, and/or required exits blocked
- no electricity or inoperable lights, outlets or switches
- a faulty or inoperable elevator
- sewer blockage
- no gas and/or water service
- no heat and/or hot water
- no smoke detector
- no exterior locks or inoperable locks
- roof leaks
- inoperable or broken windows

What is the legal definition of keeping my rental property in "good repair"?

I order to keep the premises fit for human habitation (and meet the implied warranty of habitability and the various local housing codes), landlords are responsible for making repairs to keep the property in good, safe and clean condition or upkeep. State laws and housing codes require landlords to repair specific dangerous conditions and to keep the premises up to code. Your lease may also set out items the landlord has a duty to repair, such as appliances.

Repairs to bring the premises back up to living standards are only required if the landlord *knows* about the defects or has been notified. Either a tenant, a community member or city employee can notify the landlord.

Who is responsible for structural repairs?

Landlords must make structural repairs in all cases since the tenants' safety depends on the integrity of the building. The structural repair can be minor, such as a broken step. However, minor problems may lead to serious injuries. For example, the broken step may cause an older visitor of the tenant's to lose his or her footing, fall and break a hip.

If the tenant is responsible for breaking the step, he or she is also responsible for fixing it. The situation becomes complicated if the person who fell sues the landlord. Although he or she may not have had a duty to repair the step since the tenant was at fault, he or she does have a duty to keep the premises safe. If the step was in the front of the building and the landlord knew it was broken, he or she may be liable for the person's fall.

What are my responsibilities for heating and cooling?

Rental property must have working heat and cooling systems in order for the premises to be fit to live in. Any breakdown in the systems should be immediately repaired. The situation can turn into an emergency during very cold and very hot months. Children and the elderly are particularly susceptible to extreme weather. If you do not have working heat or air conditioning and you or your family's health and safety is at risk, call the city building inspector. City codes require adequate heating and cooling.

What are my responsibilities as a landlord in terms of safety and security?

The landlord has a duty to the tenant to maintain the tenant's safety and security. In locations where there is a probability of crimes being committed against his or her tenants, the landlord should install sufficient security devices. For example, if there have been several purse-snatching incidents as female tenants get out of their cars, the landlord could install high fencing and locked gates around the parking lot to help prevent the crimes and limit his or her liability.

What is the minimum required?

Laws commonly require all rental units, including apartments, houses, condominiums, duplexes, etc., to have the following security devices installed at the landlord's expense:

- a viewer or peephole on each exterior door;
- window latches on exterior windows;
- pin locks on sliding doors;
- security bar or door handle latch on sliding doors;
- keyless deadbolt locking device on each exterior door; and
- either a keyed deadbolt or doorknob lock on each exterior door (locks must be rekeyed after prior tenant moves out).

If the required security devices are not installed, such as a keyless deadbolt lock on the front door, the tenant has the right to install it him or herself and deduct the cost from the next rent payment. Some laws also permit the tenant to terminate the lease if he or she requested that the keyless deadbolt lock, for example, be installed and the landlord fails to do so.

Tip

Tenants must make a request to the landlord for installation of a security device in writing. Laws generally require the landlord to comply with the request within 7 days or less. If there have been any intruders in your apartment, many state laws require that the landlord comply with your request within 72 hours.

What must a landlord do to secure the property?

Laws require landlords of residential property to install particular locks and security devices. At a minimum, locks are required on all exterior doors and windows. Additionally, the landlord may be required to install key and keyless deadbolt locks on the exterior doors. Sliding doors and French doors may require special security devices as well.

What locks are required to be installed in an apartment?

At a minimum, all the exterior windows must have a window latch; exterior doors must have keyed doorknobs and a keyless bolt, and sliding glass doors must have both a pin lock and a handle latch or security bar.

Am I required to change the locks after the former tenant leaves and I move in?

Yes. Laws require landlords to rekey locks so that only the new resident has access to the rental unit.

Return of Security Deposits

What is the best way to handle security deposits?

Typically, the landlord is allowed to deduct the cost of damages to the premises from the tenant's security deposit. However, the landlord may not keep all or a portion of the security deposit for normal wear and tear. The landlord may also be required to give the tenant an itemized list of the damages deducted from the security deposit.

Eviction

What should I know about eviction?

When a tenant does not comply with the terms of the lease agreement, the landlord has the right to evict or remove him or her from the premises. Generally, the only legal basis for an eviction is the tenant's:

- failure to pay the rent
- defaulting or breaking a lease provision
- refusing to move out when the lease ends

An evicted tenant is a tenant who has been physically removed from the property. The tenant's property is also removed along with any other occupants (and their property) living on the premises. Once he or she has been evicted, the tenant is under no obligation to continue to pay rent.

In order to evict a tenant who has violated the terms of the lease, such as continuing to live on the premises without paying rent, the landlord is required to follow a precise legal procedure. The specifics vary from state to state, but generally all laws require:

- a legal purpose for eviction
- notice to the tenant
- a trial before a judge
- an order of eviction
- removal of the tenant

What does the law require of me, a landlord, in order to evict a tenant?

Typically, laws require between a 3 and 10-day written notice to the tenant that the landlord is seeking to evict him or her. The notice may be called the notice to vacate, the notice to quit or some other term. Some laws allow the landlord to notify the tenant him or herself. Others require that law enforcement personnel, usually a sheriff's deputy, serve the tenant with notice.

If a deputy must serve the notice to vacate, the court clerk typically prepares the notice for a fee. The clerk then sends the notice to the sheriff's office for service.

The sheriff can either give the notice to the tenant personally or post it on the door of the rental unit.

Once the notice is served, the tenant has a short time period to pay the past due rent, (if that is the issue), or to vacate the premises. For example, if a tenant is served with a 5-day notice to vacate on a Monday morning, he or she must pay the rent that is due or vacate by Saturday morning.

Holidays and weekends are included in the tenant's time to pay or vacate before the deadline. In the example above, the tenant must vacate on a Saturday. Although Saturday is part of the weekend, it still counts as a day in the notice period. The tenant does not get to skip Saturday and Sunday and wait until Monday to pay or vacate.

The sheriff's office does not serve notices and other legal papers on the weekends or holidays. If you are a landlord, keep in mind that there may be a delay before your tenant gets the notice to vacate during holiday periods.

What is the next step toward eviction?

Once the landlord has given the tenant a notice to vacate, or the notice has been served, and the deadline passes without the tenant paying the past due rent or vacating, the landlord can file a lawsuit to evict the tenant. The lawsuit may be termed an eviction suit, a forcible entry and detainer suit (FED), or a dispossession suit. In such lawsuits, the landlord is requesting a judicial order allowing him or her to remove the tenant, the occupants and any property belonging to them that is on the premises.

Once the lawsuit is filed, the tenant must be notified of the filing. This is accomplished by serving him or her with a copy. The tenant has the right to respond or answer the landlord's suit. The deadline for a response (called the answer date) begins to run once the tenant is served. Typically, the response time is short—about 10 days.

What happens when a tenant is evicted?

The eviction order is sometimes termed a writ of possession or writ of ejectment, which gives the landlord the right to have the tenant physically removed and retake possession of the rental property.

The landlord does not personally carry out the writ of possession. Typically, a sheriff's deputy arrives at the premises with the writ and orders the tenant to immediately vacate and takes his or her possessions, under threat of arrest. The deputy stays until the tenant is completely moved out of the property. The landlord is not involved with this part of the process, since court orders are enforced by law enforcement personnel. He or she may watch and observe only.

My tenant finally vacated after I won an eviction suit; however, he left behind all his property. What do I do?

> Most laws require the landlord to keep the property for a period of time. You can leave it in the apartment or store it. Once the required amount of time has passed, you may sell or dispose of the property. For example, if you are required by law to keep the property for 14 days, you cannot dispose of it until 14 days from the time the tenant vacated the apartment has passed. You must store the property or leave it in the apartment.

The judge ruled in my favor and I can evict my tenant. Do I have to let her in to retrieve her property after the trial?

> Yes. The tenant has a right to take her belongings with her when she is evicted or before the order is served on her.

Tip
The tenant still has the right to enter the apartment after he or she has lost at trial and before he or she is served with the writ of possession.

Questions Frequently Asked by Tenants

Why would a landlord be interested in the questions that tenants often ask? For one thing, they give you a first-hand understanding of some of the problems that landlords face. Further, tenants often know the law as well as or better than landlords. What follows are some of the typical, day-to-day questions you need to be able to answer—but this time from a tenant's perspective!

General

I got a bad recommendation on an applicant from a previous landlord. Do I have to disclose this to the person who applied?

No. However, if you discriminate by refusing to rent to this person based on a previous landlord's information, you are acting illegally. For example, if the previous landlord told you that the prospective tenant had children and you decided against renting to him or her, you are discriminating based on familial status.

I completed an application and paid an application fee. If I have not heard from the landlord, have I been rejected?

Probably. If more than a week has passed, you can assume you have been rejected. Some laws give the landlord 7 days to notify an applicant that he or she has been accepted or rejected.

Some laws do not require you to enter into the lease agreement if the landlord has failed to notify you of your application's acceptance within 7 days of submission. If these laws apply to your state you will have the right to rent elsewhere. Although you are not entitled to a refund of your application fee, all security deposits must be returned to you since the landlord was late in his or her acceptance.

My application was approved but I am moving to another complex. Can the landlord keep the application fee?

If you were approved and did not sign the lease, the application may allow the landlord to keep the entire deposit. Typically, the fee is nonrefundable under any circumstances.

Even without a written provision in the application, if the landlord turned away a potential renter before you told him or her you had changed your mind, the landlord may have a right to keep the application fee as compensation for his or her loss of a renter.

I paid an application fee at an apartment complex before my application was approved and decided that same day to rent somewhere else. The landlord will not return the fee. What can I do?

Review the application carefully. Most applications contain a provision that the fee is nonrefundable if you change your mind, the application was rejected or the application was approved.

If it turns out that the landlord is improperly retaining the fee, and you cannot convince him or her to return the fee over the phone, you need to write a demand letter. The demand letter should state that you are entitled to the return of your application fee and you are demanding it be returned by a certain date or you will sue. If you are still unable to get the fee back, you can sue for it. However, the amount of the application fee may not be worth the effort of going to court.

Background Check

What do I need to know about landlords checking my credit? Can they do this?

Landlords now run credit checks on all prospective tenants. Credit reports are accessed through one of the three major consumer-reporting agencies (CRAs) listed below. Any tenant who is unsure about the state of his or her credit can contact one of the agencies and request a copy of his or her credit report. (Beginning September 1, 2005, consumers may obtain one free copy of their report each year.)

Equifax Information Services, Inc.
P.O. Box 740241
Atlanta, GA 30374
To order report: 800.685.1111
Web site: www.equifax.com

Experian
P.O. Box 2002
Allen, TX 75013
To order report: 888.397.3742
Web site: www.experian.com

TransUnion LLC
P.O. Box 1000
Chester, PA 19022
To order report: 800.888.4213
Web site: www.tuc.com

The credit report notes all late payments on credit cards, mortgages and loans. Any judgments—including foreclosures and evictions—or bankruptcies are also listed on the report. If a prospective tenant has a record of late payments or other negative history, the landlord may choose not to rent to that person.

Tip
Typically, the rental application includes a statement that by signing the application, the prospective tenant consents to a credit check. If you do not want your credit report accessed, tell the landlord and then cross out the provision in the application—but do not be surprised if your application is rejected.

Tip
Every time your credit is checked, it is reflected on the report. These checks are called hard inquires and they typically lower your score because the CRA assumes you are applying for loans or credit cards and that your debt will increase. You can learn more about consumer's rights concerning credit reports at the U.S. Federal Trade Commission's (FTC) "Web site on Credit" at: www.ftc.gov/bcp/conline/edcams/credit/index.html.

Do I as an applicant have any rights concerning credit reports?

The Fair Credit Reporting Act (FCRA) is designed to protect the privacy of consumer report information and to guarantee that the information supplied by CRAs is as accurate as possible. The FCRA requires landlords who deny a lease based on information in the applicant's consumer report to provide the applicant with an adverse action notice. If you receive such a notice, you are entitled to a free credit report (in addition to the one you are entitled to once a year) from the CRA listed in the notice.

Questions about the Fair Credit Reporting Act can be answered by calling 877.FTC.HELP. Information is also available online at www.ftc.gov.

Tip
If your application is rejected on the basis of a report from a reference-checking agency, you are entitled to a copy of the report under the FCRA. However, a reference verified by the landlord or their employee is not covered by the FCRA if your application is rejected. You are not entitled to a copy of their notes or other documents regarding the references they obtained.

Will my landlord check my employment status?

Landlords want and need to know whether a prospective tenant can pay the rent. The applicant's employer may be contacted to verify employment and salary.

If you have filled out a rental application, let the office manager or Human Resources department at your job know they may receive a call from a potential landlord.

I filled out a rental application and, although I never authorized it, the apartment manager went ahead and pulled my credit report. Is this legal?

Yes. Under the Fair Credit Reporting Act your credit report can be viewed "in connection with a business transaction that is initiated by the consumer." In other words, by filling out a rental application you have begun a transaction—the process of renting an apartment—and the landlord has the right to use a consumer reporting agency to examine your credit.

The landlord who does not have a written authorization could be violating the FCRA if an apartment was not actually available to rent. In that situation, the applicant can successfully argue that there was no "business transaction" since there was no apartment to rent at the time the consumer report was pulled.

The property manager wants a co-signer on my lease because of some negative history reported in my credit report. Does this mean I can get a copy of the credit report?

Yes. Requiring a co-signer on the lease because of your credit history is considered an adverse action and federal law requires that the property manager give you an Adverse Action Notice. The agency that provided the report listed in the notice must provide you with a free copy of your credit report.

Tip

Other actions that are considered adverse—even though you were able to rent the apartment—include:

- increasing the security deposit;
- requiring first or last month's rent when it is not normally required; and
- raising the rent (to dissuade you from renting).

My apartment lease is up for renewal. Can my landlord check my credit history without my permission?

Yes. Laws do not require a landlord to get permission, written or otherwise, to check an existing tenant's credit history. Since you are currently living in one of their apartments, the FCRA considers you to be in a business transaction.

A landlord can also pull a consumer report on a tenant that owes a debt, without the tenant's authorization. For example, the tenant who is routinely late with rent, has damaged the apartment in excess of the security deposit or moved out with time left on the lease, owes a debt, and his or her credit history can be examined without authorization.

What else can I expect in terms of a background check?

You may be asked to provide the name(s) and telephone number(s) of previous landlord(s). Either the landlord you are applying to or a reference-checking agency may contact previous landlords or other parties you list on the application in order to check your rental payment history and compliance with lease provisions.

Your criminal history is also a factor in your ability to rent. It is becoming more common for landlords to conduct background checks to determine if you have been arrested or convicted of a crime. If you do have a criminal record, advise the landlord at the time you complete the rental application. The landlord may be more sympathetic to your side of the story if he or she hears it before completing the background check.

I am in the process of a rental application and the landlord is requiring a $35 background check fee. Is this legal?

Yes. Laws allow landlords to charge prospective tenants for the cost of a background check. Landlords are not permitted to make a profit on the fee, however.

Can a landlord perform a background check without my authorization?

Yes. Landlords do not need authorization if the information is public and available. For instance, any person can check court records to determine if you have been convicted of a crime, or involved in a civil lawsuit, such as a divorce or a bankruptcy.

A greater amount of information is available publicly then you might realize. For example, records of real estate owned by an applicant are public, as well as some business filings. The military may disclose an applicant's name, rank, salary, duty assignments, awards and duty status without consent. Driving records are not confidential and if the landlord has a driver's license number, he or she can obtain information from the state Department of Motor vehicles. School and medical records, however, are not released without your express written authorization.

Police records and court records are two different documents. Court records are public records and accessible. Police departments, however, typically only release records to the individual involved in the report. For example, informal and unauthorized requests for police records using the applicant's name will be denied. On the other hand, requests for calls made to a police department concerning a certain address (an applicant's former apartment, for example) are often approved.

Discrimination

My brother just got out of a drug rehabilitation treatment center and apartment managers do not want to rent to him. Is this illegal discrimination?

No. The Fair Housing Act does not prohibit a landlord from refusing to rent to a tenant who he or she believes would pose a threat to other tenants because of illegal drug abuse or severe mental illness.

Can a landlord refuse to rent to a gay couple?

Yes. Although the answer is no if the rental property is in certain states and cities that prohibit discrimination in housing on the basis of sexual orientation. Federal law and the Fair Housing Act do not protect against discrimination based on a tenant's sexual orientation.

Can a landlord refuse to rent to unmarried couple?

Yes. Although the answer is no if the state or city where the property is located prohibits discrimination on the basis of marital status.

My husband has AIDS and the manager of an apartment complex we want to live in is reluctant to rent to us. Can the manager refuse to rent an apartment to us?

> States with laws prohibiting discrimination against gay tenants include California, Connecticut, the District of Columbia, Massachusetts, Minnesota, New Hampshire, New Jersey, New Mexico, New York, Rhode Island, Vermont and Wisconsin. Cities with local anti-discrimination laws included Atlanta, Miami and San Francisco, among others. A more comprehensive city list is available at www.lambdalegal.org.

No. The Fair Housing Act prohibits discrimination in housing based on disability, (meaning those individuals with mental or physical impairments that substantially limit one or more major life activities). Since AIDS affects the major life activities of your husband, he is considered disabled under the Fair Housing Act. Remind the apartment manager that your husband has the same status as a blind or deaf person and he or she cannot refuse to rent to you on the basis of his illness.

Can a landlord require that I prove I am a U.S. citizen before he or she rents to me?

Yes. The FHA does not prohibit discrimination based solely on a person's citizenship status. For example, the landlord has a right to know if your visa (allowing you to study in the United States) is going to expire soon, which could result in you leaving before the end of the lease.

> The landlord requesting citizenship information from prospective tenants must request the information from all applicants. The landlord cannot discriminate by only requesting documentation from certain applicants.

I am a single mother with two small children. A landlord recently told me that the only vacant apartment had been rented, when in fact it was available. Have I been discriminated against?

Yes. The landlord violated the Fair Housing Act by claiming that the apartment in question had already been rented when it had not. Making a false statement that housing is unavailable for viewing, rental or sale based on familial status is prohibited.

We have signed a lease for an apartment by the pool, but now the landlord wants to put us in a part of the complex where most of the families with children are living. Is this legal?

No. The Fair Housing Act prohibits landlords from providing alternative or different housing facilities or services to specific groups or individuals based their race, color, national origin, religion, sex, handicap and/or familial status. Your landlord is violating the law by attempting to force you to live in a certain section of the complex because you have children.

Tip
The landlord is also prohibited from requiring an extra security deposit or other fee because you have children.

I believe that I was discriminated against when I tried to rent an apartment. What is the procedure for making a complaint?

You have 1 year to notify HUD (Office of Housing and Urban Development) of the discriminatory action. You can call HUD's hotline at 800.669.9777 or make a complaint at their Web site, www.hud.gov/fairhousing.

You can also make a complaint by writing a letter to HUD that includes:

- your name and address;
- the name and address of the person your complaint concerns;
- the address of the house or apartment you were trying to rent or buy;
- the date when this incident occurred; and
- a short description of what happened.

The letter should be mailed to the HUD offices at:

Office of Fair Housing and Equal Opportunity
Department of Housing and Urban Development Rm. 5204
451 Seventh Street SW
Washington, DC 20410

How will HUD handle my complaint?

After HUD has received your complaint, an investigator will contact the person who allegedly discriminated against you and request a response. Typically, HUD attempts to mediate the matter. However, if the landlord continues to deny the discrimination and you stick to your story, the issue will be set for a hearing. Attorneys for HUD prosecute the matter on behalf of the United States government. The attorneys are not representing you personally, although you have the right to be present and get your own lawyer if you choose.

What do I "win" if the landlord is found to have discriminated against me?

If the hearing officers make a finding that discrimination occurred, you have the right to move into the housing you were initially denied. The landlord could be required to pay a fine of up to $50,000 in extreme cases of discrimination.

Landlord Policies

How do I know if there is a policy regarding tenants' behavior?

Landlords are usually up front about their expectations. Check the Prohibited Conduct provision in your lease for a list of behavior that violates the lease. It is in the landlord's interest to maintain a peaceful property, and you may have been given a list of behavior that is prohibited when you signed the lease. Also, the landlord may have had you sign a separate agreement concerning tenant conduct.

Signs are usually posted at pools, tennis courts, in laundry rooms, and on parking lots that spell out the behavior that is expected from (or prohibited by) a tenant. For example, signs posted at swimming pools set out the hours it is open, the minimum age for swimmers, as well as any glassware and toys that are prohibited.

Can I be evicted for my "bad" behavior?

Absolutely. The lease agreement prohibits most types of offensive behavior and allows the landlord to terminate the lease if your behavior violates policies. However, landlords typically give you a warning and allow you to correct the behavior before terminating the lease. For example, one loud party will probably not result in eviction, if you quieted down after receiving a complaint.

Do visitors have to follow the behavior policies?

Yes. The landlord has the right to exclude guests and visitors who are violating rules and policies. Further, the tenant can be penalized if his or her guests do not follow those policies. For example, if the tenant's friend insists on parking in another tenant's assigned parking spot every time he or she visits, the visitor friend can be banned from the premises. Or if the tenant's visitor leaves the apartment intoxicated and threatens another resident, the landlord will treat the incident as if the tenant had made the threat. Under the lease agreement, the tenant could be evicted. However, the most likely outcome will probably be that the visitor gets banned from visiting the property.

The lease agreement may give the landlord and his or her employees the right to ask visitors for photo identification and find out if the visitor is a resident or guest. If the visitor refuses, he or she may not be allowed into the complex.

Can the landlord make new policies that are not in the lease agreement?

Yes. Standard lease forms allow landlords to put new rules into effect immediately if they are distributed and are applicable to all rental units. For example, a rule that all decorations must be removed from doorways and porches must be obeyed as soon as you are informed. A notice or warning that the new policy will begin in 1 week, for example, is not required.

New rules and policies cannot require tenants to pay a new fee or additional amount of money. The tenant's financial obligations are set out in the lease agreement and cannot be modified while the lease agreement is in effect.

Can my mother bring her dog when she comes to visit?

> Unless your lease provides differently, animals are not allowed in the premises, including those belonging to visitors and guests. You can always ask the landlord or property manager and perhaps they will consent but, if you allow the dog in your apartment without consent, you have violated the lease agreement.

My landlord allows pets, but has prohibited me from getting any more. If my landlord has already allowed me to have two cats in the premises, do I have a right to a third?

> No. Limits on the number of animals, particularly cats and dogs are common. Although the landlord has consented to pets and you may have paid a pet deposit, if you bring another cat to live with you, you will be violating the lease.

I have a friend who has a service animal. Can he *and* his dog visit me at my apartment?

> Yes. Disabled individuals with service animals cannot be prohibited from bringing their pet onto the premises. The best practice in this situation is to notify the landlord of the circumstances so he or she will not think you are violating the lease if the animal is spotted on the property.

My neighbor has complained to the landlord that my dog barks during the day and disturbs him. Do I have to get rid of my dog?

> Very likely. Just as you are prohibited from disturbing your neighbors, so is your dog. The lease agreement typically requires that the landlord give you notice so you can correct the problem (for instance, find a new home for the dog).

> If the dog must go and you decide to move before the lease ends, you are breaking your lease and the landlord can demand all the rent due on the months that are left on the lease.

I own a vehicle that is not operable and it is parked in one of my assigned spaces. Can the landlord make me move it?

> Yes. If your vehicle has become an eyesore, you may be asked to move it to a less visible part of the parking lot, or remove it altogether from the property.

> Standard lease agreements do not allow unauthorized vehicles on the premises. A tenant may or may not be entitled to notice before the vehicle is towed. A vehicle is unauthorized and illegally parked if it:

> - is inoperable (for instance, a flat tire);
> - is on jacks, blocks or has wheels missing;
> - takes up more than one parking space;
> - belongs to a resident no longer living on the premises;
> - is parked in a handicapped space without the proper tags, etc.;
> - blocks other vehicles from entering or exiting the premises;
> - is parked in a fire lane;

• is parked in another tenant's assigned space;

• is parked on the grass or sidewalks;

• blocks garbage truck access to dumpsters; and

• does not have a current license, registration or inspection sticker.

Making Alterations

What are my rights to make alternations in my apartment?

Some alterations are acceptable and the landlord does not have to be notified if they are made. For example, pictures, photographs and other decorative wall hangings are usually allowed under the lease.

An issue that has become common is the tenant who wants to put up a satellite dish on his or her patio or balcony. Many lease agreements do not allow radio, television or other antenna to be erected or installed on or anywhere within the premises without the landlord's consent. However, the Federal Communications Commission (FCC) prohibits landlords from restricting a tenant from installing certain satellite dishes and other types of antennas, as long as the tenant meets FCC limitations.

Is hanging artwork on the walls an alteration?

Not usually. Lease agreements generally allow artwork, photographs and other decorative items to be hung on the walls or in the grooves of wood paneling. You must use small nails and make small nail holes; large anchor bolts or expansion bolts may be considered an alteration.

Can I hang curtains in my apartment without "altering" the premises?

Yes. Window coverings are allowed and a tenant may hang them. If you hang curtains and have to install the curtain rods, let the landlord know and assure the landlord you will repair any holes in the wall. Also, the landlord may not even mind the curtain rods at all if you plan to leave them when you move out.

> **Caution**
>
> If you want to install blinds, notify the landlord since you will be tampering with the woodwork around the window or the window frame. The landlord may consider this a major alteration.

If I make alterations without the landlord's consent, what will happen?

Making major alterations without the landlord's consent violates the lease agreement and you could possibly be evicted. A major alteration is anything from repainting a wall to changing out a light fixture to structural modifications. After the lease ends, the landlord may deduct the cost of removing the alterations from your security deposit.

I want to paint my apartment at my own expense. Is this a problem?

Painting is considered a major alteration. Additionally, paint can stain and damage the premises if it is not applied correctly. If you paint without the landlord's express consent, you are violating the lease agreement.

Example

A standard lease provision prohibits painting, wallpapering, carpeting and electrical changes.

Can I be prevented from hanging the American flag outside my rental unit?

Yes. If no flags of any kind are permitted, you cannot fly an American flag (or any other flag). You can display the flag inside the privacy of your home, but not in the common areas of the rental property.

Typically, a person has the right to fly the American flag or any other symbol as protected free speech. However, since the tenant is on private property (the landlord's), he or she has no free speech rights in common or open areas.

Can I place a satellite dish on my porch?

Under the Federal Communications Commission (FCC) rules, a tenant has a limited right to install a satellite dish or receiving antenna on the leased premises. The landlord is allowed to impose reasonable restrictions regarding installation. The most significant of these rules:

- limit the size of a satellite dish to one meter (39.37 inches);

- restrict installation to areas exclusively within the tenant's use (meaning the dish or antenna, as well as installation hardware, cannot extend beyond the tenant's porch, patio or balcony); and

- allow reasonable restrictions by the landlord to prevent damage to the property (during installation and removal).

However, the lease agreement can be more liberal than the minimum requirements of the FCC. If satellite dishes are not mentioned in the lease, you are probably allowed greater latitude in the size of the dish and method of installation.

Tip

More detailed information from the FCC on tenant and landlord rights regarding satellite dishes is available at: http://ftp.fcc.gov/cgb/consumerfacts/consumerdish.html.

Can I hang Christmas lights outside my apartment balcony?

Unless Christmas or holiday lights are prohibited, you may hang Christmas lights as long as they are not a nuisance to a neighbor. For example, if they are very bright and blink throughout the night, you may be required to turn them off at a certain time.

> The landlord, through the lease agreement, can prohibit you from publicly displaying religious symbols. Although you have the freedom to practice your religion, you are only protected from government interference, not a private individual's restrictions (such as the landlord) on private property.

Can I have a grill on my balcony?

Yes. You may have a grill on your balcony, although it is very likely you cannot use it on the balcony. Grilling near the exterior of the premises is a fire hazard and is probably prohibited in the lease. Even if the lease does not mention grills, city codes typically prohibit open fire cooking within 10 to 15 feet of an exterior wall of a residence.

Co-tenants and Roommates

What is expected if I have a roommate?

> One co-tenant cannot keep the other tenant from living on the premises if they get into a disagreement. They both have a right to occupy the premises under each of their leases.

Two or more people are allowed to rent one property. In that situation, the occupants are known as co-tenants. Landlords typically require all persons, not related, living on the premises, to sign their own individual lease covering the property. Although it is a common belief, co-tenants do not have half the obligations under the lease; they are *each* responsible for all the obligations. For example, if the rent is $500 per month and one of the tenants moves out or fails to pay, the other tenant is liable for the entire $500. Likewise, if one tenant damages the property and does not reimburse the landlord for the repairs, the landlord can demand all the costs from the other tenant.

Can someone move in with me that is not on the lease?

Not without the landlord's consent. Having another person move in usually violates the lease agreement. The landlord will give you notice that the person must move out and, if you fail to correct the situation, you can be evicted.

Standard lease forms usually state that no one else may occupy the apartment other than the tenant and the occupants listed on the lease when it is signed. Additionally, you can be limited to how many days in a month an individual can stay over as a guest at your apartment.

I am looking for a roommate. How can I make sure the person will pay the rent, clean the apartment and be fairly quiet?

A good screening tool is a questionnaire you can have potential roommates fill out. It should include questions concerning your personal preferences and pet peeves, such as whether you object to overnight guests. Other topics to ask about include:

- The hours they keep on the weekdays and weekends. (For example: Do you sleep late on the weekends? When do you leave for work or school? How late do you stay up? How much time do you spend in the bathroom?)

- Furniture and other items (For example: What furniture are you going to bring with you to the apartment? Do you have computer/stereo equipment and how much room do you need to set it up?)

- Visitors (For example: Do you have family and friends that will come over often? Will you have out of town guests? Do you expect to have overnight guests? Do you plan to entertain?)

- Working from home (For example: Do you work from home and what is your schedule?)

- Cooking (For example: Do you cook frequently? Do you expect your food to be kept separately from mine?)

- Alcohol consumption (For example: What types of alcoholic beverages do you drink? How often do you drink?)

- Smoking (For example: Do you smoke? Do you have friends and family who smoke that will visit?)

- Pets (For example: Do you have a pet? Do you object to pets? Do you expect any visitors to bring pets with them?)

- Cleanliness (For example: How important is cleanliness to you? What types of cleaning are will you do—bathrooms, kitchen, vacuuming, etc.?)

- Sharing and borrowing (For example: Do you normally borrow items such as clothes or jewelry? Do you expect to share dishes, appliances, etc? Do you expect to borrow my car?)

- Leisure activities (For example: Do you watch a lot of television? Do you like to have music on while you are in the apartment? Do you object to television? What types of music do you object to?)

- Rent obligations (For example: How do you plan to pay the rent—by mail, in person, to me, etc.? What will you do if you cannot pay the rent?)

- Repairs (For example: Can you pay for repairs if the problem is your fault? Can you be home if a repairman needs to come into the apartment? Do you have a problem talking to the landlord about repairs or other items that need to be fixed?)

- Rental history (For example: Have you had a roommate before? When and where? Did you move out early? Were you able to pay the rent every month?)

- Criminal history (For example: Have you been arrested or convicted of a crime? When and where? Have you ever had to call the police? Has anyone ever complained to the police about you?

Do I need to have a written agreement with my roommate if we are renting an apartment together and have both signed the lease?

You do not have to have one, but it is highly recommended. If your roommate moves out, you are still obligated to pay the rent—including your roommate's half—for the remainder of the lease.

My roommate and I want to enter into an agreement with each other concerning our obligations while we are renting an apartment together. What needs to be included?

Your agreement is called a Co-tenant Agreement or Roommate Agreement. The following items should be covered in the agreement:

- Term of the lease (attach a copy of the lease to the agreement).
- List move-in and move-out dates for each tenant.
- State which roommate gets what bedroom, bathroom, closet, etc.
- Each roommate must provide advance notice to the other of guests (For example: Each tenant will notify the other 24-hours in advance of an overnight guest.)
- List of expenses to be paid by each tenant and the amount (For example: Rent—$400; Utilities—50% of monthly bill; Telephone—50% of monthly bill; Internet service—$30; Cable—$40, etc.)
- Reimbursement (For example: The tenant that pays the telephone/ utility/cable bill will reimburse the other tenant's portion within 24-hours of payment.)
- Repairs (For example: Each tenant will pay the entire amount charged for any repairs for which he or she is responsible.)
- Late fees (For example: The tenant who causes the rent/utilities/ telephone payment, etc. to be late must pay the entire late fee.)
- Amount of security deposit owed to landlord (For example: Each tenant will pay a proportionate share of the initial security deposit.)
- Insurance (For example: Each tenant agrees to take out renter's insurance covering his or her items in the apartment.)
- Sublet by permission only (For example: Each tenant agrees that he or she will obtain permission from the other to sublet.)
- Eviction rights (For example: Each tenant has the right to evict the other if a tenant is charged with a crime.)
- Damage (For example: The tenant who causes damage to the apartment will reimburse the other tenant if the security deposit is withheld.)

The agreement should be dated and signed by each roommate. Although the landlord has no obligation under the Roommate Agreement, offer a copy to him or her for their files.

Subleasing

Can I sublet my apartment?

Unless your lease agreement prohibits subleasing, the law allows you to sublet your apartment. However, you cannot lease to a person that you know will not comply with the terms of the lease.

What reasons do I need to sublet my apartment?

You do not need a reason to sublease. Typically, a tenant subleases because of an extended vacation, job relocation, and marriage or family obligations.

If I sublet, do I have to notify the landlord?

Probably. Since the landlord's consent is usually required (under the lease agreement and by law) before a tenant can sublease, you would likely be violating the lease by subletting without telling the landlord and getting his or her consent.

Caution
Check the rental laws in your state. Many states have laws prohibiting a sublease without the landlord's consent.

The act of subletting your apartment in violation of the lease agreement does not in and of itself terminate the agreement. Although subletting without notifying the landlord and getting his or her consent is probably a default under the terms of the lease, the landlord may or may not decide to terminate the lease and evict you (and the sublessee). For example, standard lease forms allow the landlord to end the tenant's right to occupancy on 24 hours notice for any default. After notice from the landlord, you would have 24 hours to remove the sublessee and be back in compliance with the lease.

Does the landlord have to consent to a sublease if I find a reputable person to move in and sublet my apartment?

Not really. If the lease agreement and the law prohibit subletting without the landlord's consent, he or she does not have to consent to the sublease. And unless a clause in the lease states that the landlord may not withhold his or her consent unreasonably, you should probably assume that the landlord is not even required to be reasonable in making his or her decision. The landlord can refuse for any reason or no reason at all.

A few state laws may require the landlord to be reasonable in giving his or her consent to a residential sublease. New York law, for example, states that the landlord's consent shall not be unreasonably withheld. In these states, the landlord must consent to a sublease to a reputable person of the tenant's same character.

Commercial leases are somewhat different, often requiring that the landlord be reasonable in granting consent to a sublease.

My landlord has consented to the subleasing of my apartment. Can I sublease my apartment for the rest of the lease term?

Yes. You can sublease if you have no intention of returning to the premises. However, you are ultimately responsible for complying with the lease agreement provisions regarding termination. You must notify the landlord, in writing, 30 days before it expires that you will not be renewing the lease. The sublessee and the landlord can make their own agreement to a new lease after your original lease terminates; you have no involvement in the new lease agreement.

Who pays the rent in a sublease?

The original tenant must continue to pay the rent. The tenant collects the money for rent from the sublessee and makes the rental payment.

In some cases, the landlord may agree to accept the rent from the sublessee directly. If the landlord is a party to the sublease, he or she can agree to accept rent from the sublessee, without letting the original tenant out of his or her responsibility to pay the rent under the original lease. However, the original tenant could then argue that the landlord's acceptance of rent from the sublessee means the original tenant is not responsible for the rent any longer. To avoid any confusion, contractual responsibilities of the parties should be clarified before the sublessee moves in.

> **Tip**
>
> If you sublease, plan on collecting the rent and paying the landlord yourself. You and the sublessee should have a written agreement as to when and where the sublessee will pay. Have the sublessee agree to pay you 7 days before the rent is due. The extra time will give you the opportunity to resolve any rent issues that might arise between you and your sublessee.

If I sublet, will my furniture and other possessions stay in the apartment?

Quite often, yes. Part of the reason a sublease is attractive to a tenant is that he or she does not have to actually move any possessions while gone. Your sublet agreement should include a provision requiring the sublessee to care for and maintain your furnishings.

Is a written agreement required if I sublease my apartment?

There is no requirement for a written sublease agreement. However, without one you cannot enforce the sublease. For example, the person to whom you subleased can move out before the agreed upon date.

A written sublease protects both of the parties. You have a written agreement from the sublessee that he or she will pay the rent on time and comply with other provisions of the original lease, and the sublessee has proof of his or her right to occupy the premises for the length of the sublet agreement.

A sublet agreement should include:

1. the date;

2. the name each of the parties;

3. the address of the premises to be subleased;

4. the date the sublease begins;

5. the date the sublease ends;

6. the amount of the rent;

7. the date the rent must be paid by the sublessee to the tenant or to the landlord if he or she has agreed to accept payment;

8. the form of rent accepted (cash only, for example);

9. the amount of the security deposit the sublessee must pay and the conditions for its return (for example, you will return the security deposit when the landlord refunds the tenant's original security deposit);

10. a statement that sublessee must care for and maintain furnishings and other items left in the apartment;

11. a statement that sublessee is responsible for damage to tenant's furnishing, etc. that are left in the apartment;

12. the replacement cost or the amount sublessee owes for damage to tenant's furnishings, etc.;

13. the amount of tenant's original security deposit; sublessee will be responsible for any portion not returned to tenant;

14. the signature of both of the parties; and

15. the signature of the landlord, if his or her consent is required or he or she is a party to the sublease.

The agreement does not have to be lengthy. The items listed above can be covered in three or four paragraphs.

Tip

Your landlord may have to approve the sublet agreement under the terms of the lease agreement. If this is the case, show the sublet agreement to him or her before you go to the trouble of having the sublessee sign it.

Do I still have any responsibilities once I sublet?

Yes. Not only are you obligated to make sure the rent is paid, you are ultimately responsible for any damage to the premises while they are being sublet. For example, if the person to whom you sublet your apartment breaks the glass in a patio door, you are liable for the landlord's repair costs.

I am leasing a house. If I take in a boarder or roomer, am I subletting?

No. You are not putting your boarder in possession of the entire rental premises. He or she only has the right to occupy a room. The landlord may argue that the tenant has violated the lease agreement's prohibition against subletting by taking in a boarder. However, courts have held that an occupant is not a tenant and there is no violation of the lease agreement.

Moving In

The property manager says the apartment I plan to rent is not available for inspection before I sign the lease and move in. I have looked at the model apartment—is this an adequate inspection?

No. The model apartment is not the apartment you are renting. In this situation, once you sign the lease, you will be obligated to pay rent on an apartment you have not seen or inspected. Without an inspection, any problems that arise after you move in could be attributed to you rather than the previous residents. Tell the property manager you want to rent but will only sign the lease if the two of you can inspect the apartment first.

The property manager and I inspected my apartment, but then stated that he or she does not have time to let me walk through the entire complex and inspect the outside. Should I sign the lease anyway?

No. You should be able to walk through the entire property and inspect all areas to which residents have access. For example, you want to make sure the weight room that is advertised is a working weight room in good condition. Other common areas to inspect include tennis courts, pools, party rooms, the mailbox area, parking areas and dumpsters. If the outside of the complex is not well maintained, it is a good bet that your apartment will also be kept in poor repair.

Why do I have to pay a security deposit?

Landlords commonly require security deposits to insure that the tenant complies with certain terms in the lease agreement. For example, if, under the lease agreement, the tenant is required to clean out all appliances before moving out, and does not, the landlord can deduct the cost of hiring someone to clean from the security deposit.

Tip
When you pay your security deposit, get a receipt or have the landlord note the amount paid on the original lease and on your copy. Standard lease forms have a blank for the landlord to fill in the amount of the security deposit.

What happens to the money I paid as a security deposit?

Depending on the law in your state;

- there may be no requirements on the landlord;
- the landlord may be required to put security deposits in an escrow account; and/or
- the law can direct the landlord to place security deposits in an interest bearing account for the benefit of the tenant.

Can I be required to pay a nonrefundable cleaning fee when I sign a lease?

Yes. In addition to a security deposit, the landlord may require a nonrefundable cleaning fee. The amount is usually less than $100.

Even if you make a nonrefundable cleaning fee, the landlord can still deduct expenses for special cleaning from your security deposit at the end of the lease. Special cleaning is beyond that needed for normal wear and tear. For example, if you were a heavy smoker in a furnished apartment, the upholstery and drapes may require special cleaning to remove the odor.

Is my pet deposit refundable?

Although the term deposit indicates that the amount paid may be refundable, some landlords retain the pet deposit at the end of the lease. Before you sign your lease, ask the landlord if he or she treats the pet deposit as a security deposit (with amounts subtracted for damage) or a fee. If the landlord says all or part of the pet deposit is refundable at the end of the lease term, add that provision to the lease if it is not already included.

My landlord is charging me a pet deposit, but he or she also wants to add $25 to the monthly rent for cleaning since I have a cat. Is this legal?

Yes. The landlord can charge the amount of rent he or she believes is fair. You always have the option of not signing the lease and renting somewhere else.

> **Tip**
>
> If you do not keep the cat for the full length of the lease, you are still obligated to pay the extra $25 per month under the lease terms. Ask the landlord to include a provision that the extra amount will be waived if the cat is no longer living with you.

My roommate has a dog and paid the pet deposit that our landlord required. If the dog damages the apartment so that repair costs exceed the pet deposit, will part of my security deposit be kept?

Yes. Although the dog is your roommate's, you are jointly responsible for all damage to the apartment. You need to come to an agreement with your roommate where he or she will reimburse you for any damage caused by his or her pet that is withheld from your security deposit. Alternatively, you can ask your roommate to pay you a pet deposit, which you will return once you get your security deposit back.

My landlord has changed the locks to my apartment. Have I been evicted?

No. A lockout is not an eviction. You are still allowed to enter your apartment and the landlord has to give you the new key as well. The landlord's motive is to get you to pay delinquent rent rather than evict you.

My landlord locked me out of my apartment and refused to give me a new key since the lease says I am not entitled to one. Is this legal?

No. Laws pertaining to lockouts generally make any lease provisions that change the legal requirements of a lockout (such as requiring the tenant to be given a new key) void and unenforceable. Although the lease might say that the landlord does not have to give you a key, the law requires him or her to do so.

What can I do if my landlord refuses to give me the new keys to my apartment after he changed the locks?

You can file a court action requesting a writ of re-entry. The writ orders the landlord to give you a key immediately and allow you to re-enter the apartment. You file the request in court, the judge issues the writ and the sheriff's office serves the landlord with it. Once the landlord has been served, he must comply with the writ or risk being in contempt of court.

> **Tip**
>
> There is a filing fee as well as a fee to have the landlord served with the writ. If you cannot pay the fees, ask the court clerk for a pauper's affidavit. The judge can order the writ to be served without a fee if he approves the affidavit.

My electricity has been turned off because I am late paying the rent. Is this legal?

Laws do not allow electricity to be turned off in any circumstances when it the temperature is below freezing or a heat advisory is in effect. Additionally, landlords cannot disconnect or shut off power to a unit rented by tenant who will become seriously ill as a result.

Under no circumstances can a landlord interfere with the utilities that you are directly paying. For instance, if you pay for your electrical service separately from the rent, and the landlord interrupts the service, he or she is committing a criminal act and you have the right to go to a small claims court to obtain an order requiring the landlord to restore the service. Additionally, you can ask the court for an order terminating the lease agreement and your attorney's fee.

However, if you are in an all bills paid lease agreement where your rent includes utility payments, the landlord may have the right to turn off your utilities for nonpayment—this depends on local law. Even in this situation, the landlord may be prohibited from shutting off electricity and other utilities in extreme heat and cold. He or she may also be prohibited from shutting off electricity if you have verifiable health issues or needs. In either case, do not hesitate to call a health or building inspector if your health is endangered and explain the situation.

The landlord is not paying the electric bill in my all bills paid apartment complex. What are the tenants' options?

> The tenants can pay the electric company and deduct the payment from rent; however the best option is to terminate the lease. Laws generally allow tenants to terminate a lease within 30 days of receiving notice from the utility company of a future shut off, or notice of an actual shut off, whichever is sooner.

I live in a building divided into four apartments and the tenants split the utility payments. Can our landlord shut off the natural gas heating if one of us does not pay the rent?

> No. If the tenants of the building are paying the utility bill separately from their rent payment, your landlord does not have the right to shut off the gas connection. He can only shut off the connection for nonpayment of the tenant's separate utility bill.

My landlord is threatening to enforce his landlord's lien and seize my property for nonpayment of rent. If there is nothing in the lease about this option, can he take my property?

> No. The lease must specifically provide for the landlord to enforce a lien on your property for nonpayment of rent. Laws require that the provision allowing the landlord to enter and seize your property be underlined or printed in conspicuous bold print in order to be enforceable.

My landlord wants to increase my rent, even though I have a lease. Can he do that?

> The amount of rent that you pay under the lease agreement cannot be increased until the agreement terminates. The lease agreement is a contract and the landlord cannot change the most important provision—the amount of rent—on his own. If you have notified your landlord that you intend to renew your lease, the rent remains the same unless the landlord notifies you in advance. In a month-to-month tenancy, the landlord may increase the rent effective with the next month's rental payment as long as the tenant is given 30 days notice.

Fit for Habitation

Can I terminate my apartment lease if the landlord refuses to exterminate for mice and rats?

> Yes. The landlord has breached the implied warranty of habitability by allowing vermin to infest your apartment. However, if you have notified the landlord of the problem, he is allowed an opportunity to exterminate and put your apartment back into habitable condition.

Not all unhealthy conditions make the landlord liable for a breach of the warranty of habitability. For example, some of the paint in older buildings may be lead-based. The landlord is not required to remove the lead paint. However, under the *Lead-Based Paint Hazard Reduction Act of 1992*, the landlord must *disclose* known lead hazards when residential premises built before 1978 are leased. Landlords must also provide a pamphlet on lead poisoning to the renter before the pre-1978 property is rented.

The water pressure in my apartment is so low I can barely take a shower. Does this make my apartment unfit to live in?

> Probably not. As long as the toilets flush, you can get drinking water, wash dishes, etc., the low water pressure is more of an annoyance than a health issue. If, however, the water becomes unavailable during some parts of the day, your apartment is unfit to live in, and if the landlord does not fix the problem, you can terminate your lease.

I want the landlord to replace the regular glass in my sliding door with safety glass. If he refuses, is he violating the warranty of habitability?

> Not unless a state or city housing code specifically requires safety glass on doors in rental units. Although the safety glass might be better security, leaving ordinary glass in the door does not necessarily put your safety at risk.

My wife is in a wheelchair and I want our landlord to lower the kitchen counters in our apartment. If he refuses, can we break the lease since the apartment is not habitable for my wife?

> No. By renting you and your wife the apartment, the landlord has only guaranteed you a healthy, safe and clean place to live. His duty is to keep the property in a condition that does not deprive you and your wife of essential functions, such as cooking. Although it would be more convenient for the counters to be lowered, the landlord's refusal does not completely deprive you of the ability to use the kitchen as it was intended.

My landlord insists I pay an extra fee during the summer for the cost of air conditioning. Is this legal?

> It depends on your lease agreement. However, you should know that in some areas of the country, a landlord is required to provide cooling during high heat warnings so that it is fit for habitation. You are not required to reimburse him for his expenses in complying with the law.

> | Tip |
> | --- |
> | Extra fees for heating are also illegal unless you are required to make the payments under the lease as additional rent or a separate utility. |

My utilities are included as part of my rent. Can my landlord prevent me from running an air conditioning window unit I have purchased?

> Yes, if your lease sets a limit on the amount of energy or electricity you can use per month. If it does not, you are free to run the air conditioning unit and any other appliances. If the lease does not allow you to use the air conditioner, the landlord is still required to provide adequate cooling to make your apartment livable in conditions of extreme heat.

> **Tip**
>
> In regions where air conditioning is not common, there may be a clause in your lease that says you need permission from your landlord in order to install an air conditioner. Unless your landlord agrees to it, do not run the air conditioning unit or you will be in violation of your lease.

My landlord gave me a deal on my apartment if I took it as is. Is he free to ignore the problems I am having with the water supply in the unit?

No, your landlord must bring your apartment up to code or fit for habitation. Your apartment must have a supply of running hot and cold water. The lack of water, heat, cooling, certain security and safety measures and other unsafe and unsanitary conditions mean the apartment is not fit to rent under the law. The landlord cannot get around the requirements by renting the apartment as is; i.e., he cannot have you waive your right to the implied warranty of habitability.

> **Tip**
>
> If you rent an apartment as is, you cannot later complain of dingy paint, stained carpet, and other cosmetic issues, as long as the basic requirements of safety and hygiene are in place.

The heat is not working in our apartment and I have moved in with my mother. Am I still responsible for rent?

You must pay the rent until the lease is terminated. If the heat is not working, laws typically require the tenant to notify the landlord and allow him time to make the repair. If after notice, the landlord does not make the repair, you can terminate the lease and move out.

At a minimum, your notice should be sent certified mail, return receipt requested and include:

- a description of the repairs needed;

- a statement that a threat to your health or safety exists;

- a request that the repairs be made in a reasonable amount of time (in an emergency as little as 24 hours is reasonable; otherwise, allow for 7 days).

> **Tip**
>
> Notify the landlord immediately of the problem and that you have had to abandon the unit. He has a duty to make repairs to the heating unit in a reasonable period of time and notify you when the apartment is livable again. In very cold weather, requiring the heat to be repaired within 24 hours is reasonable.

I rented a condo in a nonsmoking unit, but my neighbor's smoke is infiltrating my unit. What are my options?

You may be able to move without breaking your lease if you can show that the second-hand smoke is affecting your health to the extent that a major life function is impaired. For example, if the second-hand smoke has caused severe asthma and you are now unable to breath without medication, your condo has become uninhabitable.

> **Tip**
> Some city codes prohibit smoking in rental dwellings. Check with your local code enforcement office to determine if you can make a formal complaint.

Even if the condo has not become unfit for habitation, you may still be able to terminate the lease under the nuisance clause. Many leases contain a clause that prohibits activities that unreasonably interfere with other residents' enjoyment of the premises. You can argue that the secondhand smoke has unreasonable interfered with your enjoyment of the premises because of discomfort or health problems.

State laws typically define a nuisance as "anything which is injurious to health, indecent, offensive to the senses, or an obstruction to the free use of property so as to interfere with the comfortable enjoyment of life or property."

If the landlord refuses to correct the problem, he or she could be liable for the tenant's medical expenses as a result of health problems due to secondhand smoke as well as moving expenses.

> **Tip**
> If you are a tenant smoking in a nonsmoking unit, the lease may allow the landlord to evict you for breaking the no smoking policy.

Does a leaking ceiling make my apartment unfit for habitation?

Yes, although minor leaks may not immediately impact your safety or health, roof leaks typically violate city housing codes making the apartment unfit to live in if the leaks are not repaired. A constant leak can lead to mold, mildew, bacteria and other health hazards. For example, the upstairs neighbor who has a toilet that constantly leaks into your bathroom is an unsafe and unsanitary condition.

My apartment is very run down but the landlord says it is "up to code." How can I find out if the apartment complex is actually safe?

Contact the city code enforcement office and ask if the complex is properly registered and certified by the city as a safe rental unit. You should also ask when the property was last inspected.

> **Tip**
>
> Before signing the lease or moving in, contact the city code enforcement office for a formal code report history on the apartment unit or building.

If the landlord has not fixed the furnace in my apartment by winter, is the apartment unfit for habitation?

Yes. City property and building codes require that rental units have adequate heating.

> **Tip**
>
> Cities have different requirements, but typically the temperature in a rental unit must be at least 60 degrees if the outside temperature is below freezing. For instance, Seattle requires a permanent heat source capable of maintaining an average room temperature of at least 65 degrees when outside temperatures are 24 degrees or above, and at least 58 degrees when the outside temperature is below 24 degrees.

We do not have heat in our apartment and I cannot get my landlord to respond to my complaints. What can I do to get the heating unit repaired?

Since adequate heating is required under city building or landlord/tenant codes, you can notify the city building inspector or the code enforcement section of your local city government. The building inspector will come to your apartment to verify your complaints. The inspector will then contact the landlord and require repairs to the heating unit. If the landlord does not comply, the city may begin imposing fines.

> **Tip**
>
> If it is very cold and there are children in the home, you should notify the building inspector immediately and emphasize that the lack of heating has become an emergency situation.

Because of a recent illness, I am now confined to a wheelchair. Is my landlord required to make any alterations or modifications to my apartment?

Yes. Because you are now disabled, your landlord should offer you an apartment that is handicapped accessible or modify your existing unit. The modifications should include such things as bathroom and tub rails, lowered light switches and thermostats and widening doors.

The windows in my daughter's bedroom in our apartment are painted shut. Does the landlord need to make them operable?

Yes. Bedrooms must have escape routes in case of fire. If the landlord will not repair the window, notify the city fire marshal. In the meantime, if you cannot unstick the window yourself, you should move your daughter out of the bedroom.

> **Tip**
>
> Generally, if an apartment unit is three stories or higher, an alternate fire exit (such as a fire escape) must be available.

My apartment is overrun with roaches although the landlord has brought in an exterminator. I threatened to report a housing code violation, but he says I am responsible for the problem. Can I make a complaint?

You can complain, but the code enforcement inspector may decide the problem lies with you. Although landlords must keep rental units in compliance with housing codes, tenants have responsibilities too. To help control roaches, rats and other vermin, you are required to keep:

• the apartment clean and sanitary

• the stove, oven, refrigerator, and other appliances clean

• put your trash and garbage in the garbage carts or dumpsters

> Most leases permit you to be evicted for failing to maintain certain standards of cleanliness and safety in your apartment. For example, you cannot continually clog up plumbing fixtures, fail to remove trash and debris or tamper with smoke alarms and fire escapes.

The heat in my apartment is not working and the landlord has provided me with several space heaters instead of making repairs. Is this legal?

No. Housing codes require a permanent heat source in rental dwellings, such as an oil, gas or electric furnace, or permanently installed baseboard or wall heaters. Electric and kerosene space heaters are not legal as a primary heat source in rental housing. Your landlord is violating housing codes.

In this situation, contact the city housing code enforcement office immediately. Lack of utilities, such as heat, typically qualifies as an emergency and the repairs must usually be made within 24 hours. If the landlord still does not repair the heating, you can terminate the lease after notifying him or her of your intention to move out.

Can I withhold rent if the landlord is cited for housing code violations?

> Rather than withhold rent, notify the landlord you are terminating the lease because the premises are not habitable. Include a statement that your health and safety are in danger because of the violations.

It depends on your location. Some cities and states have laws that allow the tenant to withhold rent once the dwelling is declared unfit for human habitation by the housing code inspector. However, withholding rent does not mean you do not pay rent. Instead, your rent is typically deposited in a city escrow account until the landlord makes the required repairs.

If you have paid money into a rent withholding account and the landlord does *not* make repairs, your money will be returned after a period of time. For example, a landlord may have 6 months to make the repairs. During that time, you must continue to pay rent into the escrow account.

I received a notice that my apartment complex has several housing code violations and that tenants will be relocated. Why do I have to move?

The city building inspectors have determined that your apartment is not fit for human habitation until the landlord makes certain repairs. Tenants cannot, by law, occupy a dwelling that is unfit.

How do I find out more about tenant relocation because of housing code violations?

Contact the person on the notice you received or the city housing code office for assistance and ask for help. In some instances, city personnel will work with tenants to find a new place to live, often making calls to apartment buildings on behalf of residents, as well as assisting with difficult problems such as deposits, move-in dates and pet issues.

> If you have been forced out of your apartment, you may have the right to sue the landlord for breach of contract (the lease) and breach of the warranty of habitability. Those types of lawsuits typically allow you to recover attorney's fee and court costs.

How do I file a complaint regarding housing code violations in my apartment unit?

You must contact your city building or housing code enforcement office. You will likely be asked to complete a form, sometimes called a request for service. Typically, an inspector will respond within 5 to 7 days, although a shorter time can be arranged in an emergency situation.

Some code enforcement offices require you to first contact the landlord by letter with your complaint and allow him or her a period of time to repair before the inspector will be sent out. An investigation of your complaint may be delayed until you comply with that requirement. Therefore, before contacting the code enforcement office, send a letter to the landlord listing all the problems and indicate a copy of the letter will be sent to the code enforcement office. Send one copy and keep another copy for your records.

What happens once I report a housing code violation?

Once you have made your complaint, a city building inspector is assigned to investigate.

The code enforcement office then writes the landlord a letter listing all the violations found during the inspection. The landlord is given a deadline to make repairs according to the severity of the problem. If the repairs are not made, the landlord is given a citation and must appear in court where he or she could be fined for his or her failure to repair.

Tip
Mark your calendar to call the code enforcement office to check the status of your complaint within 7 days from the date you first complained. Get the name and numbers of the building inspector assigned to your complaint and call to check the status with him or her as well. Continue to mark your calendar to call the inspector every 7 days until the matter is settled to your satisfaction.

Can I be evicted if I report housing code violations?

No. The landlord cannot evict you for reporting a violation as long as one exists, you have been paying your rent and there are no other issues that permit him or her to evict you.

> Retaliatory or wrongful eviction is prohibited by law. You can sue in court and recover damages (moving expenses), attorney's fees and court costs

Can I report a housing code violation anonymously?

Most code enforcement offices require the name and address of the person complaining before sending out an inspector. However, you can ask that your identity not be divulged to the landlord.

The toilets in my apartment have never worked properly. Can I move out?

Yes. Assuming the landlord is aware of the ongoing problems with your toilets and has not made adequate repairs, notify him or her in writing that you have been constructively evicted because of the unsafe and unsanitary conditions, are unable to use and enjoy your apartment and are terminating the lease.

Despite numerous complaints to my landlord and calls to the police, my neighbors continue to party nearly every night and I am unable to sleep. Can I move out?

Yes. You are being deprived of the use and enjoyment of your apartment. Since your landlord refuses to control or evict your neighbors, notify him or her that you are moving out because his or her failure to remedy the situation has resulted in constructive eviction from your apartment.

My neighbors have highly offensive posters in their apartment, with the windows open directly in my view; the landlord refuses to force them to put in window coverings. Can I move out before my lease ends?

No. You must be able to show that some portion of your apartment has become unusable due to the landlord's failure to remedy the situation with the neighbors. Although their wall hangings may be offensive, in order to argue that you have been constructively evicted, you must be able to show that because of the wall hangings:

- your apartment has become unfit for human habitation
- conditions were created that were dangerous to your life, health or safety
- the essential functions of your apartment became unusable.

I want my apartment inspected for mold but the landlord refuses to pay for the testing. What can I do?

Landlords are not required to pay for mold testing but they are required to provide tenants with a safe and healthy environment. Document the mold problem with photographs (if the mold is visible) or using a mold air test kit. Once you can show that mold is present in the apartment, make a written complaint to both the building code enforcement and health department in your city. The landlord may be forced to hire an inspector.

> **Tip**
>
> Certified industrial hygienists can be hired to test environmental air quality. However, there are many self-proclaimed mold experts willing to test your home. Always check the person's credentials; those with Internet only training and certifications should be avoided.

What are some signs that my apartment may be infested with mold?

You should look for mold that is:

- blackish-green in color ("black mold")
- yellow, green and white colored mold ("trichoderma")

Other signs include:

- ceilings and walls with peeling paint
- condensation on walls, ceilings and floors

Physical symptoms include:

- stomach aches and diarrhea
- extreme fatigue
- eye and nose irritation
- respiratory tract infections
- skin rashes and hair loss

Where do I look for mold?

If you believe there is mold in your apartment but have not been able to find it, pull out and look behind the washer, dryer and refrigerator. Mold often grows under carpeting—pull up carpets and inspect the padding and floor underneath if you can.

My family has become ill because of mold in our apartment. Can we move out?

Yes; however, to avoid owing rent on the remainder of your lease term you need to notify the landlord in writing that the premises are unsafe, unsanitary and have become inhabitable. Include a statement that because of the mold, you and your family have been constructively evicted. Copy the city health department and building code enforcement office with the letter.

Ordinary Repairs

My apartment needs new bathroom light fixtures, a hole in the wall repaired, new tile and caulking around the tub, and stove and kitchen sink repairs. Is all this more than ordinary repairs?

No. In combination, there are a lot of repairs to be done, but each one is an ordinary maintenance matter. Your landlord is required to keep the basic functions of the premises in good working order.

It is not a life or death situation, but our dishwasher has quit working and the landlord is not responding to my requests for repair. Do I have to live without a dishwasher?

> Although the landlord does not have to provide appliances, if he or she does, they must be maintained in working order. He or she is violating the lease as well as the law by refusing to make the repair.

> In situations where the repairs are small and the landlord is not responsive, the best option may be to repair and deduct. You must give the landlord notice that you are exercising your option to repair and deduct and provide him or her with copies of your receipts at the time you pay the decreased rent.

My water heater is leaking but it still works. The landlord has tried to repair it several times and now I want I new one. Do I have a right to a new water heater?

> Yes. A leaking water heater is an unsafe condition and your landlord must replace it since repairs are not working. Remind him or her that the apartment could be flooded and he or she will be responsible for damage to your furniture and other possessions. Additionally, if the water heater is a gas heater, the leak could extinguish the pilot light creating the possibility of exposure to natural gas.

> A leaky faucet or shower is typically not considered to be a health hazard and the landlord is not violating any law or breaching the lease by refusing to repair that kind of leak.

Severe hailstorms cracked the windows in the apartment units in my complex, as well as mine, more than a month ago. Is not my landlord required to replace my windows now that I notified him in writing of the problem?

> Not in this situation. Where damage occurs as a result of an insured casualty loss, the landlord can wait to make repairs until he or she receives the insurance proceeds.

> If the loss is severe, such as a large fire, and the apartment is uninhabitable, the tenant can notify the landlord and terminate the lease before the repairs are made.

Tenant's Repairs

My ex-boyfriend punched a hole in the wall of my apartment. Am I responsible for the repairs?

> Yes. The actions of anyone you invite into your apartment are your responsibility. If your ex-boyfriend illegally broke into the apartment, you can argue the landlord should repair the wall since security is obviously lax. On the other hand, if your ex-boyfriend gained entrance into the apartment because you let him in, or he still had a key, he is an invited guest and you are responsible for the damages.

Do I have to pay for a friend's damage to the complex's fence when she drove away from my apartment?

> Probably not. Although she was visiting you, once she left your apartment, you no longer had any control over her. Unless you knew or believed she would get into

an accident with the fence, you are not liable. However, if she left your apartment intoxicated, the landlord can argue you should have known your friend might drive into the fence and you had a duty to prevent her from driving. Since you let her drive, under the landlord's theory, you would be liable for the damage.

Landlord's Failure to Repair

What are my rights if the landlord does not make repairs?

If the landlord fails to make repairs that affect the health or safety of the tenant, the tenant has the right to break the lease and move out. Alternatively, (and only in extreme cases), the tenant can stay on the premises and withhold all or a part of the rent until the repairs are made. The tenant can also file a lawsuit against the landlord for breaching the implied warranty of habitability. The tenant's options are:

If you wish to deduct an amount from your rent because your landlord is not making repairs and you had to correct the problem, you must:

1. Notify him or her in writing, with the date at the top of the letter, of the problems you are facing and request repairs within a reasonable time (for example, 7 business days).
2. Keep a copy of your written notice to the landlord.
3. Contact at least two contractors for repair estimates.
4. If the landlord does not make the repairs by the deadline, hire the person with the lowest bid to do the job.
5. Keep the costs reasonable and save all your receipts.
6. When the next rent payment is due, deduct the cost of the repairs from your usual rent payment and attach copies of the repair receipts.

> **Tip**
>
> It is a good idea to take a picture of the problem and enclose the photo with your notice. This lets the landlord know you are serious about getting the repair made.

The repair and deduct remedy is for minor repairs only. It should never be used with major repairs, like new carpeting or appliances. Your rent payment will be so greatly reduced after you deduct those costs, it is likely your landlord will attempt to evict you for nonpayment of rent.

> **Tip:**
>
> If you do the repairs yourself, your only receipts are the ones for materials. You cannot put a price on your time and labor and deduct from the rent.

Can I withhold rent?

Some states have rent escrow funds where a tenant can deposit rent that he or she is withholding while the landlord refuses to make repairs. Typically, the tenant deposits the rent payment with the court when he or she files a "rent escrow action." There may be a filing fee. To file a rent escrow action, you must:

1. Notify the landlord in writing, preferably by certified mail.
2. Wait a required amount of time, such as 7 days, for the landlord to respond.
3. Complete the forms for a rent escrow action, deposit the rent with the court's clerk or administrator, along with a copy of your notice to the landlord.

The rent escrow action is set for a hearing, and if the tenant proves the landlord refused to make necessary repairs, the judge can order:

- the landlord to fix the problem;

- fine the landlord;

- require the tenant to "repair and deduct";

- order future rents paid to the court until the repairs are made; and

- return all, none or part of the rent to the tenant.

The lights in the stairwell and outside my door no longer automatically come on at night. Is the landlord required to repair the problem?

Yes. The lighting you describe affects your safety and security. The landlord must make the repairs promptly. Additionally, the landlord must replace bulbs in lighting in common areas in order to maintain the safety and security of his or her tenants.

Is my apartment required to have a smoke detector?

Yes. State laws and city housing codes require landlords to install smoke detectors in rental units. The location and number of smoke detectors required varies from state to state, but laws requiring a smoke detector outside each bedroom are typical.

The units in my apartment complex have fireplaces and I want my landlord to install a carbon monoxide detector. Is he or she required to pay for the installation?

Yes. Laws generally require carbon monoxide detectors in rental dwellings to ensure the tenants' safety. Your landlord must pay for the immediate installation of the carbon monoxide detector or he or she is likely violating building codes in your area.

Tip
The tenant is responsible for replacing the batteries in smoke and carbon dioxide detectors.

The electrical outlets in my bathroom are not grounded and I want them replaced with ground-fault circuit interrupters. Does my landlord have to make the replacement?

> Probably. Most building codes require updated electrical outlets in all rental dwellings. An ungrounded outlet, especially in an area where water is present, is a serious safety hazard.
>
> However, if you are renting an older home from the homeowner, the building codes may not require updated outlets. You should not attempt to replace the outlets yourself since electrical work must be permitted and performed by a licensed electrician.

I moved into my apartment today and the landlord cannot change the locks for 2 days. Can I change the locks myself?

> Yes. You can either install the locks or rekey them without any notice to the landlord and deduct the cost from your rent.

I want to change the locks on my apartment so my boyfriend cannot get in. Do I have to pay for the new locks?

> Yes. Generally landlords are only required to change locks at their expense when a new tenant moves in or a break-in has been attempted (or occurred).
>
> Your landlord cannot refuse the right to change the locks. Laws give tenants the right to have new locks installed or rekeyed at the tenant's expense at any time. However, the lease will require you to provide the landlord with a key to any new lock.

My landlord has not changed the locks in my apartment since the previous tenant moved out. Can I terminate the lease?

> Yes, after written notice to the landlord requesting the lock change and allowing him or her a reasonable amount of time to make the change, laws in some states allow you to move out and terminate the lease.

Breaking the Lease

When can I break a lease?

> Purchasing a home does not permit a tenant to break a lease, unless the lease specifically permits it. Additionally, other common reasons that do not allow a tenant to break the lease, including:
>
> - marriage
> - separation
> - divorce
> - reconciliation
> - leaving or withdrawing from school voluntarily or involuntarily
> - voluntary or involuntary job transfer

- loss of roommate or co-tenant
- loss of employment
- bad health
- criminal activity in and around the area

Tip
If you are in the military, or enlist while you are leasing and ordered to active duty or to relocate, you may lawfully terminate your lease before it ends. You must give the landlord notice, preferably 30 days in advance, if you are able. You will not be responsible for the rent due on the months left on the lease after you move out.

Do I have pay to for the months left on the lease if I break it?

Yes. You are responsible for paying the rent for every month left on the lease. Additionally, your lease agreement may allow the landlord to accelerate the rental payments or call them all due at once. For example, if you break the lease and leave with 3 months left on a $500 month apartment, the landlord can demand $1,500 ($500 x 3 months).

Tip
Most laws require landlords to "mitigate" damages or attempt to rent out the apartment that was vacated early. In the example above, if someone moved in 30 days after the tenant left, the tenant must pay for that month only $500.

Do I lose my security deposit if I move out early?

Probably. Not only do security deposits insure that the tenant will keep the premises maintained, they also act as a deterrent to breaking a lease. Even if the landlord does not go to the trouble to sue you for the remaining rent owed under the lease, he or she is still somewhat compensated by keeping your security deposit.

Tip
You still owe rent for the months left on the lease, even if you forfeited you security deposit. Since the lease is a contract, most laws give the landlord 2 years to sue for the remaining rent.

I had to break my lease, but I found a replacement tenant to move in the day after I moved out. Can the landlord still keep my security deposit?

No, assuming that the premises were left in good condition. If the lease allows the landlord to keep the security deposit as a penalty for breaking the lease, but you find a replacement, he or she must return the security deposit. However, the landlord has to approve the replacement tenant, and if he or she does not, he or she keeps the security deposit.

I broke my lease because I had to move. The landlord is keeping $500 of my $1,000 security deposit for the cost of finding a replacement tenant, although the apartment was left in perfect condition. Can he keep half my security deposit?

> Yes. The landlord is entitled to deduct the cost of his actual expenses in finding a tenant to take your place and occupy the vacant apartment. If the rental agency he used charged $500 to find a new tenant, then he has a right to deduct that amount (or whatever the amount is) from your security deposit when it is refunded to you.

> The cost to the landlord for having to find another tenant is sometimes called a reletting fee in the lease agreement.

Is there a deadline for returning my security deposit?

> If the lease sets out the time for returning a tenant's security deposit (for example, 10 days after tenant surrenders possession), then your security deposit must be returned to you by that deadline, minus any deductions for damages.

> If the lease does not set out a date, state or local laws may require the security deposit to be returned (minus deductions for damages) within a certain time frame. A typical deadline prescribed by law is 30 days after the tenant surrenders possession.

Do I have to make a written request to get back my security deposit?

> It depends on the lease agreement. Check to see if you must request the return of the security deposit in writing under the terms of the lease. If a written request is required, present it to your landlord when you turn in your keys so that you are in full compliance with the lease agreement.

> **Tip**
>
> The law may require your landlord to return a tenant's security deposit (minus deductions) without any action on your part. However, a written request is proof that you asked for a refund.

What types of lease violations permit the landlord to keep my security deposit when the lease ends?

> Some of the provisions a tenant must follow in a standard rental agreement in order to have his or her security deposit refunded include:

> • remaining a tenant for the entire length of the lease—moving out in the tenth month of a 12-month lease is breaking the lease, and you will forfeit your security deposit

> • providing written notice—you should inform the landlord that you will not be renewing the lease at least 30 days before it ends

> • being up-to-date on the rent—if the lease allows the landlord to keep the security deposit when you move out and are behind on the rent, you will not get it back

My landlord says he cannot refund my security deposit because he owes the electric company several thousand dollars. Do I have to wait until the electric company is paid before I get my deposit back?

No. The landlord's debts and bills do not take precedence over the return of your security deposit.

If my landlord will not give me back my security deposit, is there anything I can do?

Yes, you can file a lawsuit against your landlord for failing to return your security deposit. Generally, laws require the landlord to return your deposit if he or she kept it without a permissible reason. Additionally, the landlord may have to pay penalty damages (twice the amount of the deposit, for example), plus your attorney's fees.

> **Tip**
>
> Always send the landlord a demand letter before you actually file a lawsuit. Some laws require it, and even if it is not required, you may avoid a lawsuit if the landlord takes your letter seriously and refunds the deposit. An effective demand letter is always dated and includes:
>
> - the amount of the security deposit and when it was paid;
> - the period of the lease (for example, from January 1, 2005 to December 31, 2005);
> - a statement that the tenant gave proper notice to the landlord that he or she was moving out;
> - set a deadline for return of the security deposit (within 30 days);
> - demand a list of damages and corresponding deductions taken because of damage to the premises (if all or part of the security deposit is withheld); and
> - A statement of the law that applies, if you know it (for example, the law requires you return security deposits to tenants within 30 days after possession is surrendered).

It is recommended that you send the letter by certified mail so you will have proof that the landlord received it.

My landlord gave me a 24-hour notice to vacate and I immediately paid the past due rent. Can I still be evicted from my apartment?

No. You did exactly what the landlord wanted to accomplish by giving you the notice—you paid the rent. The landlord has no basis for an eviction. As long as you continue to pay the rent and comply with other provision of the lease agreement, you can stay in your apartment until the lease ends.

The landlord gave my teenage daughter a notice to vacate. Is this valid?

Yes, in some cases. Laws allow the notice to vacate to be given to other residents of the apartment if they are a certain age. You need to check the law in your state concerning eviction notices. In Texas, for example, if your daughter was under 16 years old, the landlord's notice to vacate has not been properly given to you.

The law in my state gives tenants 3 days to vacate but my landlord has given me a 24-hour notice to vacate. Is this legal?

In some jurisdictions, if your lease specifically provides for only a 24-hour notice, then state law does not apply. Under the lease, the landlord is acting legally and you have 24 hours to vacate the premises or to remedy the issue that prompted the notice.

I received a notice to vacate. Do I have to move by the deadline?

No. Your landlord must obtain an order from the court. Until he or she has the order, he or she cannot forcibly remove you or your belongings (unless he or she has a landlord's lien) from the apartment.

I have been served with a lawsuit for eviction. Is it too late to settle with the landlord?

No. You can settle any time before the judge makes his or her final ruling, even during the trial itself.

If you and the landlord came to an agreement before the answer was due, you can go ahead and file an answer denying the claims in the lawsuit. After denying the claims, include a description of the settlement. For example, the landlord and I have agreed to settle this case and a trial is not necessary. Then ask the court to dismiss the case.

If my landlord and I have settled the eviction lawsuit, do I need a written settlement agreement?

Yes, otherwise you have no proof of your agreement with the landlord. Additionally, if the court has not dismissed the lawsuit, the landlord can request a trial date at anytime.

What happens if I do not respond to or answer the eviction lawsuit?

You automatically lose the lawsuit and your landlord may be entitled to possession of the premises within 48 hours or less.

The landlord won his eviction suit and I have 6 days to vacate. Do I have to notify that court if we have come to an agreement on the amount of past due rent and the landlord has agreed to let me stay in the apartment?

Yes. Your agreement does not change the court judgment evicting you. Unless you notify the court, the landlord can have you evicted at any time in the future without further court proceedings. The landlord must sign a statement that he will not enforce the court's judgment and file it with the court. If he does not file the statement, then you must file it.

> **Caution**
>
> If the landlord will not sign an agreement promising to not enforce the judgment, you are in the risky position of being evicted in the future, even if you are paying rent. In this situation, you should vacate the premises although you have an oral agreement with the landlord

I know the sheriff is trying to serve me with an eviction order. Can I stay in the apartment if I continue to avoid him?

No. Laws permit the law enforcement officer that is attempting to serve an individual to post the eviction order in a conspicuous place or mail it if he cannot serve you personally. After the order has been posted or mailed, you must vacate or risk being removed bodily by the sheriff.

The sheriff served me with an eviction order and I attempted to pay my landlord the past rent I owe. Can she refuse to accept the rent?

Yes. Your chance to pay the past-due rent ended once the landlord obtained an eviction order. She is under no obligation to accept the rent and the eviction order continues in full force.

I paid my past due rent to my landlord after I was served with an eviction order. How do I know I still won't be evicted?

You can still be evicted as long as the eviction order is in effect. Your payment to the landlord does not extinguish the judge's order.

> **Tip**
>
> To make certain you will not be evicted, you must get a written agreement from the landlord stating he or she will not evict you based on the current order, and file the agreement with the court.

I have been served with an eviction order, but it is snowing outside. I cannot be evicted in bad weather, can I?

Unfortunately, you can. Despite rain, snow or cold weather, you have to move out by the date specified in the eviction order.

Glossary of Real Estate Terms

Please note: The terms described below are just part of a much larger Real Estate Dictionary available to readers of this book at www.socrates.com/books/landlording-handbook.aspx.

abandonment Voluntarily giving up one's right and interest in a particular property either by refusing to honor the obligations of that property (e.g., mortgage, taxes and upkeep) or by declaring an intention to do so in the future. One reason for just walking away from an investment might be that the owner has lost his or her job, can no longer afford the fixed expenses of the house or condominium, and has discovered that the value of the house, if it were sold, is less than the outstanding balance on the mortgage.

abatement A reduction or decrease in the value of a property that affects its market value or the amount of rent that may be charged to a tenant. Abatement usually occurs as the result of a discovery of something negative about the property (e.g., the roof must be replaced, the furnace will not make it through the winter, there is serious termite damage to the house) that decreases its worth and the price or rent it can command, or, in the case of a sale in progress, it affects the price already agreed on by the buyer and seller. The term can also refer to a decrease in the local government's valuation of a property, which in turn leads to lower taxes.

absentee owner/landlord An owner of a property who lives somewhere else and is not directly in control of that property. Tenants not only occupy the property but, if the owner has not appointed an agent, may also manage the property on the absentee owner's behalf on a day-to-day basis.

absorption rate The number of properties within a property development (e.g., a tract of land on which houses are being built; a building in which apartments are being converted to condominiums) that can be sold in a particular market within a particular time. Because the owner/buyer has probably borrowed money to fund the development, and is paying interest on that money, he or she must factor in interest costs as part of the basic expenses.

abut To share a common (property) boundary or even share a portion of that boundary.

acceptance A positive (and voluntary) response to an offer or counteroffer for a property that sets out price and terms. This positive response creates a binding agreement between the buyer and seller. Acceptance may be conditional (i.e., based on certain events taking place). For example, in buying a new residence, the buyer may make his or her offer conditional on the sale of his or her current home within a certain number of months.

access The right to enter a property. This may be restricted to certain times and to certain categories of people (e.g., those who read gas or electric meters or deliver the mail).

accessory building A structure on a property (e.g., a garage; a garden shed) that serves a specific purpose for the home or main building.

accrued interest Interest that has been earned but not yet claimed by the person to whom it is owed.

acknowledgment A written declaration by a person executing a legal document, given before someone authorized to accept such oaths (usually a notary public), stating that the person signing the document did so voluntarily.

acre A land area that is equal to 43,560 square feet. Property, particularly farm property, is often described in acres.

act of God Damage to property caused by natural forces such as rain, lightning, floods, mudslides, snow, forest fires or earthquakes.

action to quiet title A legal action that is started by one of the parties to a dispute involving the ownership of a property—for the purpose of settling competing claims and establishing one clear legal title to the property.

actual age The years a building has been in existence (i.e., its chronological age). Its effective age is a more subjective judgment; it reflects the condition of the building (i.e., how well it has been maintained). Two houses on the same street may both have been constructed 50 years ago (i.e., their actual age), but one, because of upkeep and renovation, may look almost new, whereas the other, because of neglect, may look much older than its chronological age (i.e., its effective age).

actual cash value A term used in the insurance industry to describe the valuation of a building. It is determined by subtracting the decrease in value that is caused by such factors as age and wear-and-tear from the actual current cost of replacing the building.

addendum Something added to a document (e.g., lease, contract, purchase agreement) that then forms part of it. May be used to add some provision to the original document or to clarify some aspect of that original document.

additional principal payment Making an additional payment on a mortgage. With a monthly mortgage payment of $2,000, the interest portion may be $1,750 and the principal portion may be $250. If the lender offers this sort of provision (and most do), the borrower may opt occasionally to pay an additional amount to reduce the principal (i.e., the amount owed) by more than the fixed amount of $250. Sometimes borrowers who have acquired a sum of money through means such as the sale of another asset, a tax refund, or an inheritance choose to make a substantial one-time payment of this kind. The advantage is that the total interest over the life of the loan is reduced.

adjustable-rate mortgage (ARM) Also called a variable-rate mortgage. This kind of loan has an interest rate that is determined by some outside index, such as the federal prime rate or the interest paid on government bonds. This kind of mortgage is most popular when this rate is lower, especially when it is much lower, than the interest on a fixed-rate mortgage would be. People who choose these kinds of mortgage are hoping that the adjustable rate will remain below the fixed rate for a long time—or at least until their income improves. The savings in interest on an ARM, at least in the short term, can be substantial.

adjustments Anything that, at closing, changes the value of the property (e.g., taxes overpaid or underpaid by the seller, fuel for several months stored on the premises and provided to the buyer, rent collected from tenants for the following month). A statement of adjustments is presented by the closing officer to the buyer or seller.

administrator A person appointed by a court to oversee the estate of an individual who has died intestate (i.e., without leaving a will).

adverse possession A method of claiming ownership (i.e., title) to a piece of land that is formally owned by another, by occupying it. Most governments allow such a claim, provided it is not disputed by the title-holder and the claimant has occupied the land for a certain period (the required period varies by jurisdiction).

affidavit of title The seller's statement that the title (i.e., proof of ownership) is valid, can be sold, and is subject to no defects except those set out in the agreement of sale.

after-tax cash flow The net profit of an income property after direct costs (e.g., interest on the mortgage, taxes, maintenance) have been subtracted.

after-tax proceeds The net proceeds from the sale of a property; that is, the sale price less the legal fees and expenses, the realtor's commission, any taxes paid, etc.

agent Anyone (albeit usually a real estate agent) who is authorized by a buyer or seller of property to act on that person's behalf in any dealings with third parties. The third party may rely on the agreement and assurances of the agent as being binding on the person represented.

amortization schedule A statement of the payments to be made on an amortized mortgage loan. This statement generally shows the date and amount of each payment, the portions of each payment that will be applied to interest and to principal and the balance (of principal) still outstanding on the loan after the payment has been made.

annual debt service The amount that is required to service a loan in any given year; that is, the interest that must be paid to keep the loan current.

annual mortgagor statement A document that is sent each year, usually at the end of the year, by the lender to the borrower regarding a mortgage loan. It details amounts paid for principal, interest, and (if the mortgage company pays the borrower's property taxes) taxes paid; it also notes the amount still owed on the mortgage.

annual percentage rate (APR) The total cost of a loan (i.e., of borrowing the money to buy a property) in any given year expressed as a percentage of a loan amount (e.g., 6.5 percent). It includes compounded interest. The lender (i.e., the institution or person that holds the mortgage) is required by the Federal Truth-in-Lending Act to disclose the APR to the borrower.

appraisal An estimate of the value of a property on a certain date, usually provided by a qualified appraiser, after both an inspection of the property and a comparison of that property with other comparable properties that have recently been sold.

appreciation The increase in value of a property over time. This increase can be the result of many factors, such as inflation, increased demand for property resulting from low interest rates, the condition of the market or the gentrification of a particular area.

arrears Money that, under an amortization schedule, was not paid when it was due. The mortgagee is usually given the chance to make up the arrears. If he or she fails to do so, the mortgage holder can call in the loan (i.e., demand that it be paid in full).

as is/as-is agreement The situation in which a property is accepted by the buyer (or tenant) in the condition existing at the time of the sale or lease; the seller (or lessor) is released from any liability after closing. Most agreements of sale contain such a provision.

asking price The amount at which a property is offered, by a seller, for sale. This price may change as a result of negotiations between the buyer and seller. In a tight market, a good property in a desirable location may bring more than the initial asking price as a result of bidding by numerous potential buyers.

assessed value The value placed on a property by a tax assessor for the purpose of determining property taxes.

assign To transfer interest in a property. An elderly person might decide to transfer ownership in a piece of land to children who might be more likely to develop it.

attached housing Two or more houses, occupied by different people that have a common wall (e.g., townhouses).

auction Selling property to the highest bidder at a public sale. Auctions are often used to sell property that has been foreclosed on or property that has failed to sell in the marketplace.

back-title letter/certificate In states in which lawyers are required to examine title for title insurance purposes, this document is given to the attorney by the title insurance company to certify the condition of a title as of a certain date.

backup contract A secondary offer (from a potential buyer) for a property on which an offer from another buyer has already been made. This contract will come into effect if the first offer is not accepted or is withdrawn.

balance The amount of principal that is still outstanding on a mortgage or other loan at any given time.

balloon mortgage A mortgage loan that is repaid in fixed, periodic (probably monthly) payments until a given date. On that date, either the balance of the loan becomes due in one large payment or the amount of the payments rises significantly.

balloon payment The final payment that pays off a balloon mortgage.

base rent The set rent that is paid by a tenant and to which can be added additional fees as set out in the lease (e.g., for upkeep, utilities, etc.).

bedroom community An area that includes mainly housing (residential or rental) and very few businesses. The term usually refers to a commuter town or suburb whose residents work in the central city or in more economically diverse suburbs.

bi-level Premises that are on two levels; commonly refers to a house but can also refer to an apartment or condominium unit. Also called split level.

bill of sale A document that certifies that, in return for a certain price, ownership of property has passed from the seller to the purchaser.

bi-weekly mortgage A mortgage in which one half of the monthly payment is made every 2 weeks. With this kind of mortgage, 26 payments will be made in a year; the extra monthly payment that is made each year reduces the duration of the mortgage and the total amount of interest the borrower will ultimately pay. Many people find such plans to be a fairly painless way to reduce the principal on a mortgage more quickly.

blueprint Construction plans, usually prepared by an architect.

borrower (mortgagor) A person who receives money from a lender to buy property, in exchange for a written promise to repay that money with interest. The borrower also accepts the lender's lien on that property until the debt is paid in full.

boundary The legally determined edge or limit of a property.

breach of contract In law, the failure to live up to the terms of any contract.

broker Refers to two kinds of agents: a mortgage broker, who brings potential borrowers together with potential lenders; and a real estate broker, who brings buyers together with sellers. Real estate broker is a professional designation; it requires training and licensing.

building permit A permit that is issued by a local government to allow a builder to construct a building or to make improvements to existing structures.

building restrictions Rules in the building code (e.g., zoning restrictions) that control the size, placement, design and materials of new construction.

buyer's broker/agent A real estate agent who represents the potential buyer. Agents commonly represent the seller, but potential buyers increasingly are engaging real estate agents to watch out for their interests also.

buyer's market A market in which there is more property for sale than there are buyers available to purchase it., This situation usually causes the value of available property to decrease. It most commonly occurs in over-built markets or when a poor economy results in few buyers being present in the marketplace.

buy-sell offer An offer by one owner to buy out the interests of another owner or partner.

cancellation clause A clause in a contract, such as a mortgage, that sets forth the conditions under which each party may cancel or terminate the agreement.

cap A limit. A cap is important in adjustable-rate mortgages, where it represents the limit on how high payments may go or how much the interest rate may change within a given period or over the life of the mortgage.

capital gain An increase in the value of capital property (i.e., property other than a principal residence) on which tax is payable, usually upon sale of the property.

capital loss A decrease in the value of capital property (i.e., property other than a principal residence), which the owner may use against capital gains or against regular income when paying his or her taxes, depending on the tax rules.

cash flow Net earned income from an income property after all the expenses of holding and carrying the property are paid or factored in. Also called cash throw-off.

cash reserve The amount of money a buyer of a property still has on hand after she or he has made a down payment and paid out the fees of closing. Some lenders ascertain that such a reserve exists (commonly, the equivalent of two mortgage payments) before granting a mortgage.

cash sale The sale of a property for cash; no mortgage or other financing is involved.

caveat emptor (Latin: let the buyer beware). A legal maxim suggesting that the buyer of any property takes a risk regarding the condition of the property and, that it is the responsibility of the buyer to determine the condition before the purchase is completed. Many states now have laws that place more responsibility for disclosure on the seller and the real estate broker. Potential buyers should always check on their rights with their real estate broker.

CC&Rs Abbreviated term for covenants, conditions and restrictions, which are the obligations of any real estate contract.

certified general appraiser Someone who is licensed, after training, to appraise the value of property (qualification requirements can vary, depending on the particular jurisdiction).

certified home inspector (CHI) Someone who is licensed, after training, to inspect and report on the physical condition of property (qualification requirements may vary, depending on the particular jurisdiction).

certified property manager (CPM) Someone who has met the requirements of the Institute of Real-Estate Management to manage property. The Institute is an affiliate of the National Association of Realtors.

certified residential appraiser (CRA) Someone who has met the licensing requirements to appraise the value of only and specifically residential property. See certified general appraiser.

certified residential broker (CRB) Someone who has met the requirements of the Realtors National Marketing Institute to be an agent or broker for residential properties. The Realtors National Marketing Institute is affiliated with the National Association of Realtors.

certified residential specialist (CRS) Someone who has met the requirements of the Realtors National Marketing Institute, which is affiliated with the National Association of Realtors. A CRS must have successfully completed an educational program, have an acceptable level of residential sales experience, and already be a graduate of the Real Estate Institute.

chattel A word that is not used much in common speech but is often used in real estate documents to describe personal property that is part of the property but is not fixed to the land or to a building. This is different from a fixture, which is part of the land or building. A homeowner's dining room table and chairs are a form of chattel; the chandelier above the table, which is secured to the ceiling, is a fixture. Fixtures are commonly included in the sale of a property, whereas chattels usually are not unless they are itemized in the agreement of sale.

clear title Property for which the title is free of competing claims, liens or mortgages. Also called free and clear.

closing The final procedure in any real estate transaction in which the parties to the transaction (or their representatives) meet to execute documents, exchange funds, and complete the sale (and, if a mortgage is involved, the loan). A closing typically takes place at the offices of a title company.

closing costs Expenses, usually those of the buyer, that are over and above the cost (i.e., the sale price) of the property itself, such as legal fees, mortgage application fees, taxes, appraisal fees, title registration fees, etc.

code Laws or regulations that are drawn up (often by the government) to cover a particular aspect of life in a municipality or state (e.g.,, a building code, a traffic code).

commission The amount paid to a real estate agent or broker as compensation for services rendered in the purchase, sale or rental of property. The amount is usually a percentage of the sale price or the total rental.

commitment/commitment letter A written promise, by a lender or insurance company, to make a loan or insure a loan for a specified amount and on specified terms.

commitment fee The fee that may be charged by a potential lender in return for the lender's promise to provide a mortgage to a potential borrower when that person finds property he or she wishes to buy.

common-area assessments A periodic charge (usually monthly) that is levied against owners in a condominium complex. These fees are used by the condominium owners' association to pay for the maintenance of common areas in the building. Some assessments also include fees for utilities such as central heating or air conditioning. Also known as common-element fees or assessments.

comparables A way of establishing the market value of a particular property in which another property that has recently been sold, and is similar in location, size, condition and amenities to the property in question, is used as a guide to establishing the asking price.

condition(s) Requirements in a real estate agreement to purchase that must be fulfilled before the agreement becomes firm and binding. If the conditions are not fulfilled, the agreement will usually be regarded as canceled and any deposit will be returned to the buyer.

condominium A structure comprised of two or more units in which the units are individually owned but the remainder of the property (i.e., the land, buildings, and amenities) is owned in common. The maintenance of these common areas is supervised by the condominium corporation, in which each unit owner owns a share and has voting rights.

consumer reporting agency or bureau The source to which lenders turn for the credit history of any applicant for a loan. Also called a credit bureau.

contingency A condition that must be fulfilled before a contract can become firm and binding. For example, the sale of a house may depend on whether the potential buyer can obtain financing.

contract An agreement between two or more persons (or entities) that creates (or modifies) a legal relationship. In real estate, a contract is usually an offer for property and an acceptance of that offer (e.g.,, an agreement of sale).

conversion There are two meanings: 1) the changing of an apartment to a condominium unit; and 2) the improper taking of another person's property for one's own use (e.g., moving into a person's vacation home and living there while the person is away).

co-op Abbreviated term for cooperative, a form of ownership in which the occupiers of individual units in a building have shares in the cooperative corporation that owns the entire property. Co-ops are still popular in large American cities, such as New York and Chicago, but condominiums are the more usual form of "apartment" ownership in most American cities and suburbs.

cotenancy A situation in which more than one person owns a piece of property. Title is held by the owners in one of two ways: 1) as joint tenants, where each tenant owns the land equally and, in the event of the death of one of the tenants, his or her surviving co-tenant(s) will continue to own title equally by right of survivorship; or 2) as tenants in common, where each owner owns a specific portion of the property and may sell, mortgage or bequeath that interest to a third party without the consent of the other owners.

counteroffer A response to an offer. If a prospective buyer makes an offer to purchase a property (i.e., offers a price for that property), the seller may do one of three things: 1) accept the offer; 2) reject the offer outright; or 3) suggest an alternative. For example, the listed or advertised price of a condominium is $350,000 and the prospective buyer offers $325,000. The seller makes a counteroffer of $340,000. By suggesting this alternative, the seller is legally regarded as having rejected the buyer's original offer. The buyer in turn may also counteroffer (e.g., suggest a price of $330,000).

covenant A promise contained in a contract or agreement. In real estate, this promise may be implied; that is, it may already be covered by local or national laws.

credit limit The maximum amount that an individual can borrow to buy property. This amount is set by the lender after an examination of the individual's credit history/credit report.

debt-equity ratio A comparison of what is owed on a property with its equity (i.e., the current market value of the property less the amount owed on the mortgage or loan).

debt financing The purchase of a property using any kind of credit rather than paying cash.

decree of foreclosure A court decree made when a borrower is seriously in default on a mortgage and the lender decides that the borrower will not (or cannot) pay. The decree declares the amount outstanding on the delinquent mortgage and orders the sale of the property to pay off the mortgage. The lender is then repaid to the extent possible (sales that result from foreclosure do not necessarily achieve full market value of the property).

deed The legal instrument by which title to (i.e., ownership of) property is conveyed from one owner to another when a sale occurs.

default The failure to make mortgage payments in full or on time, or to live up to any other obligations of the mortgage agreement.

defective title Ownership that is not "clean" (i.e., that is subject to a competing claim or claims). Another meaning is ownership that is obtained by fraud.

deferred interest Interest that is not paid as it is incurred but instead is added to the loan's principal.

deferred maintenance This term refers to a property that has not been adequately maintained. Its condition, and therefore its value, is depreciating.

delivery Turning over any legal document, particularly a deed, to another party, and in doing so making it legally nonrevocable.

demand loan A kind of loan that stipulates no fixed date for repayment but is due in full (i.e., principal with accumulated interest) if the lender asks for payment.

deposit Money that is paid up front by a buyer to guarantee that she or he will actually complete a transaction to buy a particular property—in effect, it is a guarantee to the seller that the seller may remove the property from the market (i.e., that the sale is "firm"). If the buyer later fails to complete the transaction, she or he generally loses the deposit. Also called earnest money.

depreciation The decrease in value of a property over time, which can also lead to a reduction in the owner's taxes (i.e., a capital loss).

designated real estate broker An individual who has a real estate broker's license and who is appointed by a corporation or institution to oversee all of its real estate activities.

designated real estate instructor (DREI) Anyone who has met the requirements of the Real Estate Educators' Association and may therefore teach courses in real estate practice.

detached single-family home A freestanding house; that is, a house that does not share walls with another house, and is designed to house just one family. Most houses in the United States are of this type.

deterioration The effects of time and wear-and-tear on a property, or neglect of that property, which causes its value to decrease unless some action is taken to counteract and correct these effects.

developer There are two meanings for this term: 1) a builder, most commonly someone who constructs a commercial complex or a residential subdivision; and 2) an entrepreneur, who prepares raw land for construction, then in turn sells the lots to one or more builders so that they may build on the land.

disclosure In some U.S. jurisdictions, the seller of a property must provide a written statement to the buyer listing those defects in the property of which the seller is aware. For example, the seller may know that the roof of the property needs to be replaced, but may be unaware that there is severe termite damage to the property. Also called vendor's disclosure.

distress The right of a landlord or lender to sell the real or personal property of a tenant or borrower to pay for arrears in rent or loan payments.

donor Someone who does one of the following things: offers a gift, makes a bequest, gives someone power of attorney, or settles property in a trust for another's benefit.

doubtful title Ownership of land or property that is questioned because there is a seemingly equal claim on that land or property.

down payment The amount of money that is provided by the buyer toward the total price of the property (not including fees, taxes or other costs). In general, the down payment plus the principal of the mortgage equals the purchase price. The down payment is customarily cash paid by the buyer from his or her own funds—as opposed to that part of the purchase price that is financed by a lender. A down payment amount that is common in the United States is 20 percent of the total purchase price. However, if the borrower agrees to insure this part of the mortgage, some lenders will accept a 10 percent down payment.

downzoning A reduction in the density, under zoning bylaws, that is allowed by the local municipality for a certain property or neighborhood.

duplex A single building that includes two separate living units. Also, an apartment or condominium unit that has two floors.

encumbrance Any right, lien or charge attached to and binding on a property. An encumbrance can affect the owner's ability or right to sell that property until such time as it is removed.

Equal Credit Opportunity Act A U.S. law guaranteeing that people of all races, ages, genders and religions must have an equal chance to borrow money.

equity The market value of a property, less the debts of that property Likely debts include the principal and accumulated interest on the mortgage, unpaid taxes and a home equity loan.

escalator clause Part of a net lease. This is a provision that allows the landlord to increase the rent payable if certain costs of the building increase, such as maintenance or utilities.

escape clause A provision in a contract that allows one or more of the parties involved to end the contract if certain events occur. For example, a potential buyer of a house may stipulate in the sale agreement that the agreement comes into effect only if the buyer is able to sell his or her current residence by the anticipated closing date.

escrow In real estate, the delivery of a deed by the seller to a third party (i.e., the escrow agent), to be delivered to the buyer at a certain time, usually the closing date. In some states, all instruments having to do with the sale (including the funds) are delivered to the escrow agent for dispersal on the closing date.

eviction A court action to remove an individual from the possession of real property, most commonly the removal of a tenant.

evidence of title A document that establishes ownership to property, most commonly a deed.

Fair Credit Reporting Act A federal law that protects consumers by establishing procedures whereby they can correct errors on credit reports; it gives consumers specific rights in dealing with credit-reporting agencies.

fair market value The price that is likely to be agreed on by a buyer and seller for a specific property at a specific time. This price is typically arrived at by considering the sales prices of comparable properties in the area, taking into consideration any special features of or upgrades to the property in question.

Federal Truth in Lending Act A U.S. federal law that requires lenders to disclose all the terms of a loan arrangement (e.g., a mortgage) to the borrower in a specific, understandable way.

fee simple The best title to a property that is available—ownership that is not subject to dispute.

fees There are two meanings for this term: 1) the fees that are charged for services provided by a real estate professional such as an appraiser or property inspector; and 2) the service charges that are required of a borrower by a lender in return for making a loan (these fees are either charged at the outset or held back from the mortgage).

finance charge The entire cost of a loan or mortgage, including the principal and interest charged over the life of the loan, appraisal and application fees, title insurance fees and recording fees.

fire and extended-coverage insurance An undertaking by an insurance company to compensate an owner of a property for a specific kind of damage to that property, such as the damage caused by a hurricane. This kind of property insurance is important to a property owner in Florida, the Gulf Coast states or the shoreline of the Eastern Seaboard.

firm commitment A promise from a lender to lend a potential borrower a specific amount of money (on specific terms) to be secured against a specific property—in other words, a promise by the lender to give the potential borrower a mortgage.

first mortgage A mortgage that, when registered, is the first to be able to claim payment from any sale proceeds. Often, owners of property take out a second mortgage, usually to "tap" some of the equity in their property. Such mortgages are paid, on a sale, only after the first mortgage has been paid.

fixed expenses These are the certain costs of owning and operating a property. The cost of painting a house is not a fixed expense but the property tax on that house is.

flip The practice whereby a property is purchased in the hope that it can be sold quickly for a higher price. Often refers to the practice whereby someone reserves (with a comparatively small reservation fee) a condominium unit in a condominium building that is being constructed (or being converted from apartments); by the time the property is ready, but before the purchaser has to go through a closing, the condominium has increased in value and the purchaser can sell it for a high price, having invested only the amount necessary to "reserve" the property.

floating rate The rate of interest that is charged on an adjustable-rate mortgage. This rate usually is set according to a specified index or is tied to the national prime rate. For example, a loan that is set at "prime plus 2 percent" will carry an interest rate of 7 percent if the prime rate is 5 percent.

forced sale A sale that is not voluntary on the part of the seller, such as a sale to satisfy a pressing debt or a sale resulting from bankruptcy. The selling price, in such a sale, is often less than true market value, sometimes considerably so.

foreclosure A proceeding that is usually instigated by a lender, in a court or not, to cancel all rights and title of an owner in a particular property when that owner has defaulted on payment of a mortgage. The purpose of the lender's action is to claim the title, so that the property can be sold to satisfy the debt still outstanding on the mortgage.

gross income The total of a person's earnings from his or her job plus any other income (e.g., interest income or dividends on stock) in a given period, before that person's expenses are deducted.

habitable A dwelling or property that is acceptable for human occupancy; that is, it is not derelict and meets standards of decency.

handyman's special A property that requires substantial work to bring it up to normal standards. Such a property is often sold at a lower price than it would be if it were in excellent repair.

hazard insurance A policy on property (or on property improvements) that covers damage by natural causes, such as fire or flooding.

high-ratio mortgage A mortgage in which the amount of money borrowed is 75 percent (or more) of the purchase price. The lender on such a mortgage usually requires the sort of insurance that is provided by various U.S. government agencies as a guarantee of the lender's risk in making the mortgage.

high-rise A tall apartment or commercial building that meets one or both of two criteria: 1) it is taller than six stories; and/or 2) it is tall enough to make an elevator a necessity rather than a convenience.

hold-harmless clause A clause in a contract in which one party releases another from legal liability for a stated risk. For example, a person who wishes to rent an apartment from a landlord may agree to sign a lease only if that lease includes a hold-harmless clause absolving the tenant from having to make any repairs that become necessary during the tenancy. Also known as a save-harmless clause.

holding over The action of a tenant who continues to occupy premises after his or her lease has expired. Also known as overholding.

home equity line of credit A kind of loan that is increasingly popular. It is secured against the equity in a property. The borrower may borrow against that equity to a certain percentage of that equity's value and then, on a monthly basis, make payments of interest only or interest plus a portion of the equity borrowed, as desired. Many such loans have a time limit (i.e., the borrower must pay back the loan, if it is not already paid back, at some time in the future). Such a loan, which is in effect a second mortgage, must be paid back immediately if the property is sold. Also known as a revolving loan.

home inspector Someone who offers his or her services as an examiner of the physical condition of property. Qualifications for this profession differ between jurisdictions.

homeowner's insurance Liability coverage that provides for both loss and damage to property. Most mortgage lenders require this kind of insurance of borrowers, and many lenders require evidence, provided each year that the policy has been renewed.

housing affordability index An analysis by the National Association of Realtors, issued on a monthly basis, of the ability of the average-income family in the United States to afford a mortgage on the average-priced home, after making a 20 percent down payment.

housing expense ratio A figure that is obtaining by comparing a family's monthly gross income with the costs of their home (i.e., the principal and interest on a mortgage plus the cost of upkeep).

housing starts An economic indicator: the number of dwelling units (i.e., houses, apartments, and condominium units) on which construction is begun in a designated area in a prescribed period.

improvements Any permanent structure or other development (usually buildings, but also streets, sewers and utilities) that enhances the value of what was formerly vacant land.

income property A ny property that is developed (or purchased) specifically to produce income for its owner, such as an apartment building.

independent appraisal An estimate of the value of a property in which the appraiser has no interest in the property (e.g., is not a representative of the potential lender).

independent contractor A person who is hired to do building or renovation work for another person but is neither an employee nor an agent of that other person, such as a contractor who works for a fee.

initial interest rate The interest rate that is being charged on a mortgage on the day that it is first signed.

installment Any regular, periodic payment, such as the monthly payment on a mortgage.

insurance A contract in which one party (the insurer) agrees to indemnify another (the insured) against possible losses under specific conditions. Such conditions may include compensation of the insured for loss of job and income, in which case the insurer would pay the insured's debts, including mortgage payments, and compensation of the insured for any damage to the insured's property caused by natural phenomena (e.g., fire, storms).

insured mortgage A mortgage that is insured against loss to the lender in the event that the borrower defaults. It usually covers both the mortgage balance and the costs of foreclosure. This type of insurance is provided by such government agencies as the FHA or VA, as well as by independent insurance companies.

interest There are two meanings for this term: 1) a person's legal right to property; and 2) the cost of borrowing money for any purpose, such as to buy property, charged as a percentage of the outstanding balanced that is owed.

interest-only mortgage A type of mortgage that is increasingly popular in which the borrower pays only the interest and none of the principal during a certain period (e.g., three years, five years). After that, the borrower makes conventional payments containing both principal and interest for the remainder of the loan's term. Such mortgages are appealing to those who want initial payments on a mortgage to be as low as possible or those who expect the value of the property to rise very quickly, providing them with a profit without substantial principal investment.

interest payment That portion of each periodic payment on a loan or mortgage (expressed in dollars, not as a percentage) that is allocated toward accrued interest as opposed to principal.

interest rate The amount that a borrower pays to service a loan (i.e., to use the borrowed money), usually expressed as a percentage.

investment property Real estate that is owned not for the purpose of residential occupation, but for the possibility that it will increase in value or that its use will provide a good income.

joint ownership agreement A contract between two or more people who have an interest in the same property. It sets out their rights and obligations, and may also set out the way in which the parties agree to manage the property.

joint tenancy/tenants see cotenancy.

judgment A decision rendered by a court. If a monetary settlement is involved, it may become a lien on the property of the losing party.

junk fees A slang term for the extra and sometimes unnecessary services that a lender may charge for on a mortgage.

landlord Also known as lessor. The owner of a property who allows another person (or persons) to occupy that property in return for periodic payments of rent. The amount of the rent payments and the terms and conditions of the rental are usually established by a lease.

landscaping The act of modifying a landscape, as well as the components used in such modification, such as changes in grade, trees and shrubs, lawns, flowers, and other plantings. The object of landscaping is to create a more pleasing appearance for the property, and one of its incidental goals is to enhance the value of that property. Landscaping may accomplish that goal, particularly if it is extensive, professional, and pleasing to a potential buyer.

late charge A penalty fee that is charged by a lender when a borrower is late with a mortgage payment.

lease with option to purchase A kind of lease in which the tenant (i.e., lessee) has the right (but not the obligation) to purchase the property during the term of the lease. Payments made under the lease (sometimes wholly and sometimes in part, depending on the lease agreement) may be credited against the purchase price; that is, they may be used as a down payment. This is an ideal arrangement for any potential buyer who lacks the financial means to make a down payment.

leasehold improvements An often complex proposition in which additions made by a tenant to rented premises may be removed by the tenant at the end of the lease if no damage to the premises results (see chattel). Fixtures present no problem in this instance, but chattels may.

legal description A description of property that is acceptable in a court of law (i.e., meets legal requirements).

legal residence There are two meanings for this term, depending on location: 1) for an American who is in the United States, it usually means street address, city, state, and ZIP code; 2) for a person abroad, it can mean country of residence.

legal title The rights of ownership that are conferred on a person when he or she purchases a piece of property. These rights may be defended against any other, competing interests.

lender A general term referring to any individual or company that provides money to a borrower in return for periodic payments of principal and interest over time. In real estate, the term most often refers to a person (or institution) who offers a borrower a mortgage (i.e., loans the borrower the money to buy property) and places a lien on that property until the outstanding loan (i.e., the principal) and all the outstanding interest on that loan are paid.

lessee The tenant under a lease; someone who leases property.

lessor see landlord.

letter of intent A formal letter stating that a prospective buyer is interested in a property. This is not a firm offer and it creates no legal obligation. A potential buyer could issue such a letter to a seller of a particular property, indicating that the buyer intends to make an offer for that property.

lien An encumbrance, or legal claim, against a property as security for payment of a debt, such as the lien involved in a mortgage.

listing agent/broker The real estate professional who acts for the seller in marketing a property. This is not the same as the selling agent, who represents potential buyers. One agent may act in both capacities for a client (e.g., be responsible for selling a person's current residence, then help them to find a new residence).

loan-to-value ratio The difference between the appraised value of a property and the amount being loaned on a mortgage.

location The factor that is often cited as the primary factor in determining the worth of a property—as in the expression "location, location, location!" It refers to the following phenomenon: if two very similar properties are located in two different areas within the same city or town, and one of those areas is more convenient to the area's most popular amenities (e.g., shopping, entertainment) than the other, the property in the more desirable area will almost certainly be more expensive.

lock or lock-in There are two meanings for this term: 1) the commitment from a lender to guarantee a certain interest rate (or other loan feature) for a designated period; and 2) the restriction that a mortgage may not be prepaid by the borrower for a specific period.

lock period The period during which a lender guarantees a particular loan feature, usually the interest rate.

lot In general, any portion or parcel of real estate (i.e., a measured section of land). Often refers to a portion of a subdivision.

lot line The legal boundaries of a property, shown on a survey of that property.

low-ball offer A slang term meaning to offer a purchase price that is much lower than the asking price. Such offers, which are often lower than the appraised market value, are frequently made when a property has been on the market for a long time and potential buyers try to take advantage of pressure on the seller to sell.

maintenance costs The expense required to keep a property in a good state of repair.

market price The amount actually paid for a property. At the moment of sale, that amount is imagined to be its current valuation; subsequently, the market price, depending on economic factors, either appreciates or depreciates.

market rent The amount that an owner can reasonably charge someone who wishes to lease a property. The determining factor is generally how much other landlords, in the same market, are charging for similar properties. Also known as economic rent.

mechanic's and materialman's liens A claim against property. Any person who supplies materials (or labor) for a property and is not paid may file this kind of claim against the property. Also known as a construction lien.

minimum down payment The smallest amount of money that a purchaser is allowed to provide toward the purchase price of a house under a lender's guidelines for a mortgage. Down payments on residential property in the United States, for many years, have typically been 20 percent of the purchase price. However, down payments of 10 percent or even five percent recently have become more common. With down payments of less than 20 percent, lenders usually require additional insurance on the mortgage. The borrower may cancel this insurance when the principal on the loan reaches 20 percent.

monthly housing expense The total cost of maintaining a home each month, including the principal and interest on a mortgage, real estate taxes, and property (and possibly mortgage) insurance. This figure usually does not include maintenance or improvements, only fixed expenses.

mortgage A loan that is usually granted for the purpose of allowing a borrower to purchase property. The loan is secured (i.e., guaranteed) by that property; in other words, the mortgage is registered on the title (i.e., the ownership record) as a claim on that property.

mortgage broker A middleman who brings borrowers together with potential lenders, thereby providing a service to borrowers who are not as informed about potential lending sources. Often, the broker collects a fee for this service from the chosen lender.

mortgage-loan servicing The lender's actions in collecting mortgage payments and allocating those payments to principal, interest, and, if the mortgage so stipulates, an escrow account for subsequent payment of property taxes and insurance premiums.

mortgagee In a mortgage transaction, this is the lender; that is, the bank, other institution (private or government), or person making the loan for property.

Multiple Listing Service (MLS) A local service that is created and staffed by real estate professionals. It brings together all property listed for sale in a given area (e.g., a town and its surrounding area or a city and its suburbs) so that real estate agents and brokers can review all available properties on behalf of their clients. The MLS also governs commission splitting and other relations between agents. Licensed real estate professionals have access to the service.

municipal address The designation (i.e., the street address, city, state and ZIP code) by which a property is known.

negotiable A term that commonly refers to something that is assignable or transferable (i.e., something that is capable of being negotiated). In real estate, the term refers to the fact that the price of a property is often the result of a negotiation between the buyer and seller, and that many of the charges on a home loan are also subject to negotiation.

net operating income (NOI) The income from a property that is left after the costs of maintaining and servicing that property are subtracted.

no bid The situation in which the Veterans' Administration chooses not to acquire a property in foreclosure when that property is in default, but instead opts to pay out the amount it has guaranteed (usually 60 percent of the principal).

no money down A slang term for the strategy of purchasing real estate using as little of the buyer's own money as possible. Can also refer to an uncommon kind of mortgage that requires very little or no down payment.

nominal loan rate The interest rate that is stated in a loan agreement such as a mortgage.

normal wear-and-tear Damage to a property that is the result of neither carelessness nor maliciousness but simply reasonable use and the passage of time.

notice to quit An announcement from a landlord to a tenant that the tenant has not followed the terms of the lease and must leave the property.

nuisance A use of property that obviously interferes with the use and enjoyment of nearby properties (e.g., noise, fumes, aggressive behavior by pets). Such nuisances may be grounds for legal action by the people who are suffering from the nuisance.

occupancy The physical possession of a building or property.

offer A statement (either spoken or written) that informs one party of another's willingness to buy or sell a specific property on the terms set out in that statement. Once made, an offer usually must be accepted within a specific period (i.e., it is usually not open-ended). Once accepted, the offer by the one party and the acceptance by the other both are regarded as binding.

on-site improvements Any work performed on a property that adds to its utility, value or attractiveness.

open-ended mortgage A loan that allows the borrower to borrow further funds at a later date with the preparation (and registration) of an additional mortgage.

open house A property that is available for public viewing during a set period. Potential buyers who wish to view the property do not need an appointment and the real estate agent usually is present to conduct tours of the property and answer questions.

open listing A written authorization from a property owner to a real estate agent stipulating that the owner will pay the agent a commission if the agent presents an offer of specified price and terms. The agent does not, however, have an exclusive right to sell; in fact, the owner may have made the same arrangement with several agents, and only the successful agent will be paid the commission.

option to purchase leased property A clause in a rental agreement that allows the tenant the right to buy the leased property on terms and conditions that are also set out in the agreement.

ordinary repairs Repairs that are necessary to keep a property in good condition, as opposed to ordinary wear-and-tear.

original cost The purchase price of a property; the amount that was paid by the current owner.

owner's title insurance A policy that protects a property owner from any defects in title that were not apparent at the time of purchase.

package mortgage A mortgage that is secured by the borrower's personal as well as real property.

paper profit An asset, such as property, that is known to have increased in value (e.g., because comparable assets have been sold and have achieved this value) but has not actually produced a profit because it has not been sold. Therefore, the profit remains speculative.

parcel A general term meaning any piece of land.

partial interest Less than 100-percent ownership of a property.

partial release The release of a portion of property covered by a mortgage. For example, a developer of a subdivision of residential properties may obtain such a release as each house is sold and payment of a stated portion of the loan has been made.

payment cap A condition of some adjustable-rate mortgages in which the level to which a monthly payment can rise is limited to a certain amount.

payment change date Under an adjustable-rate mortgage, the date on which the payment changes.

permit A government body's written permission allowing changes to a particular property when such changes are regulated by that government body. For example, local municipalities normally require homeowners to apply for a permit if they wish to make substantial alterations to the outsides of their houses, so as to make sure that these changes are not at variance with the bylaws covering the area in which the houses are located.

personal property Any property belonging to an individual that is not real property (i.e., that is not real estate).

personal residence A person's home; the place from which that person votes, pays taxes, etc.

plat A map dividing a parcel of land into lots, as in a subdivision.

point An amount equal to one percent of the principal of a mortgage. This is a fee that is charged to a borrower by a lender for originating the mortgage. It is a loan service charge that must be paid up-front when the mortgage goes into effect. Some lenders allow points to be added to the principal of the mortgage and paid over its lifetime.

possession The state of being in control of property, regardless of ownership. Thus, possession may be either legal or "wrongful."

power of attorney An authority by which one person (the principal) designates another to act on her or his behalf in commercial transactions (e.g., signing a lease).

preapproved mortgage A commitment from a lender to provide a mortgage loan to a borrower on stated terms before the borrower has found a property to buy. Most real estate agents recommend that their clients who are potential buyers secure this kind of commitment because it allows them to make a firm offer when they find a desirable property; that is, they do not have to ask a seller to wait several weeks while they attempt to obtain financing. Sometimes sellers are unwilling to wait and potential buyers may lose property.

prepayment Payment of all or part of the principal of a mortgage or loan before it is actually due.

prequalification Completion of the mortgage application process before the borrower has found a property to buy as a way of establishing how much money the borrower is qualified to obtain in a mortgage.

primary lease The main lease on a property, to which any subleases are subordinate.

prime rate The most favorable interest rate charged by the largest commercial banks on short-term loans. Such loans usually are reserved for the lender's best clients. In real estate, the prime rate is not a rate that is actually charged on a mortgage, although adjustable-rate mortgages often use it as their index. Such mortgages may offer interest rates that are always, for instance, two or three percentage points above the prime rate.

principal The term has two meanings: 1) the person on whose behalf a real estate agent is acting; and 2) the amount of money borrowed (or still owed) on a loan, excluding interest.

principal and interest payment (P&I) A periodic payment, on a mortgage, that is sufficient to pay off the accumulated interest (usually that incurred over the previous month) and a portion of the principal.

prospect A potential tenant, buyer or seller, rather than someone who is in the process of leasing, buying or selling.

qualified buyer A potential purchaser who has been preapproved for a mortgage, usually to a certain limit.

quit-claim deed A conveyance in which the person doing the conveying is stating that she or he has no interest in a particular property.

real estate The term for land and all fixtures to land, including buildings and improvements. Personal property is not usually considered real estate. A house is real estate, but the furniture in the house is not.

real estate market The real estate activity (i.e., purchases and sales) in a particular area at a particular time.

recording The act of entering a title (or titles) into the public records.

redeem To bring mortgage payments up-to-date after a serious delinquency in making those payments, and after the lender has started default proceedings. Once a borrower redeems, the mortgage is regarded as back in good standing.

redemption The process of canceling a title to property, such as happens in a mortgage foreclosure or as the result of a tax sale of a property.

redevelop To remove existing improvements (usually buildings) on a piece of land and replace them with new, more useful or more profitable improvements.

refinance The situation when a borrower pays off one loan on a property and replaces it with another loan, often from the same lender. This is done most commonly when mortgage interest rates have decreased considerably from the rate the borrower is paying on the old mortgage. Thus, refinancing is a way for the borrower to reduce the amount of monthly mortgage payments.

rehabilitate To restore or refurbish real estate.

relocation clause A condition in a lease that allows a landlord to move a tenant to a new unit, within the same building or elsewhere. The clause usually specifies that the new premises must be of the same standard and quality as the old premises from which the tenant is being moved.

renegotiation An attempt to agree on new terms to an existing contract. In real estate, there are two common examples of renegotiation: 1) when the necessary repairs to a property, as established by a home inspection, are more extensive than the seller had announced or the buyer had expected; and 2) when the appraisal of a property establishes a value or market price considerably below the price on which the parties to the contract had agreed. In both cases, the buyer will wish to renegotiate the price of sale.

renovate Another word for remodel, though it implies a much more extensive upgrade to the property.

rent As a noun: The payments that are made by a tenant to a landlord for the right to occupy premises owned by the landlord. As a verb: The act of leasing premises from a landlord.

required cash The total amount of money needed to complete a real estate transaction. This may include a down payment on the purchase price, taxes, legal fees and mortgage fees.

rescind/rescission To treat a property contract as ended or void; that is, to withdraw one's offer or acceptance of a contract. Rescission normally happens as a result of a breach of the contract by the other party to that contract.

reserve fund The fund that is maintained by a condominium corporation (or a cooperative) for future contingencies, such as unforeseen major structural repairs to the condominium building that are very expensive. A reserve fund is usually created by charging unit owners a monthly assessment that is slightly more than what is needed to cover the basic maintenance expenses of the building and placing the extra amount in the reserve fund.

rezoning The reclassification of a property, or a particular district, from one kind of use to another. An area might be rezoned from commercial to residential, which would allow former office buildings to be converted into residential condominiums.

sale price The amount of money that is paid by the buyer to the seller for a particular property. Also known as purchase price.

sales associate/salesperson A real estate professional who is employed by and works under a real estate broker.

scheduled mortgage payment The periodic payment (usually monthly) that a borrower is obliged to pay on a loan. Depending on the terms of the loan, this payment may include amounts only for principal and interest or also for real estate taxes and insurance premiums.

search A review of public records that is undertaken to investigate whether there are any problems with the title to a particular property.

second mortgage A mortgage that ranks after a first mortgage in priority. A single property may have more than one mortgage; each is ranked by number to indicate the order in which it must be paid. In the event of a default and therefore sale of the property, second and subsequent mortgages are paid, in order, only if there are funds left after payment of the first mortgage.

secondary market The marketplace where investors buy and sell existing mortgages. The purchasers of first mortgages include banks, government agencies, insurance companies, investment bankers and independent investors. The original lender often sells mortgages in the secondary market so as to have an adequate supply of money available for new loans in the future.

security deposit Money that is paid by a tenant to a landlord, then held by the landlord to ensure that the tenant meets the obligations of the lease and does not damage the property. If the tenant does damage the property, the landlord may use part (or all) of the money to make the necessary repairs. In many jurisdictions, the landlord is required to pay interest on a security deposit.

seller financing An arrangement in which a seller agrees to receive payment of part or all of the purchase price over an extended period. The debt is registered on the title as a mortgage, and the seller acts as the lender, accepting monthly payments of principal and accumulated interest.

seller's market The situation that exists when demand for property exceeds the availability of property. In such situations, a seller may set a price for her or his property that is higher than its real market value.

sever/severance To divide one property from another so that each may be sold or used separately.

simple interest Interest that is payable on just the principal of a loan and not on any accumulated interest.

single-family home/residence/unit A house or condominium unit that is designed for just a single family.

site A plot of land that is set aside for a specific use, such as for the construction of a new factory.

soft market The situation that exists when there is more property for sale than there are buyers to buy it; as a result, prices decrease. Also known as buyer's market.

spec house A new house that is built before the builder has found a buyer.

speculator Someone who buys property in the expectation that it will increase in value within a relatively short period and can then be sold at a profit.

stamp tax Charges that are levied by governments (usually the local municipality) on the transfer of ownership of property.

starter home/condominium A small house or condominium unit that is usually inexpensive and is suitable for a first-time buyer. The assumption is that the buyer will build up equity in the property and then use the equity as a down payment on a larger dwelling.

statutory lien An involuntary lien on property that is created by law (e.g., a tax lien) and to which the owner need not agree. A mortgage, by contrast, is a voluntary lien on property.

straight-term mortgage A mortgage that requires that the principal be paid in full at the maturity of the loan.

subcontractor Someone who works under a general contractor or builder, such as a roofer, electrician or plumber.

subdivision The division of a single large parcel of land into smaller parcels (i.e., lots), which usually requires government approval. The term most commonly refers to a new urban or suburban housing development. A condominium is sometimes called a "one-lot subdivision."

sublease A rental contract between a tenant and someone who rents from that tenant.

surplus funds In an enforced sale of property (e.g., a foreclosure on a mortgage), any funds that are left over after the principal, interest, and penalties have been paid. Often, these surplus funds are paid to the borrower whose default provoked the sale.

survey Usually a pictorial depiction of land, showing its boundaries and the improvements that have been made to it.

surveyor A professional who is trained to prepare accurate surveys.

survivorship Put simply, this is outliving others. Surviving joint tenants (see cotenancy) have the right to take title to land they owned with a deceased joint tenant (i.e., they have the right of survivorship).

sweat equity A slang term for the improvements an owner makes to property through his or her own manual labor. Such improvements are expected to add to the value of the property.

tangible property Assets that have a physical existence, that can be touched (e.g., real estate).

tax A government levy against real property. If taxes are unpaid, the government may attach a lien to the property. Such liens are regarded as preeminent (i.e., they are given priority over mortgages).

tax base The assessed valuation of a piece of real property. This value is multiplied by the government's tax rate to determine the amount of property tax due.

tax foreclosure The process leading up to the sale of property to cover unpaid taxes.

tax lien A registered claim for the nonpayment of property taxes.

tax map A pictorial representation of properties in a particular municipality that provides information

tenancy at will A kind of tenancy, created by written agreement, that allows the landlord to evict the tenant at any time. This kind of tenancy might come into effect for a condemned building for which the date of demolition has not just been established by the owner or local government authority.

tenancy in common Ownership by more than one owner. This kind of ownership does not involve right of survivorship; the portion owned by the deceased becomes a part of the owner's estate.

term loan A loan that comes due on a particular date, regardless of whether the periodic payments have paid that loan in full.

term of a mortgage The period during which the loan contract is in effect and the borrower is making payments to the lender. The term is not necessarily the same as amortization. Amortization is the period during which, if all payments are paid on time and in full, the loan will be paid. For example, a mortgage could be amortized over 30 years but have a term of 10 years; at the end of 10 years, the borrower must pay the balance of the loan in full or refinance the loan.

title The evidence an owner has of his or her right of possession of property.

title company A corporation that sells insurance policies that guarantee the ownership of (and quality of title to) property. Also known as a title insurance company.

title insurance policy An insurance policy that protects an owner (or lender) against loss from defective title.

total debt ratio The total costs of living for a person (e.g., debt, food, travel) over a particular period compared to her or his gross income. Also called debt-service ratio.

total interest payments All the interest that will be paid over the life of a loan.

townhouse A house that is not freestanding; it shares at least one wall with a neighboring house (or houses).

tract A parcel of land. In some areas of the United States, the term also means subdivision.

transfer tax A state tax on the transfer of real property. In some areas of the United States, it is referred to as documentary transfer tax.

trespass Entry onto (or even possession of) property that is owned by another person without the owner's consent.

triple-net lease The sort of rental agreement that requires the tenant to pay all the operating costs of the premises.

underwriter This term has two meanings or uses: 1) A person who evaluates an application for a loan or an insurance policy. 2) A company that insures another, such as large title company (the underwriter) that sells insurance to a smaller title insurance company for all or a portion of the policies the smaller company issues.

undeveloped land Land on which no work has been done to make it more useful or profitable. Also called raw land.

unit A single dwelling in a larger complex. The term is most often used with regard to a condominium project. It refers to a unit (or, in a rental building, an apartment) that is reserved for the exclusive use of the owner, as opposed to the common areas (e.g., lobby, sun deck, laundry room) that are intended for the use of all the owners.

unsecured loan A loan that is valid (i.e., the lender has given the borrower the requested funds) but is not secured by any asset . Such loans are virtually unknown; an exception would be a case in which the lender knows the borrower well, has had extensive business dealings with the borrower, and believes that the loan will be repaid.

up-rent potential An estimate of how much the rent on a particular property is likely to be raised over a given period. Such an estimate might be offered to a potential tenant as an inducement to sign a lease.

urban sprawl A slang term for the unplanned, often wasteful, and often unattractive growth of cities.

utilities Services that are needed in any premises or dwelling (e.g., gas, electricity, sewers, water) and that the owner pays for separately from any payments on a loan. In some jurisdictions, arrears in payment of bills for utilities may create a lien on the property.

VA loan A home loan, offered to a military veteran, that is guaranteed by the U.S. Department of Veterans' Affairs. It allows the veteran to buy a home with no money down.

vacancy rate A calculation, expressed as a percentage, of all the available rental units in a particular area and at a particular time that are not rented.

vacate To move out of premises.

valuation The estimation of the worth, or likely sale price, of land or property. Also known as appraisal.

variable expenses The operating costs of a property that are not fixed, such as heating costs, which can change dramatically depending on whether a winter is mild or severe.

variance An "indulgence" that is granted by a local government authority to allow an unconventional use of property. This could be an exception granted to a homeowner that allows him or her to create a basement apartment for a sick relative in an area in which zoning bylaws ordinarily allow for only single-family homes.

walk-through inspection An examination, by the buyer, of the property she or he is purchasing. The walk-through inspection usually takes place immediately before closing and is intended to assure the buyer that no changes have taken place (and no damage has been done) to the property since the buyer agreed to buy. It also reassures the buyer that fixtures and chattels included in the sale actually remain on the property.

warranty A legally binding promise that is usually given at the time of sale in which the seller gives the buyer certain assurances as to the condition of the property being sold.

wear-and-tear The loss in value of a property that is caused by normal and reasonable use of that property. Usually, in a lease, a tenant is not responsible for normal wear-and-tear in the premises that tenant leases.

wood-frame construction Buildings in which the internal elements (e.g., walls, floors) are all constructed of wood. This does not refer to the exterior of the building, which may be constructed of other materials, such as brick.

work order An edict from a local government body directing that certain work be done on a particular property to bring it into compliance with local regulations. Work orders usually are issued against property that has been allowed to become substandard or derelict.

zero lot line The construction of a building on the boundary lines of a lot. This usually is the front line (e.g., a store built directly to the sidewalk). In the older neighborhoods of some American cities, it is also common for residences to be built up to the sidewalk.

zone An area of a city (or county) that is set aside for a certain purpose, such as an industrial zone.

Index

The Complete Landlording Handbook

SPECIAL OFFER FOR BOOK BUYERS—SAVE 15% ON THESE ESSENTIAL LANDLORDING PRODUCTS AT

Socrates.com/books/landlording-handbook.aspx.

Socrates.com offers essential business, personal and real estate do-it-yourself products that can help you:

- Sell or lease a property
- Write a will or trust
- Start a business
- Get a divorce
- Hire a contractor
- Manage employees
- And much more

Real Estate Forms Library Software (SS502)

CONTAINS REAL ESTATE DICTIONARY AND MORE THAN 100 LEGAL FORMS

Simplify the process of purchasing or selling real estate and streamline your operations as a landlord. The forms in this comprehensive software will help you hire a real estate agent, make an offer on property, perform a home inspection, evaluate the best mortgage options, write a purchase contract and more. If you are leasing property, this library ensures that your landlord-tenant interactions are streamlined and legally compliant by guiding you through the process of screening tenants, writing lease agreements, collecting rent and, in extreme cases, starting eviction proceedings.

Residential Property Management Software (SS505)

CONTAINS REAL ESTATE DICTIONARY, INSTRUCTIONAL PRIMER AND MORE THAN 50 FORMS.

Simplify the process of maintaining real estate and sustaining good tenant relationships. This software ensures that your landlord-tenant interactions are streamlined and legally compliant by guiding you through finding and screening tenants, setting proper rent, writing lease agreements, handling finances, sending notices to tenants and, if needed, starting eviction proceedings.

Business Legal Forms and Agreements Software (SS4323)

If you're tired of spending countless hours and money creating and filing business documents, this complete, convenient resource may be your solution. It contains **279 ready-to-use legal forms and agreements**, most of which can be customized to meet your needs to help you legally protect your business and make your life easier.

TOPICS COVERED INCLUDE:

- landlording
- lending and borrowing
- buying and selling agreements
- employment
- credit and collection letters and notices
- transfers and assignments
- insurance
- items for personal and family use

Attracting and Retaining Quality Tenants Kit (PK209)

INCLUDES AN INSTRUCTION MANUAL WITH 10 FORMS, A CD WITH 41 CUSTOMIZABLE FORMS AND A REAL ESTATE DICTIONARY.

Learn the basics on how to prepare your property for rental, advertise to and target quality tenants and deal with showings, screenings and leases in a professional manner. Safeguard yourself from disruptive, destructive and nonpaying tenants by using the forms and following the guidelines provided in this kit.

Hiring a Contractor Kit (PK114)

INCLUDES AN INSTRUCTION MANUAL WITH 9 FORMS AND A CD WITH 9 CUSTOMIZABLE FORMS.

Find the right contractor/remodeler for the job. Learn what to ask on an interview, the importance of checking references, and how to handle the bidding and contract process. Make sure your job is done right the first time and get everything in writing.

Paint and Construction Estimator Software (SS500)

SAVE TIME AND MONEY USING THIS PERFECT TOOL TO ESTIMATE THE TOTAL AND CORRECT COSTS FOR YOUR PROJECTS.

The Socrates Paint and Construction Estimator is a simple to navigate, user-friendly program that makes use of basic diagrams and practical buttons. A detailed list of wood, concrete, other materials and labor is automatically totaled based on the costs you enter. You'll end up with the most complete, professional construction estimate for jobs both large and small.